SKIES TO DUNKIRK

SKIES TO DUNKIRK

A Personal Memoir

Air Marshal
Sir Victor Goddard
KCB, CBE, MA

WILLIAM KIMBER ·LONDON

First published in Britain in 1982 by
WILLIAM KIMBER & CO. LIMITED
Godolphin House, 22a Queen Anne's Gate,
London SW1H 9AE

© Copyright 1982 Air Marshal Sir Victor Goddard
ISBN 0-7183-0498-5

This book is copyright. No part of it may be reproduced in any form without permission in writting from the publishers except by a reviewer who wishes to quote brief passages in connection with a review written for inclusion in a newspaper, magazine, television or radio broadcast.

Photoset by Robcroft Ltd, London WC1
and printed in Great Britain by
The Garden City Press Limited
Letchworth, Hertfordshire SG6 1JS

To my late wife, Mildred,
and to A.H. and to all
who served in, or helped to
commemorate, the Air Component
of the BEF, 1939 and 1940

Contents

		Page
	Author's Note	11
	Prologue: Lindbergh's Visit	13

Part I

1	The Chief of the Attachés' Question	19
2	War Begins at Garston	34
3	Introducing Violet	44
4	The Obstacle Race	52
5	Violet and Velvet	70
6	The Phoney War	84

Part II

7	Night Sorties	92
8	Secret Operations	99
9	Der Tag	115
10	Into the Unknown	126
11	The Breaking of Command	144
12	Candle and Moth	155

Part III

13	Prémesques	169
14	Lines of Power	183
15	A King's Decision	196
16	Gort in Reverse	209
17	En Panne – À La Panne	223
18	Ad Astra	234
19	The Little Ships	243
	Epilogue	257
	Index	265

List of Illustrations

	Facing Page
The author	48
General Lord Gort with his Chief of Staff *(Imperial War Museum)*	49
Air Vice-Marshal Blount at his HQ *(British Official Photo)*	64
Blount with members of the RAF on New Year's Eve, 1939 *(British Official Photo)*	64
Dornier 17 *(via Chaz Bowyer)*	65
King George VI inspects Nos 85 and 87 Squadrons	65
The Gateway to No 1 Mess, Château Écoive	96
HQ, RAF Component	97
The author's bedroom, Château Écoive	112
Christmas Comforts	113
Hurricanes over France, early 1940 *(Imperial War Museum)*	224
Westland Lysander *(via Chaz Bowyer)*	225
Heinkel 111 *(via Chaz Bowyer)*	225
Blenheim at Condé Vraux *(via Chaz Bowyer)*	240
French airfield scene after the fall of France *(AELR Air Museum, Brussels)*	240
The little ships at La Panne *(via the Rev. Leslie Aitken)*	241
Requiem for a Hurricane *(AELR Air Museum, Brussels)*	241

TEXT ILLUSTRATION

	Page
Letter of appreciation from General Gort to the author	255

Author's Note

This book was written from memory of the events described and without documentation; official records on which it might have been based were accidentally 'ditched' in Calais harbour, I am told, towards the end of May 1940. The keeping of diaries by men of the BEF was prohibited. I had however written a draft somewhat nearer the time of the events, namely in 1957, and I have relied heavily on this draft while writing the following pages.

The book is about an epic of failure, but nearly every chapter is about an epic happening and reflects the feeling that belonged to that time.

PROLOGUE

Lindbergh's Visit

The years of Hitler's ascent to power as the Führer of the Third Reich, before his descent into war, were years of intense activity in what was then called the Air Ministry – not least in my Department. The wars in Spain and Abyssinia, the secret but rapid expansion of all so-called aligned countries from Japan all round the world and back to the Philippines, created ever-mounting problems of Air Intelligence. The increasing probability of war made imperative the need for the creation of Intelligence systems in our own combatant Commands, thus to disseminate and implement in their actions the Intelligence data which our Sections were then collating for their use. We also had the making of thousands of detailed and documented target maps. And all the time we were involved in the writing of summaries and specific reports. These activities made for long-houred days and nights for the small staff of my deputy-directorate of European Intelligence, DDI (3). And, as though that wasn't enough, in the month of June, 1939, I had to take over responsibilities for Intelligence about the 'rest of the world', too – i.e. DDI (2) – on the posting away of Wing Commander Wigglesworth. On the side would be the daily interviewing of travellers, industrialists, refugees and others who had recently had first-hand information to give to 'someone in the Air Ministry'. One such passing visitor was Colonel Charles Lindbergh. This prologue is about his unexpected visit.

Lindbergh came hurrying from Germany after his experiences there to England, on his urgent way back to the United States. Before this interview I used to think of him like I now think of Prince Philip, or the Prince of Wales – a being of stature, charm, guts and mentality of an outstanding order. Lindbergh on this occasion, however, wanted to impress his anxious views upon someone who might be instrumental through our Government towards modifying the growing intransigence of British public opinion in regard to Germany's forward policy. He was alarmed by the fact that the conquest of Czechoslovakia had stimulated England into active opposition to Hitler at the very time when (to Lindbergh) it was quite clear that the time for opposition had gone by. He wanted especially to talk to some well-placed airman who was already cognisant of German air power, and he had been advised by General Wenninger and others in Germany, I gathered, to visit me, during his three-hour stay in England.

At that time Colonel Lindbergh was still world-famous as the first man successfully to fly solo across the Atlantic. He had become recognised as a man of great potentialities. In the eyes of the leaders of the Third Reich in Germany he could become a superb apologist for the Fatherland. Although proudly American, Lindbergh was full of European influence. While still in boyhood, he had become a hero in the United States – and, indeed, throughout the world. By 1939 he had achieved stature as a man of power. This was in considerable measure due to his marriage to the daughter of a top American. On his own merits, however, he held his position as the beau ideal of America and of the world of youth. But, also, he was the object of universal sympathy because of personal tragedy – the kidnapping and murder of his son. What, in the late 1930's, could more surely represent the ideal combination of traditional hero and romantic Prince Charming than a manly, comely airman-adventurer and millionaire?

Charles Lindbergh was claimed by the Germans as a virtual prince in the Siegfried tradition. He represented in his blue-eyed, fair-skinned visage and his six-foot, athletic stature all that was specified in the Nazi worship-cult for the 'true Aryan of the Master Race'. Accordingly, Charles Lindbergh was chosen by the Nazi Government as the most potentially profitable of all the high foreign personages whom they were at that time cultivating as unofficial ambassadors for their regime. Reichsmarschall Göring – deputy Führer, head of the German Air Force and President of the German Aeronautical Society – had persuaded that body to offer to Colonel Lindbergh the award of the Lillienthal Memorial Gold Medal for 1939. The ceremony of presentation was performed by Hitler early in August and, thereafter, the honoured and fêted recipient was given, during the following three weeks, the most impressive and intensive presentation of German military might and air power that could possibly be staged in time of peace.

Charles Lindbergh confessed to me that he had been deeply and overwhelmingly impressed. Well-accustomed as he was to the gigantesque in American technological achievement and the cinematic portrayal of the fantastic, and better qualified as he was than most men to appreciate aeronautical developments and power, he had nevertheless been astounded and alarmed, unalterably convinced of German invincibility. Lindbergh emerged from that ordeal of brain-conditioning a changed man: an ambassador for surrender. He further admitted that he had been infected with the blazing rhetoric and mass fanaticism of the Nuremburg Rally, imbued with the dread might and evident determination of the Panzer (Tiger) Tank Corps, the vast and versatile Luftwaffe and the German aircraft industry; horrified (and, doubtless, subconsciously revolted) by the diabolical symphony of terror-noises artificially superimposed upon the visual demonstrations of bombing and of tank warfare, Lindbergh made his evaluation of the significance of Nazi power and blitzkrieg. Thus in desperate urgency he came to me in the Air Ministry direct from his waiting aeroplane at Croydon, to make his anxious plea.

From what he told me, the Nazis had impressed my visitor very deeply. I only knew that the Nazis had awarded to Colonel Lindbergh the best Gold Medal that could be awarded to any man of adventure – and rightly so. I was surprised and pleased when I heard that he was coming to see me. It did not surprise me that he was in a hurry; it was traditional that Americans always are, but it did surprise me then that Lindbergh had actually sought to make the British have cold feet.

Lindbergh's manner of discourse was quiet; his statements factual, but burning within him was a profound longing to convince me that Germany was utterly prepared and utterly invincible. He appealed quietly in the name of commonsense and sanity. His manner was much more English than American.

Fluently, with certainty of his facts which confirmed and amplified all that we knew of German air power and future programmes for its expansion, he poured out the impressions he had received of the massive superiority of German air power over anything that could be arrayed against it and implored me to ensure that no one in authority in this country would, for lack of advice upon the facts, be so blind or so falsely heroic as to challenge the German government. Their programme for the consolidation of western Europe, he urged, might be the only safeguard against the erosion by Marxist Communism of all that Christian civilisation had built up in Europe during the past two thousand years. His German friends, he said, wanted him to advance such arguments but that was their business – not his. His business was his own, he said – it was to do what he could to save Western humanity from a terrible catastrophe.

Looking at me earnestly through his electric blue eyes he begged me not to be, as Englishmen tended to be, foolishly optimistic and altruistic about English capabilities and intentions. For England to oppose Germany's eastward expansion with force was not merely impertinent and futile, it would certainly be calamitous and suicidal. Anyone who forced the Germans to bring their air forces into action would be, unconsciously, the enemy of his own country and a betrayer of humanity.

I did not argue with my guest; I listened. I made notes on what that brilliant and gallant young internationalist said so compellingly. He had broken his journey back to America only to make this appeal, he told me. Now he must get back to his plane.

Charles Lindbergh left with me an indelible impression of a good and noble man: German, in a sense, by his inborn love of order; Anglo-American by the infections of his young life-time of English-speaking freedom; humanitarian by reason of his airman's view of the world and of the little beings on it.

I did not know, then, that that man was to extinguish his fame in a forlorn compaign in the United States. Eventually Charles Lindbergh saw that the German Air Force had not, as he had predicted, prevailed over the Royal Air Force in the Battle of Britain; that Nazism was not to be the guardian of Western civilisation but the enemy of free peoples. Disillusioned, he left the speaking-platform of the isolationists, returned to his true profession – aviation – and performed outstanding services for the United States Air Force in war.

Another thing which I did not know at the time of that interview – and nor, am I sure, did Lindbergh – was that Ribbentrop was about to sign a pact of non-aggression with Stalin. So, before my report to my masters on the visit of this modest master-man was circulated, it appeared that he had been duped. But this was not so with that section of my staff which concentrated on German air intelligence; what they derived from that remarkable Lindbergh intrusion was confirmation of facts about which they had been in some degree of pardonable doubt because of their magnitude. Those facts had, indeed, been accepted because they conformed to the pattern of expansion which [AI 3(b)] (the German Section) had extrapolated from past assessments and which had successively proved to be correct.

I have chosen that example of Charles Lindbergh's dedicated

sincerity to illustrate the prevalent power of the Nazi protagonists and tolerators at that time. In this country, in the summer of 1939, however, the tide of Nazi sympathy which had flooded the minds of anti-communists in all countries was already at low ebb.

PART I

CHAPTER ONE

The Chief of the Attachés' Question

By the time I had looked through the papers in my in-tray that morning, 23rd August 1939, my mind was no longer pre-occupied with the news from Moscow. I had seen the headlines in the newspapers, but at that time I had no official knowledge of what had been going on between Stalin and Hitler. This was all before World War II had become inevitable.

Earlier that morning, while getting up, I had heard with the rest of the listening world, that Ribbentrop had signed a ten-year non-aggression pact with Stalin. The press photographs of the schemers smiling over the death-warrant of Poland may have heartened wishful-thinking citizens in totalitarian countries and amused the world's cynics, but for millions of thoughtful folk in all countries of the West, those pictures must have evoked disgust and forebodings. For some, the news was a verdict – war. But I had a reason for thinking otherwise. In the earlier editions of *Mein Kampf*, Hitler had shown that war with England was sure to end in the destruction of Germany, despite all appearances to the contrary at the outset.

For professional military men, it might be supposed that the highest satisfactions can only come from the experience of proficiency in battle: victory and conquest. Yet, since I entered military service in 1910 and through all the years while I had been close to it, I had never been aware that any senior officer in British military service regarded war and military conquest as representing either the failure of diplomacy, or at least, as 'diplomacy's continuation by other means'. Of course, as servicemen, we were willing to be committed to war and battle: of course, we volunteered for service in regions where war was likely or in actual progress: of course, there can be – and quite properly – human satisfaction in battle. But who in his right senses would regard the practices of war as desirable? What madman in power would really believe that in Europe, then, anything could be gained by war? No doubt, much had been gained in the past – if annexation is gain – by bluff and deception, by invasion connived at by the invaded. But the notion that Germany had anything to gain, in the long run, through committing herself to war once more with Britain seemed to me to be preposterous nonsense.

My business at that time, however, was not the preparation of British air forces for battle or the raising of their proficiency for war; it was to provide information about potential enemies for the planning of RAF operations, for the development of weapons and tactics, for the preparation of target maps and data, and, at a higher level, for advice to the Chiefs of Staffs, the Foreign Office and the Cabinet. For the past three years I had been head of the Air Ministry's European air intelligence.

The Moscow pact vitally affected my job, but that morning I had other urgent preoccupations jostling in my mind when my good friend General Wenninger, Air Attaché at the German Embassy, called me unavailingly on my old telephone number. Wenninger was no tough-necked, arrogant Nazi, nor was he an upstart sycophant like his late master, Ribbentrop, who, not long before, had been German Ambassador in London. Why should the Air Attaché for Germany want me to ring him on this day of shame? Perhaps he had something his present master wanted him to put over; something to do with the explanation that the Acting Ambassador was going to offer to the Foreign Secretary, Lord Halifax, that morning.

Although Wenninger and his wife remained rather favourite people with my wife and myself, we had seen less of them in those darkening times. I was really fond of him. He and I had much in common, both of us having been naval officers in World War I, both of us having left the sea for the air. Wenninger was straight, co-operative, kindly and good company.

Frau Wenninger was a cousin of Frau Ribbentrop. This had probably influenced her husband's selection for the post of Air Attaché. For Frau Ribbentrop, intelligent, bitter, quite unversed in the larger world, had had the wisdom to choose her charming and capable cousin to help her through the sophistications of diplomacy. From the moment of meeting Frau Ribbentrop I feared her influence upon the husband she ruled and hence upon German diplomacy in London.

While waiting to get Wenninger on the telephone, I recalled with wry amusement how scathing his wife had been when the Foreign

Office was having conversations on the Litvinoff (Soviet) plan for a triple alliance: USSR, France, Britain.

'What are you English coming to', she had asked when we met at a cocktail party, 'chumming up with those murderers, cheats and liars?'

And when we parted, Wenninger had said, mockingly, 'Goodbye, *Komrad*!'

I recalled, too, her saying at the time of Munich and Hitler's annexation of Czechoslovakia, 'Chamberlain is mad! Does he not yet know the nature of the man he is dealing with? Nothing can save Poland now. This news is terrible!' Did she then sense the inevitability of war?

On the buzz from my clerk, who warned that 'the General' was about to come on the line, I picked up the receiver and, perhaps over-playfully said, as I heard his voice, 'Good morning, *Komrad*! What's it been like in Moscow?'

Wenninger replied that it was getting very hot everywhere now, but if I wasn't feeling too hot about the news from Moscow, could I bear to come to a tea party that he and his wife were giving privately on the following afternoon at the Carlton Hotel. They wanted me to meet some special friends who were that day going back to Germany; would I mind being the only Englishman and forgive such short notice? He seemed to be hurried and anxious. I agreed to go.

Meanwhile, Chamberlain had warned the House, and thus the world, that he would give Poland a guarantee of support in the event of aggression.

Next day the thought of spending time with Wenninger, despite the dangers, pleased me. Catastrophic political events had been chasing one another since we had last met. Not being statesmen or politicians, both of us might have supposed that the world would be much better-run by good-humoured, unambitious men like ourselves! Wenninger's problem, and mine, in regard to each other, had always been to discern how each was to make the other suitably aware of the might and potentialities of the air power of his own country without disclosing its technical secrets. We had to ensure that the other really was alive to the potentialities. But we certainly had to be secretive about tactical weaknesses and expansion disabilities, production bottlenecks and vital targets. But secrecy about strength we knew to be folly: weakness was the thing to cover up. Wenninger and I never talked about our impotencies.

It was against that background of unspoken understanding and forbearance that Wenninger and I were to meet again that afternoon. I recognised that the new pact meant that Stalin must virtually have said to Hitler, 'Help yourself to Poland.' I had not then guessed that Stalin had also said, perhaps to himself, 'And so will I, with your connivance.'

At the Carlton, which then stood where towering New Zealand House now stands at the foot of Haymarket, I found a pleasant party of Germans. They included a prince and princess who perhaps were the 'special friends' then about to return to Germany.

Evidently, we were simply going to have tea in the public lounge; talk was not going to be about politics or Moscow. We spoke of friendly things. Saying good-bye to friends whom I had never met was a thin reason for meeting. But no other reason appeared and presently I withdrew from the party.

After I had taken leave from Frau Wenninger and her friends and was in the act of departing to get my things, the German Acting Ambassador arrived by the south door. I did not return to greet him for I was already on the way to the east door with Wenninger. He too disregarded the arrival of his political chief. He had seen him, out of the corner of his eye, and remarked to me upon the need to attend to him soon. He seemed to resent the intrusion.

Wenninger at once dropped the guise of the carefree diplomat and told me quickly of his dejection about what had happened in Moscow. He could see no hope, now. He had wanted me especially to come today for he feared he might not see me again. His time was up, too. But that was not the only reason why he might not see me again. Very soon, we might be fighting. What did I think?

I supposed that his whole purpose in asking me to meet him privately and not at the Embassy was to know what I thought: war, or not? This put me in an unexpected quandary. It was none of our business to give each other opinions on such matters unless instructed to do so and for a special purpose. Never had either of us asked each other questions we could not safely and rightly answer. We were not spies. If we wanted specific information there were other ways of getting it. We had been much together, I had toured all over Germany with General Wenninger and with his air force masters. So had he, with me and mine, in England. We had talked about everything except some of those things we would most like to know. But what was he doing, now? Was he taking a chance to convey to me his personal certainty about the terrible destiny to which the Nazis were driving our countries? Or was he staging an ostensibly private occasion in which, on instructions, to probe the reaction of a senior officer in-the-know whom he could get into a mood of compassionate confidence and truth?

'Very soon', he had said, 'we might be fighting. What do *you* think?'

What did I think? What could I say? I did not then believe that we should be fighting, and yet nor did I think that we should break faith with Poland.

Wenninger had virtually said that Hitler was certainly going into Poland and that we could not stop him by any guarantee. There was going to be war. What did I think? He could not mean, what did I think morally or militarily about the invasion of Poland, but rather what did I think about the Prime Minister's enigmatic and impracticable guarantee: would we British fight? Would the French? Was it really going to be World War II – or would we fall back on appeasement once more, and delay and parley until too late?

What did I think?

Perhaps a more alert and resourceful man might have parried, 'Answer *me* one, first! Has your Führer forgotten all that he wrote in *Mein Kampf* about the mystical certainty that if ever Germany went to war with England again, Germany would be destroyed?' But that posing of a substitute question to be answered first, which you haven't the wit to think of at the time, has earned a special name in diplomacy – a *pensée d'escalier* – what you wish, as you go down the stairs, you had said while still in the presence.

'Wenninger, we will *fight* you out of this!' I said, and noticed how he took it, as a certainty: as inescapable fate . . . Nothing to be done. His face already lined with anxiety, filled with pain. But I myself, did not believe that it would come to physical fighting in battle. I simply believed that Poland would not after all be invaded.

I believed that, faced with the certainty of our intervention, Hitler would switch. I believed that Germany had no vital strategic need to go into Poland. Had Hitler's military people believed in air power in the way that I did, with the air power resources which they could deploy, using the Army as an adjunct to air power, Germany could secure the Ukraine without violating Poland. Maybe that plan was no better, morally. But politically it would be better for us, I thought. I could not say so, and it would not have mattered one iota if I had.

On the other hand, I had no doubt that if Poland actually were invaded, the British certainly would declare war. Despite the realists who knew our powerlessness to prevent, physically, the invasion of that country, democratic Poland was fast becoming to the British public another 'Little Belgium'. The so-called Soviet Socialist Republic of the Ukraine was another matter. England could not have cared less about that region. It was the Ukraine where Germany certainly would go eventually and could go then, Moscow pact notwithstanding. I hated the ruthlessness of the prospect but wished that Germany would side-step Poland and go where Hitler really meant to go.

Those thoughts did not go through my mind then. They were my background. I knew what I felt.

Wenninger looked ill with distress at my saying, 'We will fight you out of this!' and I felt that I had done wrong in saying anything, and in implying more than I meant. I put my hand on his arm and said, 'It will not come to actual fighting . . . We shall be at war with you and, yet, it will not *be* war! Don't be afraid that the worst is going to happen.'

In his anxiety the kindly Wenninger lapsed from his usual careful English into short interrogations. Why did I say that? Why not 'actual fighting'? He thought that there would be. Could I please explain? But at that moment the First Secretary, a guest at the tea-party, suddenly appeared and intervening peremptorily said, in rapid German, 'General Wenninger, speak to the Ambassador at once, please!' He was referring to the Acting-Ambassador, Theodore Kordt, who, as we had seen in those last few moments, had unexpectedly come into the lounge.

Wenninger excused himself and left us abruptly, before I had answered his questions.

Supposing that he might come back, I waited in the hall. Looking back into the lounge, I saw the party leaving by the Pall Mall entrance. Determined to get Wenninger on the telephone later, to tell him to read what his Führer had said in *Mein Kampf* about the English in war, I went out by the Haymarket door. I could see that Wenninger understood that what I was about to say was that Hitler was inwardly terrified of fighting England, and would hardly dare to do it. His inner prompting was right: he would be beaten in the end if he did.

Years afterwards, when one looks back at a point of crisis, and recalls some fact of indiscernment or lost opportunity, one may hope to see it in a softer light. Perhaps this incident never was significant. After all, it was a precise statement of what, in fact, was going to happen. Yet it could have been a last straw in a load of a million opinion-factors which made Hitler suppose that the English people would not go to war over Poland.

At the moment of separation from that troubled German friend, I sensed no great potential harm in what I had said. In my mind, I was still carrying what I meant; I had not then perceived the importance of what I had not said.

As I walked thoughtfully out of the east door of the Carlton, through the traffic to Charing Cross, I became more aware of my chagrin at not having had the extra seconds in which to convey to Wenninger my basic idea that it was Hitler who, on his own showing, would not go to war. Optimistic, as ever, I supposed that I would straighten it out on the telephone before any harm was done.

But the Wenningers did not go back to their Chelsea home that night. They went to Berlin. That tea-party was their farewell, not to a prince and princess, but to me. This parting would bring Frau Wenninger and Frau Ribbentrop together again in Berlin. With some unconscious bending and amplifying, those half-expressed opinions of mind might go to Ribbentrop and Hitler as though they represented informed opinion from the centre of British air power. Supposing the same sort of thing to be happening the other way round, in Berlin, any such view expressed by my opposite number in the German Air Ministry about German reactions to vital exigencies would certainly be reported by the Ambassador and would automatically go to members of the Cabinet. Such evidences of German intention would surely add weight to other evidence of the same kind.

As the potential gravity of my frustrated talk occurred to me, I decided that I would have to report my fears to my friend and colleague at the head of Security in the Air Ministry: the 'grand old man' of the Air Staff, Archibald Boyle.

*

Archie Boyle, who was soon to become Director of Intelligence in the Air Ministry, was a Civil Servant. Once he had been a regular major in the Royal Scots Fusiliers and a trusted friend of Major Trenchard when both were young men before the First World War. If not universally loved he was certainly universally respected. His business, as Head of Security, was chiefly concerned with assessing the attitude of people, including the shady ones and the twisters,

British and foreign, who had associations with air power.

Boyle had been brought by Trenchard to the Air Ministry when he, Trenchard, was welding the RFC and the RNAS into one service – the Royal Air Force, the first of all independent air forces. There, in the Air Ministry, Boyle had stayed for over twenty years, a living rock of commonsense and good judgement. By 1939 he had become the doyen of the Air Staff. He had Trenchard's massive stature, his rugged directness and his kindly humanity. Unlike Trenchard, Boyle was not particularly interested in ideas: he did not get excited about the looming potentialities and menace of air power, and he took no part in the perennial inter-service arguments about the role of, and military control of air power. Because of his job and his appointment as one of the three Deputy Directors of Intelligence, he was my closest colleague. His short title, DDI (1), meant that he was the chief watchdog, not only of the Air Ministry itself but also of the Air Force as a whole, and of all the Air Attachés. He was the 'father' of our own attachés in foreign capitals, and the mentor and regulator of foreign Air Attachés in London. It used to be said of him, 'What's not Boyle's business is nobody's business!'

On the day after the Carlton tea party, when I found that the Wenningers had fled, I began to feel guilty. My initial impetus, to tell Boyle about it, had begun to wilt. There was more than one reason for that. Boyle liked to hear what people were thinking about problems of the day. He would surely demand an explanation of the Moscow Pact; he liked to pretend to know nothing. He would expect me to have the situation weighed up. I had not got it at all clear – whether it was a real *volte face* and a combination of dictators versus democrats, or whether it was purely a swindle. So I put off going across the passage to see him and we did not meet that day.

By the next morning, hindsight was already filling gaps in my foresight about the Moscow Pact and I felt better able to stand up to the challenge I was likely to get from Boyle. I remember deciding that I should tell him that, like everyone else, I was astonished, because, if one thing was settled in those turbulent times, it was that Communism and Naziism were sworn enemies: it was not possible that Stalin and Hitler could seriously promise mutual tranquillity for ten years – as they in fact had done. If we knew anything, we knew that they were bound to fight: it was only a matter of time and the question was not whether, but when. So what was the sense of the pact? But I should not, I knew, get out of it by putting the question back. Boyle, always cagey about giving an opinion on such things, would simply retort, 'Well, you tell *me*!'

But I knew I must have a talk to him. I had to introduce a difficult topic: I had to make a confession. To us, General Wenninger was one of many attachés constantly seeking information, constantly asking for permission to visit Air Force establishments and aircraft factories. It was the job of attachés to know all that they could find out. Indeed, it was in the best interests of our security that they should find out facts of strength which could deter and which could not be exploited to our disadvantage. But there were many security restrictions; the Secret List was swollen by our concealed strengths. The existence of RDF (radar) and the armament of our new Hurricane and Spitfire fighters – eight forward-firing guns – were certainly not among the disclosable 'strengths' at that time.

That may now be judged a tragic mistake, for, in these days of determined deterrence-by-strength-in-technology, we seem not to be so secretive of real capability. But whether or not it was wise to declare all strength for war to potential enemies, it was surely unwise to declare weakness or even to suggest weakness. Boyle, hearing from me what I had said to Wenninger – and, like Wenninger, not hearing how I had intended to qualify it – would at once detect that I had committed the crime of suggesting weakness, and that I had done so to a man avid for a weakness that he could quote authoritatively.

Although Wenninger was only an attaché to us, an equal, one of the cogs in a technical machine, he was much more than that to the masters of the Third Reich. He was the man-on-the-spot for air power in England, and air power was the crucial factor in the war considerations of the British cabinet. It had not been and still was not the dominant force in our military preparations against war, but air power was certainly the chief deterrent to a declaration of war by the British Government. The German Government would rightly suppose that the willingness or the unwillingness of the English for war would depend upon their estimation of relative potencies in air power. Would 'the decadent English' face war? Would the Air Ministry – the Air Staff advisers to the Cabinet – induce the already terrified Chamberlain to go back on his guarantee to Poland and relapse into another frenzy of pacification and appeasement as and when Poland was invaded in the very next week? (For, blitzkrieg, as we now know, was planned to begin in the following week; Wenninger must have known that, when we met at the Carlton.)

The question was a 'sixty-four-billion-mark' question. Who

could answer it? Ribbentrop would have to answer it. But, surely, he had already done so. Did Hitler accept that advice? Who would reassure him? General Keitel, his chief military adviser, would. And so would Göring, his chief air mentor. But how would they know? They would *not* know, in Ribbentrop's estimation, for they did not know the English as he did – or thought he did – nor did they know Whitehall as he did. But who would know what went on in the minds of the Whitehall air advisers? Who better than General Wenninger? General Wenninger, then, had been called back to Berlin to answer the question. The question was – would the English fight? And the last answer he had received from his highest friend in the Air Staff was, 'It will not come to actual fighting.'

My cogitations were not fortifying me for the interview. How could I tell Boyle that I had said what I had said? Boyle, rugged Britisher that he was, would have apoplexy. How would I begin?

The preliminary line of argument which I decided to put to Boyle was to show that Stalin as much as Hitler had his own reasons for wishing to see Poland destroyed cheaply. This I felt I could do fairly convincingly. It had not then occurred to me that violent partition of Poland between two voracious aggressors was the secret of that historic monument to cynicism.

It was none of my business to know the answers to any of these political questions, of course. But we had been given no clue to the inside facts from any of the Foreign Office telegrams which automatically came day by day, nor did the press leader-writers offer any enlightenment. In those exciting days, everyone had 'views' and I was expected to be aware of the state of the game.

That same day the British and Polish Governments virtually spoke my thoughts aloud in a formal pact of 'mutual support in the event of aggression', signed between them. The date was 27th August.

Unaware of the imminent announcement of our unusually swift diplomatic riposte to the Moscow pact, I went along to Boyle's office to pass the time of day with him – to 'swap lies', as he called any exchange of hunches or hearsay.

Boyle looked up as I came in, smiled quizzically and said that he supposed that I knew that Wenninger was in Berlin. I answered that I had been told that he wasn't in the Embassy nor at his house in Chelsea.

Boyle then said, still smiling, 'What was it you actually *did* say to Wenninger at the Carlton? Wenninger seemed not to be sure about your meaning.' Then he stopped smiling.

So he knew! – though how, I did not immediately guess. Wenninger and I were alone and out of earshot during that brief, anxious exchange. London hotels were not wired for concealed microphones. Surely Wenninger could not have rung up to ask somebody – say, Charles Medhurst, the Director of Intelligence, our boss – what I could have meant? Medhurst rather studiously avoided contacts with attachés, especially attachés of the German Embassy.

Forgetting that I had really come in to confess my misgivings, and slightly nettled by being thus suddenly put on the spot, I temporised and asked whether Boyle had been at the party in disguise, for I had not seen him there.

Boyle said he had gathered that I was the only Englishman there and I parried that that did not rule out the possibility of a surreptitious Scot from eavesdropping: had he been behind a pillar? To which Boyle replied that it seemed that *I* was the person who was trying to hide ... something.

Then I remembered another occasion when Boyle had mysteriously known the details of a telephone conversation I had had with the same man. It was when I had been fixing a series of visits to German Air Force stations by an Air Staff Mission. Wenninger had assured me that the Chief of the German Air Staff had said that I could choose to go wherever I liked. I mentioned two very vital places (about which we secretly knew something, but not enough) and said I would like to visit them. This caused serious embarrassment in the German Air Ministry. Boyle, I then recalled, had had a recording, not of my conversation with Wenninger but of what Wenninger had repeated of it to the German Air Ministry on the telephone when, in urgency, he (Wenninger) had broken his Embassy's rules on telephone security. That was before the days when telephones were fitted with electronic scramblers and unscramblers at each end. So – it then dawned on me – after that Carlton talk, Wenninger, or his wife, or someone – perhaps the Acting Ambassador himself? –had telephoned that unfinished conversation to Berlin, the same evening. Was that the reason for Wenninger being recalled? Probably not. The probability was, rather, that it had been planned that the Embassy should be reduced to a minimum staff that night. But surely Wenninger would have told me that he was departing that night, had he known?

On second thoughts, surely not!

I began to tell Boyle of the brief talk I had had with Wenninger. I got to the point where I qualified the assurance that we *would* fight with the fateful conjecture given as certainty that it would not come to actual fighting. Boyle, who had been standing facing me, turned away. He waited for my explanation. He did not want to know why I said it, or what was to follow. His fears were confirmed. Nothing else was significant.

'And so you *did* say that we would not actually fight with the bastards!'

'No! Archie, I did not!' I quickly replied, 'but evidently that is the construction Wenninger put on what I did say. You have had a tapping of his report!'

He turned from the window and looked at me with compassion and understanding and said, quietly, 'My poor old fool!'

After a pause, nothing being said, I assented.

'Yes,' I said, 'and there's no practical value, except to me personally, in saying anything more. It would ease my mind to tell you what was in it!'

Boyle heard me while I explained my conviction about Hitler and 'the English'.

'That's all very well, from *your* point of view,' said Boyle, in a fatherly way. 'But you forget that you stand for something very significant in the eyes of these Nazis – not that Wenninger, poor chap, is a Nazi, as you well know. They regard you as the Head of European Military Intelligence in this place, with particular regard to air power. They suppose you to be a principal adviser to the Chief of the Air Staff – Head of the Royal Air Force – on matters concerning air warfare in Europe at large. Hence you virtually advise the Government on matters of top policy and hence, they may well suppose, you are likely to know what the Government have in mind, what they are likely to *do*, about war. The fact that the Government has a great muddle in mind is something which the Hun doesn't quite know for certain. Although Hitler hasn't much respect for Chamberlain, I gather from what you say that he probably believes that there is some special logic in the English and that it takes an Englishman – one like you, perhaps? – to understand it and elucidate it.'

I could not have shrunk much smaller.

It was then that I remembered Vachell, our Air Attaché in Berlin, and the irritations I had felt about the credence our own Cabinet

Ministers seemed to place upon reports he had made to our Ambassador there – reports which had been repeated by the Ambassador and circulated with the daily issue of Foreign Office telegrams without my staff having a chance to comment. Vachell's reports were splendid, taken the right way; they showed exactly what Göring and other German air officials wished the British Government to think and believe about the German Air Force; they were excellent resumés of highly important and indicative conversations. But as factual guidance to the truth, they were as misleading as they could be, coming as half-truths from a most dependable observer, Group Captain John Vachell, who was most skilfully permitted to have a good view of half-truths to substantiate what he reported.

It is well-known that the prophet who speaks from a foreign land gains credence more readily than the humdrum Staff adviser at home who happens to know the facts and the trends. What is not so well known is that the man-on-the-spot is often wrong in matters of secret international tactics because of the insidious social and mental conditioning in which he is unconsciously the victim.

Baldwin, as Prime Minister, continually based his utterances about the relative strengths of air forces, Germany's and ours, on erroneous statements from the Embassy in Berlin, rejecting the figures and advice upon trends which my staff provided and which were based on facts of indisputable authority and verification.

This pernicious reliance on what the man-on-the-spot was deceived into saying to his Ambassador, and thence, unchecked, to the Government, caused us in the Air Ministry to campaign for and eventually establish, a branch of the Imperial Defence Committee which came to be called the Joint Intelligence Bureau. In that (new then) entity, all departments concerned could concert facts and derive common beliefs. But the Foreign Office telegram system for purveying hot news and views from the man-on-the-spot still persisted. How pernicious this system was in every respect is still not recognised because it never became generally known that both Mussolini and Hitler, separately, had their own means for knowing, daily, the contents of incoming and outgoing Foreign Office telegrams. That this treacherous trade persisted for two years, unchecked up to the time of which I now write, may be incredible; but that does not alter the truth of it and the explanation it provides of Hitler's quite unmagical yet persistent clairvoyance of British policy and next moves.

But I stray from the dilemma which was confronting me in Boyle's office: the dawning of consciousness that although I might not be a key adviser to the Government of my own country in regard to war and peace, I might have come to be so regarded in the country that was to become our enemy in war.

'In Germany', Boyle went on, 'they are likely to take a great deal of trouble to put really intelligent men in a position like yours ...'

'If they can find them and spare them!' I interjected.

'What I mean is, they know that secret intelligence is of first rate importance and that we have a great reputation in that field. Therefore, they naturally assume that what comes from you, comes from a highly intelligent and well-informed man. It may not be acceptable. It may be deliberately slanted to mislead. But if it suits their book, and fits in with other evidence, they will take it as dependable. If *you* go and tell your friend Wenninger, who trusts you, that a British declaration of war does not necessarily mean that there must immediately be fighting ...'

'But I didn't say that Archie!'

'No, of course you didn't. But that is how he has taken what you *did* say, you may be sure! And that is just what Kesselring is confronting – a fanatical Hitler who half believes, and wants to believe and has been advised by Ribbentrop, at least, for the past three years to believe, that the "effete English" don't want to fight and *won't* when it comes to the point. After all, everything Chamberlain has done – as distinct from what he has said – has tended to confirm that hope and prayer of Hitler – whatever he may once have believed in his heart, if he any longer has one. So when you, from a central point inside the machine, seem to confirm the monstrous presumption, how is it likely to affect Kesselring's final statement on air power probabilities? Remember, he's dealing with a fanatic who has ranged his army and air forces for the destruction of Poland and who means to go ahead with it, knowing that it is bound to succeed!'

Boyle was only telling me what had been wrestling in my own mind for the past two days. Those thoughts had been grappling ineffectually with the equally strongly-based conviction that Hitler was a 'brinkman'. Again and again he had come through a crisis. But this time Hitler seems to have made up his mind to invade Poland and to put that country out of action. He had already accepted Keitel's advice that Germany should not fight a war on two fronts, east and west. Hitler's experience of Chamberlain had convinced him that England would not fight and that France was divided. Consequently France would be relatively easy. Chamberlain might go to the length of making a promise to support Poland but such a promise was only intended to frighten Hitler and he would not be frighted by Chamberlain.

*

I learnt later that Hitler had recalled his Embassy from London because he had already decided to invade Poland as a logical part of his pact with the USSR; his army and air forces had already had their orders.

For that reason any misgivings that Archie Boyle or I may have had about the construction which General Wenninger might have put upon what I had said to him were without significance. Hitler, presumably, neither asked the Acting Ambassador, Kordt, nor Wenninger, whether the English would fight – he knew already that while Chamberlain was Prime Minister they wouldn't. And while there was a risk of war, the Conservative Government would stay in power.

In those two prognostications Hitler was, as usual, correct.

CHAPTER TWO

War Begins at Garston

On 2nd September 1939, the morning after the German Army invaded Poland, Archie Boyle and I converged at downgoing stairs on the third floor of one of the many buildings in which the Air Ministry was then scattered about London. This one was the main one in Whitehall. The scattering was a fortuitous bane: it was not an example of Parkinson's Law and it had no defence purpose. We were recent intruders upon the Home Office. Previously the Air Staff had been in Kingsway, much too far from Whitehall for close co-operation with the Cabinet and the Defence Services. Munich had made that plain. During the past few weeks we had been re-establishing our staffs, above ground and below ground, as fast as we could. The double-floored basement of the building had been reconstructed, under thick concrete, as an intelligence focus and centre for the general direction of air operations. Boyle was on his way there. I was on my way to 'Z' – a secret place in the country.

The ever-genial Boyle and I were both unwontedly burdened. We had armfuls of 'secret' files in their bright pink jackets, and minds full of questions and doubts. The day of decision had arrived and we were mentally at the moment of transition to war. It was surely only a matter of minutes before war would be declared. Poland had been invaded. That was the signal for instant response. What were we waiting for? Presumably for the French Government to act in concert with ours. Or was Chamberlain, I gloomily wondered, going to wriggle out of his solemn pact? Not that I wanted war, nor that I dreaded it: I had not accepted that it was actually going to happen. But the prospect of it *not* happening, then and at once, suddenly became appalling. What if the Prime Minister ratted? The dread that filled me was not of war but of another declaration of 'peace in our time'. Conventional thinking, maybe. Chamberlain's feared alternative – London in moaning, flaming butchered ruins within the hour – was a mental picture that may have been agonizing his mind. It did not enter mine.

Despite his smiles and buoyant manner, I guessed that Boyle, too, was heavy-hearted. Naturally we must as usual affect to be gay and unconcerned. Walking down the stairs, side-by-side with him, I broke the silence by making a derogatory suggestion that Boyle was on the way down to needless bomb-proof cover in the lower basement, in fear of an attack which I had often told him was not going to happen.

'Going down to your funk-hole, Archie?' I asked.

'... and you to your rustic retreat?' he countered. 'Now that you find you're wrong about there being no war, I hear you're making sure you're not going to be in it till it's all over!'

He knew that I must be on my way to a secret place which had no name – and even that enigmatic letter 'Z' was still almost unmentionable.

'Are we going to have a war?' I asked.

Boyle did not reply. We continued down the stairs in silence. At ground-level we parted, I to go to a waiting car to take me to Z, he to the basement intelligence and operations centre.

'Well, have a good war, Archie – if any,' I offered as a parting shot.

It was at Munich-time that Z first came into existence, but only as a shadow. Despite all evidence to the contrary, the cautious presumption was that under the first strike by the German Air Force, the Air Ministry might be destroyed. There must therefore be an auxiliary Air Staff branch of the Air Ministry to continue as a link between the government (if any remained) on the one hand, and the Royal Air Force Commands and their vital resources on the other. I had recently handed over European Air Intelligence and Target Planning to one successor, and only that morning the Rest-of-the-World Air Intelligence to another. Thus I was freed to assume responsibility for bringing Z – the 'shadow' Air Staff – into action.

This mysterious organization was a skeleton intended to be manned by survivors from an about-to-be-wrecked air operations centre in Whitehall – the very building I was quitting as I parted from Boyle. I had had to do the same thing, at the notice of a midnight telephone call, when Munich came to crisis. This time, the notice was shorter but at least I did know the name and location of the place which I had to reach by car, and what to expect to find there. For Z was to be set up once more in the Building Research Establishment, then at Garston, a few miles north of Watford.

I did not know then that the evacuation of London by all its children had been decided upon with two factors in mind, each as unlikely as the other. The first, that the possible primary act of the Germans would be to send their entire first line strength of bombers supported by all their fighters, over London. That was the knock-out blow theory. The second theory was that the effectiveness of that attack would be at least as effective as the Zeppelin attacks had been in World War I. They were the only statistics then available and apparently sixteen casualties were produced by each live bomb dropped. That meant that the casualties resulting from the knock-out blow would be at least three million coming from one attack by the whole of the German air force bombers.

My quiet master and Director, Charles Medhurst, had told me that morning that the Civil Service staff of the Ministry of Works, who then took care of the housing of all the Government departments of State had the administrative arrangements for Z in hand for some time. The Deputy Chief of the Air Staff, Air Marshal Sir Sholto Douglas, who had given me my orders for Z, had told me that he would be coming out later in the day; meanwhile I was to see that everything on the Service side was properly organized. 'And, incidentally, see that they've got me a reasonable billet!' he added, with cheerful menace in his voice.

Sholto Douglas* was one of the ablest, coolest men I have known. Great clarity of mind and independence of thought marked all his Service judgements and actions. If ever his judgement erred more than a little it could have been in regard to his own remarkably powerful metabolism, for he was already showing signs of a future Falstaffian grandeur of figure. Certainly he had excellent judgement of men, wine, and other matters demanding insight and subtle discernment fortified by experience and moral courage. This faculty he applied to air power. He was a spacious man of wide interests and he needed space for living.

I had his needs for *Lebensraum* in mind as I approached Z in that car loaded with files, office things and personal kit. Naturally, I wanted to get rid of my kit first, and so decided to find my allotted billet – and Sholto Douglas's, at least – before I got immersed in administrative botherations. There was bound to be a crop of eviction troubles in the Research Establishment. There had been at 'Munich-time'. When a quiet body of scientist-researchers have to be turned out of their laboratories into the garden, with all their equipment; and when, at the same time a hundred and fifty or so

---

*Air Chief Marshal Lord Douglas of Kirtleside.

strange officers, clerks, radio operators, cooks, Service police, etc., and their equipment, have to be installed in their place, all unprepared and unrehearsed, and all in some state of psychological disturbance or dismay, there are bound to be some queries.

Having identified myself to the civil police and Service armed guard at the gate, I entered the grounds and found a Civil Service official waiting. I wrongly presumed that he had charge of the arrangements for installing 'Shadow' Air Staff under my direction, and for the logistics of the situation: communications, transport, quartering and feeding. In fact, he was an assistant clerical officer with subordinate duties.

'We've taken over the local infants' school for the Raff chaps,' he said, looking at me doubtfully. I was in the uniform of a group captain with four stripes on each cuff and was wearing my 'brass' hat. I was not unconscious of my own authority. My appearance was, I thought, reasonably benign, but I had never looked at people of my sort, dressed like I was, through young civilian eyes. It is true that I thought that this young man would call me 'Sir': indeed, I thought (but did not say) that he *should*. But that slight awareness, however, of shortcoming was lost in the gorge-swelling emotion I felt when I heard that young fellow's collective noun for the men of the Royal Air Force – 'Raff chaps'. I made no comment. Clearly, this young clerk meant no harm, and this was no time for teaching minor etiquette. One must try to be decent. After all, there was a war on, or nearly. There would be worse for us both to bear than minor breaches of conventional manners of deportment. My face probably displayed profound distaste as I asked, 'How many men have arrived?'

'A hundred-and-fifty.'

'Got all their kit with them?'

'Kit?' The clerical officer did not understand.

'Clothes, bedding, messing and cooking equipment,' I prompted.

'Hasn't arrived yet,' the clerical officer replied. He wasn't able to tell me then what I learned later that night, that the railway people had, quite reasonably, sent the whole consignment of barrack furniture and equipment to the only station they had by the name of Garston. It happened to be in one of the suburbs of Liverpool.

I was saying that I would like to go to my billet and get rid of my personal stuff when we were joined by a young officer in flying officer's uniform who saluted. The clerical office said that he had shown 'this chappie' where the officers' billets were, and that he could take me there. I began to fear the worst.

We drove about a mile-and-a-half to the outskirts of Watford where rows of quite superior, identical, semi-detached junior commuters' and artisans' houses presented the ready-made if undistinguished billeting area selected for the thirty Air Staff and Signals officers appointed to Z. These were to be mainly of squadron leader, wing commander rank. Some, more senior. In the allocation of houses as billets, deference had fortuitously been shown to seniority: the list happened to be typed in that sequence. So the Deputy Chief of the Air Staff – Sholto Douglas – was to go into No 1, I was to go into No 3, next door, and so on, down both sides of the road, Very orderly, very simple, but totally unsatisfactory. This whole concept horrified me more than any visualization I had so far conjured up of the supposedly imminent devastation of London which might begin (but in my opinion would certainly *not* begin) to happen within that very hour. I had hitherto not been conscious of my mind boggling at any situation. I think that my state of being then began to enter 'boggledom'.

I knocked at No 3. A pleasant, rather worried woman showed me to the bedroom I was to have. It had a double bed, a washstand, a wardrobe-cum-chest-of-drawers and a chair. All very clean. The pleasant woman said she could do me breakfast with her husband at 6.30 and high-tea at 5.30.

I visited No 1, to see how Sholto Douglas would fare. His room had a double bed, washstand, wardrobe-cum-chest-of-drawers and a chair. All very clean. The pleasant, rather worried women said that she could do breakfast for him at 8.0 and high-tea at 6.30.

Out of curiosity more than interest I visited a few others on the even-numbered side of the road. They were similar except in regard to meal-times which varied depending upon night-shifts, school attendance and whether or not the husband would agree to sit at table with an officer.

We drove away, that flying officer and I, without depositing my kit.

It would be easy to say that I was suffering from an attack of class-conscious snobbery. As a matter of fact, I was suffering acutely from an inferiority feeling. I did not know what to do. I, personally, should have been quite happy to share the accommodation, routine and society of that private household, but none of it was going to be suitable to the circumstances of my job. The officers of Z were to be at Garston to take charge of the war – the war-in-the-air.

That I, personally, did not think that this would happen was beside the point. I was acting under orders. According to the authority for Z, Garston would come into action only after London had been devastated. The German Air Force was then expected to deal similarly with the Port of London and other ports within reach of their bombers. The air war then would be the only war that could be fought in a big way until 'the invasion' began. The fleet would be kept at Scapa, Orkney Isles, or at some remote zone of ocean, 'in being' until the German fleet came out.

As I have said already, I could not believe that any of that was going to happen. After concentrating on the notion that I ought to imagine it all happening; that tomorrow it all *would* have happened, I found that I could not believe that there would be much prospect of Z functioning effectively. But whether or not I could see our little organisation performing miracles of co-ordination, I could not see thirty or forty harassed staff officers in charge of the conduct of the air war amid chaos and havoc, quietly walking to-and-fro daily to share the disrupted bomb-scared lives and war-scare gossip of thirty housewives and their husbands till bedtime. The whole idea seemed to me to be false. The routine of the commuter would not be happening if the knock-out blow really took place.

'What d'you think of that billeting plan?' I asked my young flying officer companion.

'Just like the Civil Service, Sir. Very straight forward and according to the regulations – quite unworkable!' he said; then added, 'I was afraid you'd think I'd fixed it!'

'Well, what *would* you fix?' I asked.

We neither of us knew the answer to that, and I found neither he – nor anyone else at Z – had a large-scale map of the area of which houses of substantial accommodation could be identified. 'Everything', he said, 'had been so secret. Nobody was to know where Z was, or that it was going to be anywhere – or even that it was going to *be*, at all.'

What we needed for billets were nearby houses with telephones – houses capable of quartering half-a-dozen or a dozen officers and providing facilities for their messing together. It dawned on me, then, that the practical thing to do about billeting was not to prepare for the worst, but for the best. To act, in regard to quartering, on the supposition that London would survive.

It happened that I had childhood memories of Garston. Walter Bourne, co-founder of Bourne and Hollingsworth of Oxford Street, lived with his wife and seven children at Garston Manor. I remembered they had extended an already spacious, many-roomed mansion, to include a ballroom and more bedrooms for guests. The Manor had everything that could be desired in the way of convenience, amenity, dignity, seclusion, comfort and proximity to Z. Just where it was, I could not precisely recall. As a child in summer happiness, and as a young midshipman on leave in World War I, I had loved that place, and all that happy, loving family to whom it was home. I was filled with nostalgia at my remembrances of Garston. The Bournes, I knew, had gone long ago.

I stopped the car as we passed a new road-house on the Watford Road, and the two of us went in.

'Who lives at Garston Manor?' I asked the landlord.

'My chief does,' he said.

'Who's that?'

'Why, Mr Benskin himself!'

'Splendid!' said I. 'May I use your telephone?'

'In the box in the hall. Want the number?'

He gave it, and I rang. A lady answered.

'Mrs Benskin?' I began, and gave her my name. 'I'm an old friend of the Bournes. I am just ringing to say that I will be sending an officer in to see you in a few minutes with a list of the names of some senior staff officers who will be coming to stay with you, tonight and until further notice. Will you please say nothing of this until my officer arrives with a note from me?'

'Oh, yes,' Mrs Benskin replied with equanimity, 'but, of course! Perhaps you can't just say about how *many* officers?'

'A dozen,' I hazarded firmly, and added, 'They'll want dinner at about eight, if that is not too inconvenient. You will like them.'

'Thank you,' she replied, 'I'm sure we shall. We will be ready. Do not bother about sending the names now. You must be very busy down there.'

'Thank you very much, Mrs Benskin.' I rang off.

So she knew! Of course, the whole countryside *would*!

My brusqueness was quite uncharacteristic, I hoped – just the outcome of anxiety and haste, not of constitutional bad manners and lack of feeling. Indeed, Mrs Benskin's immediate acceptance, without demur or fussy question, brought tears to my eyes – unseen, I hoped, by the flying officer beside me. It is no ordinary thing to command a woman to give up her home to an invasion of strangers. Instant, unquestioning acceptance created an overwhelming moment. What a woman! What a relief! In fact, that commandeering proved to be a very happy arrangement for all. Trust a brewer's wife to know about hospitality and good fare. But I never met the lady, then – nor have I met her since – to thank her for the way she responded. She was, no doubt, but one of thousands of women with houses great and small who acted thus. That day, I was to meet another whom likewise I remember with gratitude, and also with reverence and awe. Englishmen who had not known such women have not known an essential aspect of the creation of England's greatness.

With a tinge of conscious self-abnegation, I decided that Garston Manor, of which I had such fond memories, should be the Operations Staff's mess. I would have to find another local mansion for the Intelligence Staff, which was more numerous. There was no time for all this, but I must make it, somehow.

'I remember,' I said to the Benskin landlord, when I got back into the bar, 'a big abbey sort of a house in lovely grounds somewhere nearby – over there?' I pointed, interrogatively.

'That's the Lady Knutsford's place. More over *there*, beyond the trees,' he said, correcting my direction.

Lord Knutsford had been the great champion of the London Hospital in the day when public hospitals were kept going by private charity: he raised millions. He was the prototype of the then flourishing trade of charity money-raising. But he did it for love. The landlord told me of his death, not long back.

We returned to Z.

I sent the flying officer over to the Manor, with a list of names of officers who were to be the Benskin guests. (Before long, all on that list were to become well-known names as commanders in war.) Then I walked down the branch lane, the other way, about a quarter of-a-mile, to Munden Park, and asked for the lady of the house. The fact that she had recently lost her husband was a consideration I had weighed and discarded.

An old lady, and grey, she came towards me in questioning, smiling dignity as she moved over a marble floor strewn with Persian rugs. Her hand extended to me, she said, 'I believe you have come to ask me to do something for you? What is it to be?' Her face was sad but yet bright and kind.

'Well, Lady Knutsford,' I said, after introducing myself, 'I want to ask if I may see any accommodation you are not using, and whether it would be reasonable to present you with a billeting order for a bunch of officers.'

This lovely old châtelaine then led me through a number of rooms, upstairs and down, each with the dignity and spaciousness of a civilisation now menaced with sudden destruction while already quietly dying of taxation.

'You must take your pick,' she said. 'My old butler will help to take care of you, but my other men are all gone or going to the war – territorials and reservists. Try not to make it more than ten of you,' she added, 'for I fear that our things will not go round. You see, you are not the only invaders. This afternoon I am to receive fifty children from East London homes, and a number of school teachers.' She spoke without emotion, as though such an event was an ordinary happening. 'The evacuation of London, I have just been told, has begun. I don't quite know where we shall put them all. But we will manage!'

The evacuation of London! I had forgotten. Perhaps that was why Chamberlain was holding fire – not willing to bring down 'fire and brimstone' on London until its many thousands of children were clear.

Four of us only dined at Munden Park that night. All that afternoon and evening we had been setting up our 'shadow Air Ministry'. We would be going on with the job all night. By the following morning we had it in some sort of working order. We then became, as it were, a spare wheel; mounted and running as a fifth wheel to the coach. All the 'war' transactions of the Air Staff in Whitehall had to be repeated to Z and studied there so that at any moment we could, in some fashion, assume their executive role.

On that Sunday morning, our first morning at Z, the BBC announced that the Prime Minister was to speak at noon. What he was to announce was not declared. We had our own hopes and fears, but few had doubts. At breakfast time, the old lady invited her airmen guests to listen with her. When I returned for the fatal broadcast, I met her walking back from the village church.

We listened to Neville Chamberlain wearily, for what seemed like half an hour, wrestling with recent history in Europe, telling us and the listening world of the ordeal of his government's failure to arrest the progress of an obsessed madman. At last, he came to the dreaded end – dreadful whatever it might be. It was that this country and Germany were, once more, at war.

No sooner had Chamberlain ended speaking than we heard a known but unfamiliar sound – the moaning wail of air raid sirens.

That eerie sound was not coming over the country air through the trees from Watford; it was generated right within that quiet room; within the radio set. The melancholy, wavering vibrations were being transmitted, as had been the Prime Minister's sombre words, through the Prime Minister's own microphone in No 10 Downing Street, but fortuitously; the wailing siren was in Whitehall.

Old Lady Knutsford looked wanly at me and said, 'At least the Germans let Mr Chamberlain finish what he was saying!' She folded her hands in her lap and waited. The radio remained silent. Then she rose. 'Let us have a glass of sherry,' she said.

The anticlimax was not long in coming. The Duty Staff Officer at Z telephoned that he had spoken to his opposite number in the Air Ministry. The cause of the alarm was, as everyone else was to know, an Imperial Airways liner unexpectedly coming in by an unusual route from over the Thames Estuary.

Historically, that alarm was the first ever to be signalled in response to a radio-pulse echo from an aircraft believed to be a raiding enemy. Many months were to pass before anyone was allowed publicly to admit that such an air-raid detection system as 'Radio Direction Finding' had been brought effectively to our protection during the post-Munich period.

During that night we were awakened by the wailing of the Watford sirens. I offered the old châtelaine, through her bedroom door, escort to the basement. She bade me regard her not as cowardly but lazy, and to go below on her behalf and tell the assembled people there what to think about.

I did that, and the cook brought in urns of tea and cups for more than sixty of us. When I met our hostess next morning I congratulated her on the splendid air-raid accommodation and underground catering, and remarked that her household of Londoners looked to be more than fifty young people.

'Yes', said Lady Knutsford, 'by mistake, the Home Office and the London County Council sent me two lots. But we shall manage.'

CHAPTER THREE

Introducing Violet

My only experience of squadron command in war operations had been in Iraq, then eight years back. That was a war against insurgent Kurdish riflemen on horseback, in support of the Iraqi army. That was typical of Service life; no sooner had one become a bit of an expert in something than you were sent off, at a moment's notice to hold responsibility for lives or actions in new circumstances right outside your experience.

So, when on that bright Sunday morning I was suddenly told on the telephone that I was to go at once and take staff charge of the operations of the Royal Air Force with the army then on the move to France, I had a moment of surprised elation followed by an awareness of unpreparedness, not to say incompetence. For I was to be virtually Chief of Staff to a Commander unnamed, whom for certain I did not know. I was told that his title was Air Officer Commanding, Royal Air Force Component, British Expeditionary Force. I wondered why he had picked on me, whoever he was, or if he had.

My orders were to report to Air Headquarters, RAF Component, BEF; where that formation might then be located the message to me did not say. I at once dropped my role of understudy to the Air Staff and hastily packed.

Now that the prospect of war in France had come as an actuality I regarded it with both excitement and dread. Excitement naturally; dread because I knew that success on land would follow success in the air and that the French Air Force was no match for the Luftwaffe in any single aspect. There may, too, have been a more personal dread. As a very young man in World War I, I had been in the local background of the carnage and mire of the Battle of the Somme which went on and on, from the end of June to the middle of November, to back up the French who were then confronting the nearly victorious Germans at Verdun. War in France was not a glamorous memory for me. All the same, I was certain about the final outcome of this war and I believed Hitler to be uncertain in his own mind for the reason already given.

I guessed that my new boss was to be Air Vice-Marshal Charles Blount (pronounced Blunt). His reputation was in keeping with his name – Charles for charming, Blount for what that name meant. For I was aware that he had latterly been commanding No 22 Group – the Army Co-operation Group of Lysander squadrons dotted about England, near army bases.

My immediate concern was to get to the right place quickly. The question was, what was the geographical name of the right place? Drawing a bow at a venture, I decided to ring Charles Blount and ask him whether he was expecting me to come to him. If so, perhaps without breach of security he could tell me when and where he wanted me to come. This worked. Blount said, 'Yes. Come to Farnborough in two hours' time, or sooner if you can.' He added with an unexpected warmth in his voice, that he would be delighted to have me. Charming but unlikely, I thought. I did not then know that already he had made his plan for my future employment.

My thoughts as I drove to Farnborough were mixed. There was a problem. I knew why, despite earlier determination to the contrary, we were after all sending an expeditionary force of two corps to France which was pretty well all we could then muster. I had also gathered that if possible it was eventually to be built up to an army of three corps. Up to a few short months ago such a project had not been on the cards: it had been specifically ruled out. Previously it had been agreed by the French and British cabinets that the role of the French Army would be to hold the elaborately fortified Maginot Line and that the British contribution to that role would be limited to a Royal Air Force striking force of three wings and twelve squadrons and a mere two army divisions. Bomber Command was to despatch their group of twelve Light Bomber Squadrons to be based behind the French Army in an area centred on Rheims. For those particular squadrons to be of any effect against a German invasion of France, they would necessarily have to be based in France: they had not the range otherwise to reach targets in Germany.

There was no agreement with Belgium or Holland. Our only other, and very recent, commitment then was to support Poland.

The British Army's task, it had been agreed, was limited to home defence against German invasion of the United Kingdom. The Army was to remain in readiness to meet that invasion which was expected to follow a German seizure of the Channel ports. The Belgian Army was not expected to hold the German Army at bay.

It should be remembered that at the time that agreement was made the German Air Force greatly exceeded the strength of the French and British Air Forces combined. Which way the Italians might jump was a material factor but was not likely to be a decisive one: theirs, we knew, was a shop-window air force.

Although an Eastern Front had been envisaged when this agreement had been reached early in 1939 there had been no question then of Poland being involved nor was the Russo-German Pact then perpetrated.

After this arrangement had already been reached between the French and English Governments, that cunning little German Minister of Public Englightenment, Goebbels, briefed by Hitler, had been declaring for French ears that the British were prepared to fight to the last Frenchman. Goebbels' gibe soon achieved the desired result. It had run rapidly through an already frightened France, precipitating political agitation. The popular argument ran as follows: to make sure that Great Britain came into the war at all the French people knew instinctively that it was imperative that English blood should be spilt on French soil at the outset. This meant not airmen of the Air Striking Force but more soldiers. Fresh inter-governmental talks were then instituted in March and the United Kingdom Cabinet after much deliberation, finally ordered the Chiefs of Staff to prepare physically to send an army of two corps to France on the outbreak of war.

For such a force of two corps, the Army would receive an initial allocation of air forces of two wings, each of three army co-operation squadrons, and two wings of two squadrons of fighters.* There was also to be a wing of two long-range reconnaissance squadrons and a communications squadron. This made thirteen squadrons in all plus headquarters, depots and ancillary units – all to go to France.

In August 1939 the war plan for the Air Force held almost nothing in reserve for a commitment to an army-in-the-field – in short, a BEF. The one army co-operation group, not being a part of the three main commands, was available for action – but in England not France. It was not on a fully mobile war footing; it was

---

*In the event, only Nos 85 and 87 Squadrons left for France in September to join the Air Component, although other fighter squadrons joined the Advanced Air Striking Forces. It was not until November that two Gladiator squadrons joined us, Nos 607 and 615.

intended to be a training organisation rather than a fighting one until invasion should loom. It stood low in priority, if not lowest.

The Air Force, struggling with its own expansion, was hopelessly over-stretched. Air defence had priority of claim but the single command of the Air Defence of Great Britain had gone – chiefly for lack of trained staff officers. Thus, the Air Ministry had once more to co-ordinate the three operational commands at home – bomber, fighter and coastal commands.

I arrived at Farnborough sooner than I, or anyone else, thought possible. It was stimulating to be on historic Air Force territory again. The old Headquarters of 22 Group is better known now as a sky-line feature to Farnborough Air Display millions. It is that pleasant collection of red-roofed bungalow buildings on the low hill which stands near the north-eastern end of a most famous runway. Now, that two-mile tract lies like a sword across Laffan's Plain. Then, it was still the unsophisticated grassy home of British military aeronautics, a private land of hope and glory. This hill was the 'nursery slope' where Colonel Cody – American turned English – prepared for his first take-off in the first British military aeroplane. Farnborough, one-time base of the Balloon Battalion of the Royal Engineers, was the very home and centre of army aviation; it was a place of pioneering and of tradition.

I went straight to Blount's office, knocked and walked in. The entry was mistimed. I almost walked into a strange-looking brigadier whose battered sponge-bag of a peaked-cap was over his ears. Startled, he turned sharply round as I entered. The inertia of his heavy peaked-cap caused it to continue to point towards Blount while his face was coming my way, Then, off it fell, revealing a pink head less adhesive than it was when that peaked-cap first came into use.

The distracted owner of the cap was evidently in full spate of protest to the AOC (whom I had not yet properly seen, let alone saluted). As he stepped to retrieve the headdress, he continued to protest his case. Alas, his dental equipment was as insecure within his head as his cap had been upon it. The top plate struck the floor as it fell and bounced to rest upon the cap. As though accustomed to such untowardness, the indignant man grabbed his teeth with his right hand and the cap with his left, in which he was already holding a short, stubby cane.

Embarrassed much less than were his spell-bound observers, but determinedly Servicelike in his imperturbability over minor accidents, the departing brigadier tucked both cap and cane under his left arm and fell silent. Facing Blount for the last time he brought beside his bald head a clenched right hand to the salute, then he turned to the door, crammed into his mouth what that hand concealed and reached for the door-handle. It was, however, I who let him out. For that service he vainly tried to thank me, his jaw moving up and down, while two rows of teeth rested in detachment in the skull-like smile of death.

There was a long silence in the room. Servicelike we stood our ground, composed. This was an occasion; I was meeting Charles Blount – my AOC – and Ben Capel, both for the first time officially. The occasion was grave and urgent; I collected myself into a salute. That broke the spell. We laughed a little, wickedly but sadly, and the meeting lost its grim formality. Blount said, 'Poor devil! He hadn't seen an aeroplane to touch, or an airman to speak to, for over twenty years. He knew nothing about army co-operation!'

'I suppose, Sir, you don't think I know very much more,' I said.

'Well, no, I don't,' Charles Blount replied, 'but at least you *look* as though you did. And now I must tell you straightaway that I am making Ben Capel, here, my SASO, and you'll be AOA. You'll find that work, administration, much more up your street.'*

'SOA, surely!' I countered, emphasising the first letter.

'How d'you mean?' asked Blount. 'Oh, you mean that you are not an air commodore and therefore you can't be called *Air* Officer in Charge of Administration.' He mused a moment, then added,

---

*The SASO's job was to help the AOC to look after the fighting. He thus had under him the Operations Staff, the Intelligence Staff and the Cypher Staff. Together they formed the Air Staff and that explains the title he was given of Senior Air Staff Officer. The Signals branch of the RAF provided the 'service' of signals and received its orders mainly from the SASO; it comprised radio and telecommunications; the latter contained plain language R/T and morse code W/T.

The job of the Air Officer i/c Administration (AOA) was to relieve the AOC of all the work of administration so that the Air Officer Commanding (AOC) could give his maximum attention to fighting the battle in the air through the air staff. Thus the AOA was established to be an air officer of at least air commodore rank and senior to the SASO. He had under him the Organisation Staff, the Personnel Staff and the Armament Staff, the Engineering Staff and the Equipment Staff (the last three last mentioned staffs have now been included in the Engineering Staff) and the following services: medical, chaplains, works and buildings, rations and catering, RAF police and land and air transport.

The reason for the SASO being an air commodore and the AOA being a group captain and thus only an SOA is explained in this chapter.

The author.

General Lord Gort, VC, Commander-in-Chief, British Expeditionary Force, France, with (on right) his Chief of Staff, Lieutenant-General Sir Henry Pownall.

decisively, 'No, I'm not going to have you as *Staff Officer* in Charge of Administration. It will be an important part of your job, sometimes, to tell generals where they get off. You'll be *A* – my AOA; let's say no more on that! So far as I'm concerned you *are* an air officer. Don't let's bother with words. AOA you'll call yourself. I'm glad to have you.'

Then he had an afterthought. 'Oh – on the subject of words, I need hardly say that this whole operation is to be treated as secret. I can't tell you any facts about dates, yet. One extraordinary fact I have just learned from the Army's Movement Tables, not issued, is that from the moment we leave here all units take code-names. Ours is Violet, of all things. I s'ppose it's one better than Buttercup or Daisy – but really – having to go to war with a name like that. I suppose we'll get used to it.' He seemed more amused than injured by the epithet. Capel muttered that the name was wet.

Then Blount pressed the bell-button on his desk and said, 'Thank you. My PA will take you to your room.'

My joining interview was over.

Charles Blount, impetuous, brisk, was laughingly determined not to keep the rules nor to obey the Air Ministry in this 'small matter' of my appointment which had, in fact, already loomed too large. So I began my apprenticeship in administration of Air Forces deemed to be 'in the field'; I began under a false title which I continued to use for the ensuing six months. I expect a good number of folk who care about such things – as indeed, I did – wondered at my brazenness in styling myself Air Officer in Charge Administration when I did not hold the rank which that long title signifies.

The officers appointed to fill the 'establishment' of my administrative staff were in several cases, I soon found, like me, without experience in army co-operation. This was a strange way of forming an AOC's headquarters and a strange order in which to move to battle. Fortunately, fighting in France seemed still not to have begun.

On the very next day, I managed to rob my old staffs, both at Z and at the Air Ministry, of two experienced 'army co-operators', one of whom was the calm and capable Wing Commander Donald Hardman who proved to be my teacher, guide and salvation. The other was Wing Commander Claud Pelly who went to the Air Staff as Head of Intelligence and kept me informed of the Air Staff's intentions.

I was as curious as you must have been. What in the world can have been going on when I entered the AOC's office?

Well, I have already explained that the Air Force in 1939 was hopelessly over-stretched. Thus when it came about that the war plan was drastically changed a certain once-famous officer of World War I was appointed by the Air Ministry secretly and unknown to Charles Blount or to the officer concerned, to be Senior Staff Officer (SASO) in the headquarters of the Air Component of the Expeditionary Force. In that eleventh-hour preparation of an Air Headquarters for a previously unscheduled expeditionary force there had been no time to find out whether officers in the Reserve List of Group Captains were, in fact, the men they once were.

This particular officer, at the age of twenty-one, had a superb record as a fighter and a commander; he was holding the rank of acting brigadier-general in the RFC. To be a general at twenty-one was phenomenal. But, when, twenty-one years later, this same man turned up at Farnborough, he was found to be phenomenal in less effective ways. His flame had died, and his frame had withered with his fame. No flair for his task; shrunken in his khaki uniform of World War I and carrying the red tabs of a brigadier-general, he was unaware that twenty years previously the title, brigadier-*general* had been abolished in the Army; he was unaware, too, that Army rank titles could no longer be used by Air Force officers.

Nothing would persuade this one-time gallant warrior to accept the fact that he was rated not as a general, but as a group captain and that the appropriate dress was a blue uniform with four stripes on the cuffs. This was a pathetic situation for all concerned; clearly the man should not be where he was. But so frantically was our small service stretched that Charles Blount was told by the Member of the Air Council for Personnel to make the best use he could of the man.

So the painful farce continued amid the stress of mobilizing, for embarkation and for battle, a force of squadrons which themselves had instantly to be replaced by new squadrons for the training of new army formations. After a few more days of inappropriate and unconstructive explosions by and around the superannuated hero, it was decided that Z could be robbed of me. Hence my sudden posting and Blount's fulfilment of the threat he had given to the Member of the Air Council for Personnel. While I was on the way, Blount told Air Commodore Capel, his Air Officer in Charge of Administration, that he (Capel) should become SASO and take over the air staff at once and that I, on arrival, should take his post of Air

Officer of Administration – AOA.

What I had intruded upon, when I burst into Charles Blount's office, was the final interview of the AOC with his unwanted SASO. What the man's name was I never discovered. Nor did I try. But it was a sad though laughable situation.

CHAPTER FOUR

The Obstacle Race

Not many hours later I was flying to France over a stretch of stippled azure, bright as the clear sky above. I had a feeling of holiday, so peaceful did the Channel Isles appear, the coast of France so reminiscent of past holidays. My destination was Le Mans. No likely starting point for anything except a motor race and – though I did not know it then – that was what it was, in a sense, to be.

My excursion with Donald Hardman was for the purpose of joining the C-in-C's Movements staff. (General Lord Gort had been glad to give up his post as Chief of the Imperial General Staff to become C-in-C of the BEF in France.) The Movements' task was to move a British Expeditionary Force of two corps and an Air Component Force by road and rail from the Atlantic coast of Brittany to the traditional English battlegrounds of Normandy, nearly 400 miles away, and Donald Hardman and I were to look after the Air Component. The motor race which we were to be organising might become a contest with the German Army to secure the French hinterland of the English Channel and its vital ports – an event which might end in a bloody land-battle if it was not frustrated by air devastation while the race was still in progress. I, personally, did not believe we should have any interference by the Germans; they were concentrating on the Poles.

Since 1066 – indeed, before that in Roman times – the logistics of the Channel crossing had always loomed larger in military speculation than the tactics of fighting when invasion was complete. On this occasion, for the first time, the British plan for invasion of the Continent had disregarded all possibility of employing the narrow sea ports of Calais, Boulogne and even Le Havre, because of German air power.

Although we had knowledge that the German High Command was thoroughly imbued with the need to avoid being forced to engage in war on two fronts simultaneously – west and east – this had not been allowed to affect Movements staff's plans. It was, however, for that reason, of course, that the High Command in Germany had insisted upon that unlikely pact with the USSR; it was to ensure inaction by the USSR, and consequently by France, while Poland was being destroyed.

But we had no knowledge that the German General Staff already well knew the Anglo-French plan. Two days before the invasion of Poland began (which was after the Movements staff had had their plan agreed) Archie Boyle had told me of the arrest of two clerks in the Foreign Office whose sole job was to duplicate for circulation all the incoming and outgoing Foreign Office telegrams. Those telegrams were full of information and intentions. I used to receive copies of them daily. So also did one or other of two porters in the German Embassy. No wonder Hitler had such uncanny insight into Anglo-French mentality and intention. That arrangement had been going on for years, without detection.

When we landed on the race course at Le Mans I knew that we were to go to a place which would be secretly indicated on traffic road signs about the town. Eventually, after following successive '403' pointers, we found the last one on the door of the *Mairie* – the Town Hall. Spacious and dignified was that building, but lacking any furniture with four legs and having only two telephones.

The Movements plan which had been hastily but meticulously prepared in Whitehall before the USSR pact with Germany was published, entailed transplanting some thousands of separately listed and dispersed units and military formations. They were to move from a hundred or so different starting points in the United Kingdom and Northern Ireland, through five major ports between Southampton and Glasgow, through three major ports on the Atlantic coast of France – Brest, Nantes, St Nazaire. Thence they were to travel by west-to-east roads and railways spreading over 25,000 square miles of Northern France, to areas in Normandy that none could with certainty define. This lack of definition of journeys' endings was in the very nature of the case inevitable, for who might say where the land-battle would be raging by the time the British Army arrived on the scene?

In the view of the planners, the British Army could not expect to join up alongside the French in the battle zone – wherever that might be – before the German Army joined the French in actual battle. For that reason the leading formations of the BEF were planned to move in the wrong order for logistics, in the right order for battle; that is, fighting formations first, administrative formations after. It was not at all convenient for the Army to move like that, but since the enemy might be met in a headlong clash at any moment, the fighting feelers – the armoured car formations – must be in the forefront from the start. If it was difficult for the Army to make a long movement like that in the wrong order for administration, it was much more difficult for the Air Force squadrons moving with them. Then, all major movements and supplies for soldiers and airmen alike were sea-borne and groundborne. Airborne forces were not included in our Expeditionary Force for the simple reason that they did not exist then in quantity. But German airborne forces were already spearheading the swift conquest of Poland.

Neither Hardman nor I had seen the Movements plan for the BEF. But we were content that it existed and that it included the ground echelons of the Air Component which had been duly moved to ports and embarked. So secret was the plan that its schedules of movements, cryptographically expressed in a series of coded timetables related to a secret zero hour, had been in few hands outside the Movements staff of the War Office where it had been evolved. Indeed, I gathered that almost no one actually to be moved in accordance with that plan had seen it before becoming immersed in the flow of it. And there was good reason for the road movement in France being by night only, without lights. By the morning all units in the Movement Order, who were moving by road in France, had to be under cover.

Every unit in that plan had a code name. Every port, town, and village had a number. Every road and railway was disguised in a cipher. The whole system was unsystematised by being split into many sections. Thus the code indices had to be separately secret, and sparingly issued to the Movements officers who would take station on the various routes. They alone would be able to check the units as they moved through advising them as to where they were to go on the next stage. Adjusting their position or rerouting them according to requirement or emergency.

Knowing one's destination on that move was not just a problem; it was an impossibility. Consequently no one knew his destination – neither by geographical code names nor by name. While the move was in full progress General Gort was with the Grand Quartier Général of the French Army (GQG) awaiting final confirmation about where precisely the British Army should go.

Indeed, the planners did do a very great deal to prevent the enemy from discerning what the plan was or meant should they be able to get a copy of it hot from the printers, for the key to the code names and cipher numbers was printed elsewhere. Without the key, the Movements schedules were incomprehensible. They were nearly incomprehensible to the British officers who had to use them, even with the key.

Despite its difficulties, the plan would have worked like clockwork but for several typically French adverse factors. These had effects as disconcerting as German bombers might have achieved had they participated in the operation. For the French also had their own precautions for security. These had, perhaps over-cautiously, been kept to themselves. By edict it had been required that, on the outbreak of war, all signposts and place-names should be removed in the areas likely to be invaded. This affected the greater part of the movement area; in fact, we became the actual invaders.

Another measure issued by the French Government was intended to frustrate the 'Fifth Column' of enemy informers known to be operating throughout the country. It was an *ordnance* by the police and post office authorities which required that all telephone conversations must be conducted exclusively in the French language. Telephone operators who were unable to understand what was being said by telephone users were immediately to disconnect – to *couper* – any conversation. These two measures proved to be, each in its own way, a marvellous hindrance to every British column, although probably not to the Fifth Column observers.

Another French safeguard of a different kind was the mobilizing in Brittany of a whole French army. As our forces began to arrive in the west of France, GQG decided to move that army (then in reserve) from Brittany to a region south-west of Paris, by rail and road. This quite stupendous movement of an army took place, employing all possible routes diagonally across railways and roads allocated to the British Army. Consequently, the promised increment of at least twenty telephone lines to the Town Hall at Le Mans for the use of the British Advance GHQ failed to materialise.

For about fifty staff officers all with urgent things to see to we had *two* telephones. One of these two lines we agreed to use for only outgoing calls, and for this we would stand in a queue giving way to reasonable priorities' claims only. The other telephone we used for incoming calls. To meet the extra burden which would fall upon the Le Mans exchange by reason of our extra twenty lines, the French operators were to be reinforced, as soon as they could be got there by what they called 'English Tommies' of the Signals Corps. The foreign language ban would then be put in abeyance so far as they were concerned. But there would be no guarantee that any telephone conversation would ever be permitted to clear any difficulty before the circuit was cut. As I think of this situation after all these years there creeps over me a feeling of paralysis. I am loth to strain credulity, still more to revive pains long forgotten, but my story demands the inclusion of some reminiscence of Le Mans telephony. Imagine me, then, awaiting the coming through of a call booked an hour before to my linkman, Bob Musgrave-Whitham, in the Air Ministry.

The bell rings. I am sitting on the only chair by the only table, supporting the only telephone in a large room with a queue of waiting staff officers behind me, all of whom are awaiting calls. The one that comes through happens to be mine.

English Operator: Your Air Ministry call, Sir. Speak up!
Me: Bob? . . . Oh, he's out, is he? . . . George Stanton. Goddard, here. You know what Bob wanted to know from me about unit Cockchafer. No – chafer! Well tell him . . .
French Operator: Parlez Français, ou je coupe!
Me: En bien. Pardon. Je parle à Londres . . . George, écoute! Il faut parler Français. Unit Hanneton.
Sqn Ldr Stanton: Yes, I've got that, Sir, Unit *Hanneton*.
Me: Hell! The blighter's cut us off!
Intruder: Are you Advanced GHQ?
Me: *(Horrified at the breach of security)* Well, steady on!
Intruder: Well *are* you? Speak up!
Me: *(Nettled)* This is the outgoing line. I was talking to the Air Ministry.
Intruder: Blast that! What are you? For Heaven's sake, get me someone who will *do* something!
Me: Tell me *who* you want and *what* you want.
Intruder: Look, I'm Brigadier Jackson, commanding 'Honeybee'. I am supposed to be on route 217 approaching town 6291, I would like to know precisely where my General has got to. Last night my outfit was cut in half by a Frog column of ancient armoured cars and horse transport that went streaming through for an hour and a half, bound for God knows where. I tried again in daylight today but again got foiled by the French Army. I am speaking from an *estaminet*, the

	number seems to be CRO IT 27. Get some one to ring my GOC wherever he may be (he's on another route) and tell him I can't get through short of opening fire. No one speaks any known language here. Their French is rotten. Can't understand a word of it.
Me:	You say you're Honeybee on route 217 approaching...
French Operator:	Il faut parler Français seulement. Je coupe!

And he did, much to my relief, But I reported all that he had said to the appropriate army staff officer. Some conversations may have been more usefully productive than that one. I cannot recall that any of mine were.

On the third day and night of this pantomime, I flew back to Farnborough to find out what was going on in France, and learned that we had been allotted twelve airfields, all unknown except in regard to their position on the map. I flew to have a look at them from the air and found that some squadrons were already on the ground, aircraft dispersed, camouflage netting on. None of the fields had any hangars; not one was a properly prepared airfield with resources laid on. They were not even of grass turf, but of clover! After a day of rain, they would be unusable. No supplies of any kind were yet available. The Air Force was certainly ahead of the Army but to no useful purpose.

I flew back to Le Mans.

By then, the Army staff at Le Mans knew the general destination of the army. It was to move to an area surrounding Arras with a front on the Belgian frontier near Lille, with the French Seventh Army on the left flank, and the French First Army on the right.

As I looked at the map upon which the deployment of our army was set out I discovered that not one single one of the airfields allotted to the Air Component of the BEF was in the area allocated to the British Army and I recognised the military and administrative implications of this anomaly. None of the units for whose administration I was to be responsible would be accessible to any of the British Army systems of supply and maintenance services. This was a nightmare situation. The Army was responsible for supplying all the common needs of the whole of the BEF including some of our more uncommon needs. Pay, rations, petrol, oil, fuel of all kinds from high octane aviation fuel to firewood; works services, tentage, quartering, canteens, postal services, billeting, furniture, kitchen equipment, stationery and all kinds of consumable stores – for all those things the squadrons and units of the Air Component attached to an army in the field were to be entirely dependent upon the Army. In those respects our Army was our foster-mother. It was their job also to provide anti-aircraft protection as well as ground defences, and the security and provost services were theirs too. In all those respects the Army was our foster-father.

Feeling like Alice needing consultation with the Red Queen, I sought a high master. The very man I needed had just arrived on a flying visit: the QMG. I went to him and told him that he would be sorry to hear that all our airfields were outside the BEF area. He replied cheerfully that I could not have given him better news. That would be a great load off his mind. I would have to get French Army rations for all my people. 'They'll give you' he said – much relieved to have something to joke about – '*vin très ordinaire*!'

'But seriously, Sir,' I said, 'what about pay for the men, quartering, billeting? What about works services, hangars, dug-outs? What about fuel, ammunition, defence? Everything? All we have got for the squadrons beside the aircraft and crews, are some spare parts, some technical maintenance personnel and their kits, some doctors, a few chaplains, and an assortment of staff officers and clerks for a variety of headquarters, parks, and depots and so on. I don't yet know the numbers but I suppose that we shall have about ten thousand mouths to feed, bodies to house, hands to pay – not to mention the aeroplanes. For them, we shall have an enormous amount of construction to do . . .'

'Yes, Goddard, it *is* serious,' the QMG replied, cutting me short. 'I'm very sorry about your plight. I don't know *what* you'll do. There's absolutely nothing I can do for you, once your people are out of our area. As for works services with Sappers, there'll be nothing doing at all. I can't give you a man. The French have a Maginot Line of forts up to the point where France meets Belgium. On the Belgian frontier there's nothing but a ditch. Every Sapper we can lay hands on is going to be employed in constructing a Maginot Line of our own – of sorts. I'm afraid you'll have to fend for yourselves. Sorry!'

At that point I rather lost my temper with the QMC. 'But you must represent to General Gort that the French should provide airfields for the Air Component within the BEF zone.' And I vividly remember QMG's somewhat withering reply.

'*Must*, Goddard? You know perfectly well what the book says.' (He was referring to the *War Manual for Air Forces co-operating with the Army*, which, years ago, I had had a hand in writing.) 'It says that the Air Component of a field force will be located exclusively in the administrative area of an Army force in the field and that any unit of the Air Force not so located is an administrative responsibility of the Air Force. I appreciate your position, but don't talk to me about *must*! I know what I must not! If you can't cope, you must tell Charles Blount. It's not for me to fight your battle. I've got enough troubles of my own. But I will stretch a point. I can fix for you to have a much bigger imprest account than you normally would have. Even without francs you'll get the French to do a lot for you if you ask them nicely. It's their war as much as ours. Only, don't tell them they must!'

That is roughly what the General said, and he was right. He could not have said or done better. But he left me with, again, that feeling of creeping paralysis which after a while gave way to my built-in optimism.

This Movements Plan, as I have already said, was made before the Nazi regime in Germany had made their outrageous pact with Russia allowing both parties to the pact to deal with Poland first. Nazi Germany never had any intention of interfering with the British Movement into France, but the Army plan had to allow for that interference. Fortunately, the Movements Plan did allow for unforeseen delays. Fortunately, regimental officers disregarded the prohibition which the Movements Plan had put on daylight moves by road. So, though it was a long way round, we all managed to get to the end of our journeys on time. Fortunately, too, for the squadrons of the Air Component, the French unit commanders nearest to our own airfields showed generosity and compassion to our squadrons. Fortunately, again, our squadrons liked French rations and their *vin ordinaire,* and our aeroplanes liked the French/Arabian petrol and oil which they drank up happily. So all was well, in the end, and what is more, there was no war.

*

If resourcefulness is an English characteristic, that may largely be because of the contradiction it implies; it is a quality which has no scope, virtue or reality except when a man is apparently destitute of the resources which a situation demands. Resourcefulness develops out of habitual resource-emptiness. This is historically and typically English in matters of conquest and war. For want of the proper resources, the air units of the BEF were compelled to exploit every makeshift they could devise for themselves. No miracle of organisation or of procurement was to be expected from an air force administrative staff cut off from all its expected army sources of supply.

My little office in Maroeuil near Arras and GHQ became a mecca for every senior malcontent holding responsibility for providing impracticable services: medical, pay, quartering, equipment, fuel, rations, signals, transport and works services. Having blown off steam and found no prospect of remedy through me, they found elsewhere the means for achieving the impossible – that is to say, within themselves, in their enterprising subordinates and in the scattered units for which they held staff responsibility. Regulation-bound by habit as they all had been, they suddenly recognised that regulations mainly existed only to regulate fools. With the minimum of by-your-leave and the maximum of urgency, they acquired all kinds of quarters, buildings, châteaux, facilities, credits and indigenous services.

Having no creative 'works' staff of our own, Donald Hardman purloined one rather small Sapper captain with a motorbike who galvanized French local contractors into all kinds of constructional activities in a hundred different locations. Having no proper airfields and no prospect of any being built for us by the Army or by French contractors – for airfields with runways are colossal undertakings – we had to make do with the soggy clover fields we had been given.

After a few weeks, we achieved a lucky gift from the Army in the shape of a Territorial Sapper brigadier – Appleyard, by name – who had just come from being chief engineer in a famous road-construction firm. He undertook to make twenty new airfields for us by the end of spring. That was a long way ahead: it might be too late, but we were beginning to assume that the French preferred to remain in winter quarters behind their Maginot Line and that Hitler certainly preferred to have time to secure his position in the east before becoming committed to full-scale war in the west.

Appleyard went over to London and called on the managing directors of five well-known road-construction contractors and told them what he wanted: namely, five completely equipped airfield-construction companies. Each company was to carry the name of its own firm. Each firm was to equip its company completely with all the paraphernalia for major earthmoving, road construction and living accommodation. They were, in fact, immediately to produce five little private armies. Appleyard undertook to provide the uniforms, the NCO's stripes, the officers' commissions and the shipping to carry the battalion over the water in ten days time. The contractors had to do the rest.

I cite Appleyard as a major example of the kind of universal resourcefulness which gradually transformed hard impossibility through hard imagining into hard reality while Flanders, that winter, froze the hardest of all.

The great road constructors formed their volunteer companies and put them into uniforms. The foremen had sergeants' stripes, the charge hands were corporals, the managers were captains and the directors who came were majors. That was Appleyard's arrangement. They got their pay. Over they came to France, and built their own hutted camps, set to work – soldiers and navvies too – on soggy tracts of farmland, soon to become iron in the bitter freeze.

When spring came, half-a-million tons of concrete had set in broad runways. Thousands of acres of flat ploughland fields had been transformed into great areas of rolled grassland whose green carpeting had grown out of four thousand tons of seed shipped from all over the world, and so the Air Component of the Army was in virtual possession of twenty great new airfields. Professional and artisan constructors, they learned their soldiering on the job and when the time of retreat caused them to down their spades; to ditch and blast – in short, to 'bitch' – their bulldozers; they took up their rifles, bayonets and machine-guns, and won fame for their fortitude and skill – as well as for their nominal regiment, the Royal Engineers – as soldiers in an epic rearguard defence of Arras. Their fighting spirit, built upon a loyalty of a civilian order – an allegiance quite other than the traditional 'home' loyalty of the county regiment –was founded upon their own awareness of leadership and proficiency, of team achievement in technological construction, under the names of those five road-constructing firms. In all my experience of the inculcation of soldierly qualities in men ruthlessly thrust into uniform and 'shanghaied' into foreign hardship, I have found none to excel in spirit, efficiency and gallantry those five companies of earth-working amateur soldiers.

That airfield construction saga gives but one example of resourcefulness born out of no prepared resources. Like to it were other achievements of extempore creativeness and dauntless determination brought into being in the battle-lands of Northern France during those gloomy yet glowing eight months of twilight war.

Before the tidal wave of blitzkrieg broke upon our static preparations and swept us all away, the inglorious, indefinite period of *para bellum* or phoney war had its compensations in sheer overcoming. Radio and telephone systems, radar and radio direction-finding stations, fighter-control centres, aircraft hangars, repair and storage parks, medical, recreational and welfare facilities, all gradually came into being through restless initiative and striving in this grim war not of conquest but of provision under menace; not of over coming an enemy but overcoming circumstances and self; a struggle in discomfort and deficiency against winter, against time and against all precedent and likelihood. I have no recollection of making any positive contribution to all that range of achievement but I do remember being daily astonished by examples of obstacles giving way before the will of those determined to overcome them.

But that was only one side of the life of the air forces with the Army. Besides administration and construction on the ground, there was continuous, though desultory war in the air. Unknown to most and indeed scarcely heeded by the majority of those who actually did know, the fighter and long-range reconnaissance squadrons of the Air Component of the BEF were, day by day and night by night, in lively and deadly operation, with guns, with cameras and with flares, but without bombs. At that time of 'no fighting', both sides were, in fact, fighting in the air for knowledge of the other's dispositions, constructions and movements; fighting in the air against intruding reconnoitrers. Single vapour trails at great height would give silent witness to us below that all that we were doing upon open ground was seen daily by the enemy as it progressed.

At first we had insufficient Hurricane fighters to challenge the Dornier intruders, flying at 300 miles an hour, 45,000 feet up. Our biplane Gladiator fighters, when they arrived in November, constantly alerted and climbing to their 'ceiling' height of 35,000 feet, had little prospect of reaching a level for combat on clear days. On cloudy days, if the Dorniers came over at a lower level, the chances of interception were still extremely slight; not until the eve of the battle did we have any effective radar system giving early-warning of the approach of enemy aircraft, telling their position, course and speed in the sky. Even had the fighter squadrons known in time, and had they had the height capability to make an interception, the best that they could have hoped to deliver was a brief volley of machine-gun fire; for the Dornier 17s could easily outpace our Gladiators. As time went on, the Air Ministry, the War Cabinet and the C-in-C of Fighter Command, Sir Hugh Dowding, were induced to spare successive Hurricane squadrons, one at a time for a day at a time, to exercise with ours; to learn our communications system, and with luck to gain fighting experience.

During November the Hurricanes had some success in shooting down reconnaissance Heinkels, and I recall one occasion when news came to Maroeuil of one of our fighters shooting down a Dornier 17. I was delighted as much for David Atcherley's sake (commander of 60 Fighter Wing) as anyone else's; and of course for Blount's. Perhaps in the light of what I was to learn the next day I should not have felt quite so elated, but nevertheless for me that event marked the beginning of the long climb to victory in the air.

The day after that happening I was to be making a visit to David Atcherley at his Fighter Wing Headquarters about taking over a French landing ground in the Seventh Army area. Naturally, conversation turned to the shooting down of a Dornier 17 and I learnt that the French Air Force had taken over the wreckage of that aircraft. For it had crashed in the Seventh Army zone. They also had the solo pilot, but he had died in hospital that morning.

Atcherley and I discussed the problem of taking over the landing ground from the French Air Force Command and we went together to fix it with the proper people at their General Headquarters.

The Atcherley twins, by the way, both then wing commanders, had long been legendary figures in the Air Force. They seemed to typify the spirit of the flying service; they put lively initiative in priority of place over that subservient sort of discipline which peacetime Service life engenders. The chasm which often widened dangerously between those two standards of conduct they bridged precariously by a gay buoyancy of life not prescribed by Service regulations. Partly French by birth and by domicile when young, David Atcherley was immediately *en rapport* almost *en famille*, with the French Air Force. It was a delight to see the effect of his presence in that formal headquarters, on the latent enthusiasms of French airmen, already elated by the shooting down of a Dornier 17 in, as it were, their own backyard.

The outcome of that crash, however, was as astonishing as it was sobering. To be confronted with evidence of strange and terrible forces, then in action and in potentiality in Germany, mysteriously concealed and yet exposed in the death of one young man, was to be suddenly awakened to the actuality and hidden purposes of war.

Ostensibly, the Dornier was on photographic reconnaissance. It was loaded with complex equipment of a technology in which the Germans were then supreme. When employed in its primary role of bombing, as I had known it in the time of the Spanish Civil War, and when manned as a bomber-leader plane, a Dornier 17 carried a maximum crew of three. For reconnaissance, the crew might be two.

On the occasion that we were considering, the pilot had been flying alone. That was the first of many points for interest and speculation: why was he alone? In fact, that was not unusual, but the question gave rise to other questions: Why did he have to crash-land? Was his plane really vitally crippled? Did he intend to crash with both engines stopped – switched off, in fact? Was that all done solely to prevent fire from destroying what he carried? Could he not have landed properly on his wheels and remained intact? What was the plane's defect?

All those questions were evoked by the background enigma: why had he carried with him on that flight, in an innocent-looking large envelope in his map-case, a rudimentary map – a map, pencil-drawn on a coarse yellowish sheet of paper, seemingly a tear-off from a roll of 'under-lining' of the kind which wallpaperers use? None of those questions did the pilot answer before he died.

Here was a problem that was rare, but not unique. Indeed it was a riddle of the kind often found in fiction but seldom in fact. It was later shown to be a version of the strategic plan Plan Yellow, the masterplan for the eventual invasion of Britain after conquest of as much as possible of Holland and Belgium and after defeating the Allied armies. The revised plan, although not specifying a new subsidiary aim to isolate the British Army after it had made its planned advance into Belgium, provided for that very happening, since it involved the engaging and defeat of as large a portion of the Allied armies as possible in Northern France and Belgium, thereby creating the right conditions for the continuation of the war against England and France. (There was to be an episode similar to that of our Dornier in the middle of January. A German naval plane made a forced landing in Belgium, carrying staff officers. Presumably their destination was a Naval Headquarters in the region of

...ce-Marshal C. H. B. Blount at work at his headquarters at the RAF Component ...where in France.

...t looks on with interest while members of the RAF receive their Comforts Funds ...n France, New Year's Eve, 1939.

The Dornier 17

His Majesty King George VI inspects Hurricanes of Nos 85 and 87 Squadrons Air Component

Frederikshavn or Kiel. How they came to make a forced landing in Belgium is a mystery. They were carrying war plans about the imminent implementation of Plan Yellow which they tried —or ostensibly tried — to burn before they were rounded up.)

Thus, once again, as Plan Yellow plainly declared, the British Isles were to be confronted by the immemorial strategy of her successive Continental enemies — the quest for the Channel ports. Once more, if that plan was not a 'plant', the major aim was to be to seize the gullet-pipe of England and so achieve victory through starvation.

I was not then in the Air Staff; the conduct of operations was not my affair; I was an administrator. Such matters were for the General Staff and the Air Staff. They would be dealt with by the Intelligence Staffs, in the first place or — as the French would say —the *Deuxième Bureau*. (Naturally I reported what I had seen to Claud Pelly when I got back to Maroeuil.) Not only was it not my business, I knew nothing of it.

The sketch diagram I was looking at, held out somewhat guiltily by two French staff officers, was a dynamic representation of a vast dynamic plan embodied in only five lines and a few symbols. There were three sweeping, curved lines, arrowheaded and numbered at their tails. They swept like trails of three aircraft in formation, diverging from a focus low on the right across a dog-legged pencil line. That last was the boundary between 'cold' and 'hot' war: Germany's frontier with her neighbours. Thence, the arrowed lines swept curling like the crest of a breaking wave, surging towards the fifth pencil line; the line of Plan Yellow finality for the armies: the coast-line of Belgium and of Northern France.

I had seen none such as that before, drawn by a German hand. It seemed to have been drawn in haste and in anxiety. It seemed to lack authority. But there, presented in that diagram, was another series of enigmas, certainly for me though perhaps not for any military traditionalist. Against the background of my own prejudice, already once belied, I saw in the strategy represented in that map, a certain implication which was personal to Hitler. If that cryptic diagram was, in fact, the plan for blitzkrieg (when it should come) had Hitler, I wondered, changed his mind?

My fixed belief, based on what I took to be good evidence, was that he was inwardly determined upon the conquest of France, and France only. When that was achieved, England, he might hope, would be ready to conform. That would be as good as conquest —

indeed better; for in his inner belief, England was invincible by Germany (as I had long supposed). And that was not the only consideration. Hitler's advisers would surely demand the complete subjugation of France before the invasion of England was staged, and they all abhorred the prospect of war on two fronts again. So it was not illogical to suppose that the plan I had glimpsed could be a 'might be' and was not a 'must be'.

After we had been allowed a momentary glance at that strange and grimly simple diagram, it was refolded and the French staff colonel put it back in its envelope. With a wry smile at its irony for Germany, he monotoned the standard slogan, *'Taisez-vous! Méfiez vous! Les oreilles ennemies vous écoutent!'* Then he explained, for his own future protection, that the 'enemy' ears he hoped would hear the least about this unofficial presentation were the ears of his next higher authority at GQG who would already know that the British fighter pilot who had done the shooting-down had, within an hour of landing, gone with his fighter commander to the crash and had been allowed to see the tangled wreckage of his first war victim. There was something slightly questionable about our being shown the treasure – or was it the trap? – that had been shot out of the sky while in such unlikely porterage.

The inference I drew from that brief sight of the map of the Nazi German intentions was two-fold – either of which might be the truth. Either the pilot of that Dornier 17 was pro-English and was a traitor. Or else, that map was intended to show Hitler's intentions with a view to frightening the English into surrender. It was tragic for the pilot of that Dornier that he was shot down so that his plan should fall into the hands of the French Seventh Army instead of the British. The result was that the plan found its way to GQG and perhaps to the French Prime Minister but not to GHQ and thus to Chamberlain. Not that it would have made any difference.

So we came to the real purpose of our visit – to talk about the transfer of the use of a French occupied airfield to our fighters.

We said no more about the Dornier. It was none of my business to think about it or to talk about it when I got back to Maroeuil. Yet I did talk about it to Claud Pelly and I did think about it. I knew nothing about what already might be reliably known to the Allied governments or to their higher commanders about German military plans. Probably there was nothing of value in that gratuitous sketch map. But it affected me. It had brought home to me a probability or a possibility: England as the main military objective whether or not she might surrender – England, with her army in France destroyed? Bypassed? Captured? Those sweeping arrows gave no indication of pause for battle or divergence from the straight run through.

My contemplation of the matter was as superficial as a daydream. Perhaps quite fancifully and wrongly I surmised that what that pilot had said without words was, 'I have seen the German Army's plan of advance. This sketch is what it looks like. Those numbers are the army corps which will make the sweep to the Channel coast when blitzkrieg is ordered. I offer it with my life. Make what use of it you can.'

That notion was easier for me to accept than that the young man was ordered to get shot down carrying a strategic indication, whether or not that strategic indication was true. But if the alternative was also true, his compliance with orders was hardly less heroic. Of one thing I was certain; that pilot knew what he was doing, and it was a pity for his sake that his gesture was wasted.

It has been held by historians that Hitler was giving way to an unstrategic vanity by swinging south to capture Paris instead of concentrating upon the sweep to the coast and completing it, first. Maybe the evidence on that point is incomplete. Maybe it was not vanity but superstition. Maybe he held to his belief that, France defeated, 'England' would not continue then to be standing alone but supported by an invisible and invincible force. Be that as it may, the countermand which he imposed on his armies was one of the inscrutable factors which substantiated his superstition of England's invincibility by Germany.

His decision, in military eyes, was a fatal one. Had that northern sweep been carried through, as certainly (if there are any certainties in war) it could have been in the first week of June, the invasion of England could have been mounted there and then, before Fighter Command had had time to double its available Spitfire squadrons, or Bomber Command to develop its anti-invasion strategy. Precious months were lost to the victorious German Army thanks to the bait of Paris to a crazy man, or thanks to a nagging certainty at the back of Hitler's mind. I wonder which?

While our fighter squadrons in France were taking almost negligible toll of the German high photographers – one only but a prize one – our long-range Blenheim reconnaissance squadrons were suffering heavily from Messerschmitt fighters and anti-aircraft guns. We were soon appalled to find that, in clear weather, none of our Blenheims returned. For the sake of the slight knowledge hitherto gained by fair-weather day observations, such losses could not be justified, and daylight sorties over the strategic areas behind the German lines were discontinued. In cloudy weather, dodging in and out of misty cover, the Blenheims could see little of value and photograph even less, and even though they presented but fleeting targets they still could be, and were, shot down by anti-aircraft fire from the ground. This deadly shooting prevailed, we gradually learned, even when the Blenheims were deep in clouds. To fly low, hedge-hopping and zig-zagging, might defeat the defences and, in fact, often did; but it defeated also the purpose of the reconnaissance by reducing the effective range of flight and stultifying photography.

Thus the Blenheims were forced into the night and to chancy photography by the light of magnesium flares. After thus disclosing their whereabouts, they were, too often, effectually barred from direct return to their bases by defending fighters. The German searchlights were too efficient in their tracking, even though they had not the aid of radar. Our casualties in actual numbers were in ones and twos, night after night. But the sorties were only in threes and fours at most. Casualties of those proportions, when employing only two squadrons of eighteen crews each, soon became insupportable.

By March, the only practical way we had of making any deep reconnaissance was on the 'through-run' principle. Instead of making a circuit from its base in France back to the same starting point, each Blenheim would enter Germany from the west and fly out from the north, then over the North Sea to a bomber base in Lincolnshire. After debriefing and a sleep, the crew would fly its Blenheim back by the safe route to its base in France.

It was not my business – not then – to know what value was brought to GHQ by all this scarcely-heeded, undaunted tenacity of the night reconnaissance crews. I had to know about the killed and the missing, and see to their replacement. I also had to know about how the squadrons were faring under the strain, for the life of a squadron in all its ground activities is a reflection of the life of its flying crews: they live for and by each other. The commanders of wings let me know, so far as they could, how their squadrons were feeling. But you can't really know things like that without doing the job yourself – being with it, as the saying goes; being of it and in it.

My job was mainly to see that material needs were supplied. In that sense, the word material is stretched to include men –

replacement trained-men: 'bodies', as the younger people in the Air Force referred to their own kind, then. That they were far more than bodies needed no saying. But from the administrative supply point of view, men were necessarily counted as such. If their psychological and spiritual needs required special administrative arrangements that, too, was supplied through other 'bodies'. But the real man himself was in his own keeping under the care of his commanding officer, and 'care' had its chief significance in its word *caritas*. Because of that fact, casualties and command combined to cause staff officers to act with more humility than otherwise they might. The daily slipping-away-from-sight of men into a casualty list demands a ministering that goes beyond administration.

But the time was coming when those Blenheim pilots after long months of almost fruitless night-reconnaissance would become the carriers of vital and dramatic news. For, unknown to me until almost the day the thing happened in April 1940, I was to take over after all the role for which I had first been appointed. The Air Ministry's decision was being defied by Blount. I might have guessed that the arrangement would not last indefinitely. But I was too much occupied with what I was confronting day by day to have any thought for the probability that Ben Capel would, on the eve of battle, be taken away.

CHAPTER FIVE

Violet and Velvet

After their initial separation into echelons in the Army movement plan, the sections of our command headquarters that were directed by the Air Staff and the Administrative Staff, came together as a hived-off part of the GHQ of the Army. They set themselves up for work in the premises of a busy little velvet-making factory. This unlikely place was in the village of Maroeuil, three miles from Arras and GHQ. There we sank our identity into the delicate code-name, Violet, and feverishly wrestled ourselves into an organization. At the same time, Brassard – Gort's GHQ – was establishing itself in and around Arras. Although the Air Force was theoretically and almost as religiously separate from the Army as is the Navy, our headquarters was 'one of the Army's services', in effect a component part of GHQ; Blount in effect was the commander of one of the Army's services.

That word 'services' is used in too many ways. One of the Army's *own* 'services' is the Signals Service. The entire signals communication system of the BEF was under the command of a major-general of the Royal Corps of Signals. He managed the whole affair as a command, but also his business was to split up that command into bits, and to allot them to the service of all and sundry, at their will and behest. Everyone had a call on the Signals Service. So it was with the Air Component; it was under its own commander but everyone had a call on some part of the Air Force Service.

Well, somehow we settled in to the factory's offices. At first I shared an office with Donald Hardman whose calm and humorous manner, yet stern firmness of purpose gradually produced a coherent organisation; a system of administration which had the physical means for ensuring that the Army co-operation squadrons could co-operate with the Army, despite their isolation which was, even after moves, in many instances beyond the reach of Army resources. Squadrons and their wing headquarters, their aircraft supply and equipment parks in the eastern area of confrontation were establishing themselves as best they could, while living, without pay or money for local purchases, on French Army rations.

In the far west, three hundred miles away, the great air stores depot at Nantes in Brittany was being set up for supplying the needs we all might have for any replacement, repair or whatever.

Meanwhile, resourceless, I was drawn quietly to wonder by the ingenuity, cheerfulness and sagacity of the men of that stranded and dispersed air force; our units achieved the seemingly impossible in face of apparently insurmountable obstacles of language, no money and incomprehensible French civil administration, despite the fact that British Army administrative services could not be extended beyond the confines of the area allotted to the BEF. That the French at that time would not give up the few established air bases that existed in our Army's limited zone must not be blamed upon them, for the so-called airfields provisionally allocated to the Air Component had, in fact, been accepted in principle by the Air Ministry in the discussions which had taken place so hastily in the final weeks of crisis, in the summer. Unfortunately our gentleman's agreement with France to do no intelligence studies in that country prevented our knowing the hollowness of the assurances we British accepted. But we are harking back to the causes of our nightmare situation.

By the late autumn of 1939, Charles Blount began to accept two probabilities; one about the nature of the war on hand, the other about the nature of his major preoccupation in the winter months ahead. First, he accepted that the war was not likely soon to become an Army co-operation war. So far, it had been a war limited on both sides to tenuous air reconnaissances for intelligence purposes only. It was likely to remain so. Neither by fighter-aircraft nor by anti-aircraft gunnery were we achieving any frustration of enemy air reconnaissance over the British Army area, nor were the French over theirs. The Germans were hardly hampered at all in surveying our territory, but we were paying dearly for the slender information we obtained. Failure in denial of the use of our skies to the enemy and our inability to use his was, in a word, due to our archaic biplanes and insufficient Hurricanes – our time for ascendency had not come. We were in the aftermath of the 'ten-year rule'; no preparation for a war occurring in less than ten years; therefore no new equipment.

How were we to stop the Germans photographing all our dispositions? The Gladiator squadrons, with great capacity for combat of manoeuvre, provided no deterrent to the swift and high-flying Dorniers. Our Hurricane fighters were capable of

Dornier interception, but they were hard-pressed, and the losses were mounting. No more Hurricanes could be spared from Fighter Command for they were essential for the air defence of England against what was inevitably to come if the war became real and unrestrained. They were precious. As for Spitfire squadrons, they were hardly existent as operational units then. They were also having their teething troubles.

So, in air defence we were sadly deficient of the necessary tools. What could be said of the other aspect of our work – penetrating the enemy's air defences, his skies and his disguises on the ground? High-speed, high-altitude, long-reconnaissance aircraft to out-match the enemy's Messerschmitt fighters, did not exist in the Royal Air Force. The Mosquito miracle of innovation and the long-range, unarmed Spitfire photographers had not then flown into the realm of imagination, let alone the drawing-board and the factory. The mother of their invention, necessity, was slow in perceiving.

We had entered the war fully imbued with the lessons of the last war; that is to say the lessons of the victorious end of the last war. Air superiority was our watchword. How to penetrate from a position of inferiority – we had not given much thought to that. To win the air battle first was foremost in our thought: high speed and invisible reconnaissance had not been in our mode of preparation for that battle.

Lacking enough of the right equipment, Blount turned the heat of his zeal on to the commanders of his Fighter Wings and his powers of persuasion on to the commanders of his Blenheim Reconnaissance Wings, all to achieve the next-to-impossible. He accepted that the armies were not soon to be going to battle. He knew that the air forces must go to battle ceaselessly for Intelligence. He was determined not to fail for want of trying anything and everything. Failing demonstrable efficacy of equipment, he would have phenomenal personal efficiency, winter and storm notwithstanding. Ineffective as the primary equipment of his squadrons was for its tasks, he saw no reason for their being further handicapped by lack of administrative resources.

Thus, administration gradually became Blount's dominant interest. He was going to see to it that every administrative excuse which might be offered for the slightest operational inefficiency would be invalidated by making the administration administer as never before. Every day Blount would make a tour of units, inspecting; finding and hearing of deficiencies and complaints.

Violet and Velvet 73

Every evening back at Maroeuil – or Violet, as everyone called us and our place of business – he would survey in conference his latest catch of snags and deficiencies. The session consisted chiefly of his subjecting me and the heads of services to a grilling on a hundred points of defect and want, fifty of which probably had no substance in fact or were well on the way to being remedied already. In this torrent of drive, dissatisfaction and drive again, we all became torn, worn and somewhat weary.

One Sunday afternoon in late November, after nearly a month of rain, the sky was blue and the air keen. Charles Blount came back to his office from a tour and picked up his telephone to speak to Ben Capel. 'Give me the SASO,' he said to the operator.

'Gone out, Sir,' replied the operator.

'AOA, then,' said Blount.

'He's out, too, Sir.'

'Well, give me the Chief Signals Officer.'

'*Everybody's* out, Sir,' said the operator

'Where?' demanded the AOC.

'Gone for a country walk, Sir,' said the operator.

Blount put down the receiver and reflected. His mind went back over the past months of toil. He became conscious of the fact that his staff had been working in those cramped offices – when they weren't chasing trouble somewhere else – day-in-day-out, Sundays included, from early in the morning till late in the evening and often long into the night, without a break, for three solid months. That fact slowly dawned on his restless mind. He recognised that he, too, was weary. He went out and sat on the steps in the sun.

I happened to be the first back, with Louis Jarvis, Senior Personnel Staff Officer – one of the most whimsically humorous men I've known. Our thoughts were far away from Blount's business as purveyor, custodian and shrivener of Air Force officers and men, as we came to the end of our outing and a near view of the main entrance to the administrative block of our velvet factory. Neither of us had noticed that the hatless figure sitting on the steps, head on hand and contemplating space, was our commander. We were talking about sailing and holidays we had spent together when the Jarvis family lived in a thatched house at the head of Wroxham Broad. They provided the moorings for my half-decked racing cutter, and the evening attraction for the men who used that handy boat. We became aware of the identity of the sitting figure when he turned his head towards us.

'Where d'you chaps think you're going?' he enquired languidly.

'Hello, Sir,' I replied with surprised guilt and feigned unconcern, for I was the instigator of the spree. 'We were thinking of going to work!'

'Going to *what*?' asked Blount, with mock incredulity. 'You can't go in there! There's a strike on. I'm picketing the place.'

He stood up and smiled broadly. 'That was a bloody good idea, Victor,' he said. 'We've been getting things a bit out of proportion. I'm fed-up too. I wish to God this ruddy war would start!' Then, after a reflective pause he added with a wan smile, 'Thank heavens I'm not one of my staff!'

'If you ask the SPSO nicely,' I said, looking at Jarvis, 'he might grant you a week-end leave.'

'Leave?' echoed Blount. 'What's that?'

From that day until blitzkrieg, we had our Sundays off. And on that night the great winter frost began. Except for a brief and slushy thaw when the King came, hard weather and dry continued through to the spring. I recalled no winter like it for severity, in my lifetime.

*

Winter's frost began its severe regime back in November. No premonition by long-distance forecast had warned us that it was to persist, on and off, until the spring. By the middle of the first week in December, Flanders mud was hard-congealed and this unwonted firmness underfoot was welcome to us all, more especially to airfield users. The sudden news that the King was in France and would next day be making a tour of inspection of his army in the field was doubly welcome, on its own account, and again, because it brought with it a rarity – a spice of excitement. Naturally, the event put us all into something of a flurry of preparation. We had but a few hours to concert a general plan in which the maximum number of men of all formations should appear, well turned out, on parade.

The coming of the King was right from every point of view; to present him with a succession of static parades seemed wrong because it was so completely out of context. Formal parades and meticulousness about dress regulations were on the way to becoming archaic memories; circumstances had been too difficult, too diffuse, too dispersed, too busy for the peacetime routine of inspecting men on parade; inspecting them on the job was going on all the time while preparing for battle. Had the King been given that to do – inspecting the men preparing – it would have been in context and the King would have found it more agreeable. It was quickly decided by Gort and Blount that there would be two Air Force parades; one for representative aircrew with their aircraft on one of our own airfields near Lille, and one for ground personnel on an unoccupied French airfield near Douai. The former place, Lille-Seclin, we had recently enticed over from the French Armée de l'Air for one of our fighter wings. Comfortably within the BEF zone and furthest forward towards the Belgian region of our Army's expected first battleground, Lille-Seclin was to become, all too briefly, the 'Biggin Hill' of the Battle of France.

The second place, the field near Douai, was *terra incognita*; I, at any rate, had never been aware of it as a place at all; certainly not as one that we British could use. It belonged to the French.

Ben Capel was deputed to present the Seclin parade to His Majesty on the first day of the Royal tour; I was to present the one at Douai on the second day, 6th December. On both occasions Charles Blount was to be with the King, a member of the Royal entourage seeing all and being seen by all.

Millions go to see a King, but when the King comes to see you, it's a different matter and it makes you think about the principle of it. It goes without saying, of course, that a Sovereign must see his Army, and of course the troops must see their Sovereign. But when you think of it, you know that what is needed is that every man should become personally aware of the conjunction – of the King and himself being together – and that the King should become aware of each man with him. This shows the likeness of the military calling to that of religion; both should be personal throughout from head to foot – modern theories notwithstanding. For no force or nation, nor any organisation of man's mind, can transcend the limits of the personal, however exalted the names invented for omnipotence, or however vociferous the claims of majority-controlled democracies.

Everyone knows that Royal parades are traditional, but it is not generally known that they are vital. Nor, alas, is it widely recognised that 'royal' means 'real'. The real purposes of kingship must be served. An army in the field needs to realize allegiance. So does its king. Shakespeare's 'touch of Harry in the night' was one of his Agincourt ways of serving the royal purpose among soldiers, serving it privately, for the King, only – a way that any British-born king might naturally prefer. But that intimate approach, man to man, only suits the meeting of a king and small numbers; it could not serve a monarch limited by democracy and confronting a quarter of a million men in the space of a few hours. Nor can intimate talks, incognito, in darkness, be contrived into the service of mass publicity, and service of that requirement was an essential part of the purpose of the Royal visit, alas.

Ideally, it should be enough for King and Army to be at one; by that means King and country should be kept as one in war. But the time for that is long past and on this Royal occasion no truly real purpose could be wholly served: only could the appropriate noise and gestures be made. The King could no more see the men at work comprehensively than the men could see him at work, comprehensively; for a King's real work consists largely in *being*. This need for the King *being* is higher than the need for him to be *doing*, perpetually and perforce always – and to be seen to be doing. So, on this occasion in France, instead of the arrangements being as the King had asked should be arranged for him – that he should be able to see and talk to the men while they were doing whatever they *were* doing, wherever they were – the occasion had, as I have said, to be one of many formal parades. The King, limited by time, space and democracy, complied, but reluctantly. Alas that a sovereign can no longer be a sovereign in himself.

An adverse circumstance of this Royal visit to our army in the field was that the Army parades were ordered to take place literally *in* the fields and the fields had long been frozen hard when the hasty plan was made. But on the night of the King's arrival in France a sudden thaw set in and rain began again. The fields became incipient quagmire as heretofore. The roads, too, freed from binding frost, erupted through their thin surfacing of tar and quickly turned to muddy slush.

The Air Force parades were to be different in one vital respect. They were to be within hangars or, in my case, on a firm spread of tarmac covering the area between the line of hangars and the airfield – in short, on the apron, a square of one acre.

The King's arrival at the Douai field was fixed for 4 p.m.

The timing allowances in the GHQ plan, for getting the successive parades ready for inspection, were liberally extended. That was military custom, age-long. It persisted still, regardless of the squandering of time and the damping of enthusiasm which result. Optimistically but quite deliberately, I had decided that, for my parade, half the normal time of preparation would suffice, and that 3.30 would be quite time enough for the two-thousand men drawn from our northern units to begin to form up on the apron. I meant to arrive, myself, at 3.20 and watch remotely until at eight-minutes-to-four (or should I say fifteen-fifty-two?) it was time for me to take over. Punctuality is rightly a Royal politeness and the King would surely be 'spot-on-time'. He was to be inspecting an infantry division nearby at three o'clock.

The driver of my car was a quiet Breton schoolmaster; beside him was Cossins, my batman. We were splashing along the muddy lane leading to the selected, 'unknown' airfield. We were in very good time, but near the Douai airfield we found the way blocked by a line of slow-moving staff cars. Evidently, they were trying in vain – or so I supposed – to pass an obstinately obstructive, horse-drawn farm vehicle ahead. That was a familiar pastime of the region. I resolved to overtake the queueing column of cars. I noticed, by the way, but unconcernedly, that the back windows revealed that the waiting cars were carrying soldiers with red hatbands. I bade my driver 'honk' his way through, and on the wrong side. We hustled past the first three cars, spraying them with muddy water from the squelching verge as we bumped and skidded our somewhat dicey course beside them. The fourth car in the queue had a familiar back view. It was the AOC's Humber. Through its rear window I could see the smoke-blue forage-cap and fair-haired cranium of the Air Vice-Marshal himself – Charles Blount.

What the devil, I wondered, was *he* doing there at that time of the afternoon? He should have been with the King. Uncomprehending still, but with a spasm of belated subservience, I signed to my Breton to slide into the queue of cars, behind the AOC's. According to my map, we should be within a few hundred yards of the entrance to the airfield; no need to bustle rudely by; I had heaps of time and could, I decided, refrain from dowsing Blount's car with a shower of puddle-water.

But what was all this cavalcade of generals? Surely not an unscheduled reception party for the King at some place nearby? Perhaps they had got lost on the way to another parade? Or, perhaps they hadn't! I was beginning to perceive the obvious. Perhaps the King was in the leading car, arriving early by more than half an hour. I looked at my watch and regarded the second hand. It was moving. The watch said 3.20 as we pulled into line behind Blount's car.

There seemed to be no farm wagon obstructing us ahead. Instead, I glimpsed armed motor-cyclists with provost armbands and white-topped caps. At that moment, the leading vehicle turned off into the entrance of the airfield. A Royal Standard was fluttering from its bonnet. That seemed ominously strange to me but I did not as once accept its meaning.

I looked at my watch again. It said 3.20. No mistake about that. 'The King's not due for half an hour,' I said aloud.

Two of the motor-cyclists dismounted and stood by their machines on either side of the entrance, at the salute, as the stream of cars with generals and equerries and ADCs turned off the road. I then saw that, as I already knew must be so, the leading limousine was not only carrying a Royal Standard, but also the King!

Over the airfield, a quarter of a mile away, were the hangars. On the apron I could see scattered groups of airmen and lorries from which more men were leisurely jumping down. The field between the cavalcade of cars and the apron was largely covered with little lakes of thawed snow – water. The unhedged airfield road, aiming to the left of the airfield buildings, was clear ahead. The King's car could be at the parade ground in two minutes, going at its then stately, slow pace.

'Turn off and go full speed for the hangars, there!' I said, pointing and using bad French to my impassive Breton. '*Vite!* – *avec toute vitesse ou nous serrons* . . . be bogged!' The only way to make that mushy crossing was to do it at full throttle, like a seaplane taking-off.

With whirring back wheels and flying sprays of muddy water from the wings, we dashed, swerving by the water pools toward the apron 'shore', four hundred yard away. By great good fortune, I was spared the indignity of being marooned in the water-logged fields; we bounded onto the tarmac and stopped. I jumped out and impetuously bellowed, 'On Parade! The King is here!'

If you have not been brought up as a military person you may not know how it feels to be in that kind of situation. But if you have experienced a fairly normal sort of nightmare, you may have an idea of my state, in which the wish for obviously necessary action produces perversely negative response. Nearby groups of officers and airmen seemed only to show astonishment at my ducks-and-drakes cross-country water-splashings for no apparent reason. Was there not a perfectly good road by which to arrive? More than that, they seemed to indicate by their lack of response to my loudly audible command, that they supposed that I had gone round the bend. It was for sergeant-majors, not group captains, to bellow 'On Parade!' They hardly moved. They knew the timetable. The King was not due for nearly three-quarters of an hour. What reason could there be for this sudden commotion? To most of them I was a strange being, putting up a strange performance.

Another loud yell from me to look where I was pointing had the desired effect. Along the unfenced road over the airfield, those who heeded me saw with their own eyes the slow cortège of cars heading its way to the building and hangars. By then they could even see that the leading limousine had a larger-than-usual fluttering standard. Those with the more discerning eyes and minds apprehended the phenomenon. Immediately there were cries from sundry commanding officers, calling for their sergeant-majors by name to get their men on parade.

It had not been my intention to become involved in the preliminaries. I had intended to watch, unobserved from an office window, the always fascinating if over-slow procedure by which men of the Services are subjected to a routine for forcing order out of chaos in a quite archaic manner. The process is not without sanctity. In another way, it is deplorable. Everyone is stirred by a first rate, full-dress parade with bands playing – onlookers and participants alike. But men of the Royal Air Force more often than not, feel intellectually unflattered by the system employed to get the required precision and snap which is held to be evidence of cohesion and allegiant unity. They think that the same effect can be got quicker with much less 'bull'. On this occasion the view of the rebel-thinkers was to be justified. The scene I had planned to watch evolving slowly was in turmoil.

Scattered mobs of officers, NCOs and men sorted themselves out into the planned disposition of units which their officers had received only that morning and which they had never rehearsed. As I watched this rapid crystallization out of a swirling mess, I quelled my inner urge to go and hold up the King's approach till we should be ready. I stayed where I was, fascinated. I cannot say that I am a military ritualist; when presented with a spectacle of the absolute order and precision which are generally accepted as criteria of *esprit de corps* and the hall-marks of soldierly self-control and discipline, I do not experience orgasmic exaltation. Nevertheless, a parade that is right and ready thrills; and is deeply satisfying to one who likes to see things looking as they are expected to look. I could only marvel at the sudden transformation of chaos into an orderly stillness whose only trace of motion was glitter. Later, I remembered my needless fear of total disgrace.

I had been wearing the King's uniform for more than thirty years; since the then King's grandfather was King. It did not occur to me to suppose that the King was at fault, or that he too could take pleasure in seeing a mass of men in the raw of disorder, then getting into shape. It didn't even occur to me that the King would not expect to find things ready if he arrived as early as that. I had a conditioned mind. I had altered GHQ's parade timing instructions – GHQ had ordered that our men should parade at 3.00, I had ordered 3.30 – and things had gone awry, so I felt guilty. I had a feeling of genuine dread – confronting one's dread lord!

The main fact of the situation from my point of view was that I was in command. To any observer at that moment, no one was in command. Having myself been 'under command' from the age of twelve-and-a-half, I had a considerable degree of built-in subservience. My unrecognised fear was, no doubt, concerned with what would be thought, not of the state of the men, but of the state of my command. In the other half of my mind I was remembering my first personal encounter with that Royal personage when a boy. We collided on roller skates and fell in an entangled heap in the skating rink at Osborne. (That was the place where naval cadets used to go before they went on to Dartmouth.) Prince Albert, as he then was, was distinctly nettled. After to-day he would again associate me with the word 'shemozzle'.

I need not have worried. Airmen accustomed to independence act coherently and with intelligence in an emergency. Despite their phobia for parade-ground fetishes they acquire an instant readiness for rising to an emergency – or at least that is my nostalgic recollection of the species, coloured perhaps by this occasion.

The approach road took the slow crocodile of gliding limousines round the far side of the hangars and the cortège passed out of sight. It was 3.23 by my watch. If the King had planned to delay coming into view, would he not have stayed out of sight from the airfield altogether? Surely. So, in one minute they would re-emerge!

The stillness of readiness was yet to come. At that moment there was a clamour of commands, a clatter of rifles being slapped on their straps or clanked on their butts; a clicking of bayonets; a stamping of feet, rapid callings of numbers.

As orderly spaces appeared through which to move, I made my way across the apron towards the rising ground beside the middle hangar where the Royal Standard would come fluttering into full view.

Then all was still.

Not quite 3.25, my watch then said.

On that higher level, six cars drew up in line. Confronting them below their level in a sunlit vista, were arrayed two thousand airmen, sized, in open-square formation, standing rigidly in that steady feet-apart position, misleadingly called 'at ease' – their gleaming bayonets fixed on slanting rifles, butts to the ground.

The GHQ time allowance of one hour for pre-inspection and re-inspection before a Royal parade had been curtailed to four minutes.

The soldier beside the driver in the King's car jumped out as the car stopped and smartly swung open the door.

The King stepped out in the service dress of a field marshal.

That was my moment. I was standing at the centre of the clear, fourth side of the open-square parade. In stentorian voice I called for the Royal Air Force to come to attention, then to present arms for a Royal Salute. As two thousand bayonetted rifles took the last slap of two thousand airmen's right hands, the trumpeters sounded off their unrehearsed but well-phrased fanfare. The King and all officers who held a sovereign's commission – his generals, his air marshal and others with him, and all his commissioned officers on parade – stood at the salute.

Officers of warrant standing and officers without commissions or formal warrant, anonymously termed NCOs, and all the other airmen standing in ranks, in generality unnamed except as *other ranks* – all stood stock still, assenting in the Royal Salute. Again the moment of silent, dancing glitter from two thousand shimmering blades.

That was the King's moment.

It passed, and I advanced and announced the state of the parade – that is to say, its composition.

Then the inspection began.

In prospect, a parade – even a Royal parade – is a chore, if not a bore. Nobody wants it; least of all the inspector, if he is wise. But in retrospect it brings a certain re-assurance. On that Royal occasion it would have been a disappointment to the assembled men of the Royal Air Force had they failed to present the startling demonstration of *esprit de corps* which they actually did present. And each man saw George VI and was seen by him; each man could have felt the atmosphere of kingship, and his own liegemanship as his king passed by.

As we walked away from the tarmac the King, after giving me thanks for the event said, 'Were you in that car that went splashing over the field as we were arriving?'. On my admitting it, he remarked that I need not have worried; Charles Blount, he said, had told him that tea was arranged. They were going to take 'a quick cupper', while the parade formed up.

That was enterprising of Blount, and over-trustful; I had all the tea-things in the back of my car! Praying that Cossins had found the room where tea was to be served, I asserted with similar truthfulness that it should be ready, then. We went in and found that it was.

'Ineffable' is a long word to associate with tea, but there is something about the prospect and the realization of a cup of tea which, like that word, passes understanding. Everyone had been tense. King George himself was tense. Surely, he would have been much upset by the change of plans; he was a stickler for duty, precision and programme. What had happened to cause the change, I did not know, but at the sight of the tea-table he smiled. Then he said that as he then had plenty of time to spare he would like to talk to 'some of your officers and men'.

He remained silent awhile, contemplating his steaming cup and then made a remark which at first surprised me: 'I hate parades,' he said, 'especially when you have to wade in mud!' Looking down at his immaculate field boots, he went on, 'These had to be cleaned in the car as we came along to you, after I decided to cut the rest of my inspection of the 4th Division. They were lined up in four ranks, half a mile long, in a field that had become a marsh. They were all pretty well bogged-in!'

So that was the reason for his arriving so early.

I was surprised by what he said on three accounts: first, about hating parades; second, that he had cut an inspection of thousands of waiting men, after hours of preparation; third, that he spoke with almost no stammer. I had nothing appropriate to say. I restrained myself from muttering automatically the standard air force cliché of those days – 'Bad show, Sir!' King George VI had been through all the same military training as I had, Navy and Air Force; he knew it was a bad show, on everyone's account.

Sensing my embarrassment and perhaps his own need not to be misunderstood, he added the opinion that nobody should make a fuss about mud when the occasion was quite a muddy one, but the whole idea of a parade was ruined if the conditions for it were not right for the purpose. An essentially smart occasion, a ceremony meant to be brilliant and precise, demands the right milieu. What the King hated was not parades as such, rightly arranged; what he hated was being foisted upon unsuitable parades which had in turn been foisted upon hundreds of thousands of men in unsuitable circumstances. Trudging in mud and silence, with no band playing, before men who could not show their paces, was not his idea of a ceremony of kingship and soldiering.

As I have remarked already, what he had wanted was the sense of being with the army in the field, identifying himself with them, like 'Harry in the night' and experiencing their experiences. This was not that – nor did he quite say all that in words, but he conveyed it in feeling. There really is something ineffable about having been schoolboys together.

I recalled then, as I recall now, a newspaper picture of that king taken while he was visiting a factory. The picture showed him talking to a machinist operating a drilling machine with his left hand. The caption below as in inverted commas, 'I see,' said the King, 'you are left-handed! They made me use my right hand.' That was all.

That 'they', coming from a king, was what caught my memory. By using that word for unnamed authority, he virtually declared that he had been under a kind of authority which he did not love enough to name. For this Royal parade occasion, 'they' had insisted that the King must fill his time reviewing parades of a kind that are somewhat unlovable. His saying 'I hate parades' covered a lot of unspoken thoughts. But did we not all hate parades in which we did not really parade? Unless, of course, they suddenly became an exciting challenge as ours had been that day.

The 4th Division's loss was our gain. Besides the fun of 'putting up a surprisingly good show' – to quote the jargon of those days – many of our people had a talk with that victim of democracy's arrogance, that fellow-sufferer throughout the greater part of his life under 'stiff-upper-lipped' disciplinary practices, that modest exponent of military good sense and kingly kindness whose sagacity was then beginning to emerge, even in that early stage of his unsought, unselfish reign.

CHAPTER SIX

The Phoney War

The 'race to the front', described in Chapter Four, was an obstacle race over a course set by a friendly French government seemingly acting as though it wanted the British Army to abandon the contest. Theoretically, it was a race in which the German Air Force and Army were also expected to compete. They, however, failed to participate, and so when the contest petered out as the BEF came to an unexciting halt in half-deserted villages and farms around Arras, we had to settle down to a quasi-peacetime form of domesticity.

To me, the region where we found ourselves was not strange nor yet was it welcoming; in the days of the Battle of the Somme, twenty-four years before that time, it had been my 'war country'; it was still a country at war – war with itself; a land of agriculture in a losing contest with coal-mining; an area of poor villages, poor farms, potential mud, incipient revolt, all vainly suffused by suffering and sadness.

We had to have somewhere to live, that is to say, somewhere to eat, sleep, relax, gossip and amuse ourselves; we needed quarters. I have mentioned how 'Q' staff at GHQ allotted to Blount for his headquarters area the village and neighbourhood of Maroeuil. Blount's staff was not very numerous in staff officers but when they and their clerks, the radio operators, telephonists, drivers, despatch riders, police, cooks, and batmen were all totted up the total would not be far short of 300 men. The BEF had no women. Fortunately a concentrated tent encampment was barred as being too obvious from the air. Invisibility, camouflage – passive aspects of security – were the watchwords for that, so far, bloodless campaign, and this fact is worth a passing glance before we go further into our settling down.

The main fact of the political situation remained generally unknown. It was that Hitler, Daladier, Chamberlain, each in his own mind had decided that if *he* could prevent it there would be no fighting war – no hot war, nothing more than a walk-over against France which would be easier than the crushing of Poland. That was to be made possible, Daladier assenting, by treachery. Unknown to us, the military zones and the administrative system of France were riddled with traitors in a highly developed fifth column of French Nazi sympathizers. They did not like what they knew about communism as practised in Russia. Against these hidden men the population of France was warned by many placard notices. But those exhortations provided no protection against the French enemy whose official position and official allegiance were merely a working camouflage for his covert actions. That espionage system was well able to penetrate our dispositions and intentions sufficiently to construct an accurate picture of what was going on from day to day.

Whether, in the circumstances, security was necessary or not, we were of course professionally bound to practise it; it is inexcusable to be lax; the practice of rigid security measures keeps people on their toes. So, with security as the main excuse for our dispersion, and needing no justification for commandeering buildings of the largest size in our area, the officers of Blount's staff settled into a vacant château two miles from Maroeuil – the Château Écoive.

Now that we have arrived at the winter quarters to which the principal characters in this story were to belong, we might dwell a moment at its dignified Louis XIV rectangular facade in grey stone with granite steps to its central front door. The building dwarfed the hamlet which clustered about its walls. The château was empty, the hamlet seemed empty – no one came out. I remember seeing in that place no living soul. The gaunt château became our home.

After we had been in a few days, successive little groups of officers arrived. Soon our château became over-populated and the hiving-off process began. It fell to me to get rid of everyone bar the two 'policy' branches of the staff – the air staff and the administrative staff. One might have supposed that that was a task so easy as to be in no need of mentioning, but eviction always seems invidious to the evicted. Each in turn – the Principal Medical Officer, the Chief Equipment Officer, the Chief Signals Officer, the Senior Engineer Staff Officer, the Senior Chaplain, the Chief Press Liaison Officer, and the other heads of services – represented to me his own personal importance to Blount; how essential it was that he, as head of this or that, should be at the AOC's elbow, night and day. That was a healthy sign in one respect but not in another. Part of my business was to see that people did not use the Mess as a means for lobbying the commander. Thus Château Écoive became No 1 Mess. Four other officers' messes were formed in and around Maroeuil.

When our eleventh-hour air headquarters was formed there was said to be not one trained airman, cook or batman left on the books of RAF Records for posting. I had one such untrained batman allotted to me at Farnborough, nominally as 'my own'. This willingly conscripted man from Somerset, Cossins by name and a stonemason by trade, was graded as an aircrafthand and was one of the four who had to run the domestic life of Château Écoive. There was no cook among them. Of course, with normal perspicacity, units very soon hired French cooks from their local villages. There was no deficiency of perspicacity in No 1 Mess, but we were fatally handicapped by our ghost. The locals, if there were any, were said to believe that our château was haunted. So we could not find cooks locally and we employed Cossins (stonemason) and Beasley (shoemaker) as our joint *chefs de cuisine*. They knew less about cooking than they did about flying and neither had ever flown till they came to France. They learned as they earned. They earned 3/4d (i.e. 17p) a day and learned an equivalent amount about the art and technology of cooking. Nevertheless, we who lived in that gaunt place enjoyed our meals despite the ludicrous quality of the cuisine.

We might have remained unaware of the depths of our gastronomic standards in Château Écoive had some of us not gone to take part in a staff exercise with the staffs of the French GOC-in-C 7th Army – General Giraud – where we experienced the quite different atmosphere and regimen of a French general's headquarters staff at meals. This particular French general was later to come to fame as the kidnapped general – kidnapped in Vichy France by British agents, shanghaied over the Mediterranean in a British submarine, and placed (then quite willingly) in command of recalcitrant French forces in Algeria at the start of Operation Torch – the invasion of Northern Africa. Giraud in his headquarters near the Calais coast seemed to be a monument of sagacious and imperturbable isolation.

Giraud's 7th Army's job – if and when some fighting should begin – was to make a dash up the coast, through Belgium and on into Holland, and there he was to turn the flank of the advancing German Army; for it was a foregone conclusion that when, eventually, the German Army moved, its first moves would be into Holland and Belgium. It was a staff exercise on this swift movement that we had come to share, for we would be swinging forward beside that 7th Army when the time came.

My mental image of Giraud, after all these years, may have

become a little confused with that of General de Gaulle. To me, they now seem to have been similar in appearance, manner and bearing: typical examples of the St Cyr-trained, dedicated, self-assured intellectual, severe-father type of military leader; tall, unbending, coldly courteous, dignified, aristocratic, highly professional and academically so. War, for them, was not a game of co-operative skill so much as an intellectual art of mechanistic discipline. Both those men had a strongly developed sense of authority, neither (I thought) any sense of fun. Giraud's qualities as a soldier have been praised by judges more competent than I, but if his discernment and ordering of affairs in matters of cuisine and wine are valid as criteria, he must have been a first-rate general. If I had to use a single brief expression to characterise this man's attitude to warfare and to gastronomic welfare, I should make it religious dedication.

We who came over from Maroeuil-Écoive had our own standards in staff exercises, as indeed we had in Mess life. Although we looked as wise as we were able to look, we could not fully savour and assimilate the military fare provided primarily for French minds during the staff exercise. This grave and meticulous presentation and discussion of an elaborate and bold plan of advance kept us uncomprehendingly quiet for two days in the stately château where Giraud was then quartered with his staff. The proceedings were entirely conducted in rapid technical French but, we gathered, despite all difficulties of having British allies on their right flank, the French 7th Army got through to Holland on paper and in time, before the Germans could get there, and so the 7th Army could outflank the German Army, perhaps. At least, we judged the exercise well-conducted. This favourable opinion may have been influenced by the supreme excellence of the General's table and cellar. Knowing as I did too much about German power and French weaknesses, I found the exercise quite unconvincing yet enthralling; the cuisine and wines entirely convincing and enchanting.

Of course, some weeks later, there had to be a return of talk and hospitality at Maroeuil and Château Écoive. The Air Force General of the French 7th Army and his senior Staff Officers had to be invited over to AHQ and to luncheon – we used that word – in our Mess. The General, himself, could not – or did not – face it. His Chief of Staff came and brought with him two colonels and a major.

Although it was none of my business to see to meals in mess, it was a matter of enforced interest to me; Blount turned to me to rectify every point of administrative inefficiency, and our messing was certainly one that cried out for help. Then, also, my own batman, Cossins (the stonemason) was joint-chief cook. It was up to me not so much to strive to please our visitors from the 7th Army as to avoid seeming to insult them. Therefore, despite my lack of official justification for interfering, I did represent to Ben Capel (President of the Mess Committee) that, lest during the forthcoming luncheon the scheduled bully-beef-in-batter came adrift in the cooking, his menu should dignify the dish with the title, 'Old English beef and Yorkshire pudding'. My stronger suggestion, however, was that the last thing on the menu should be the best. There are times when people need to forget. Whatever else happened, or did not happen, at the end we must have excellent coffee. I therefore offered to provide a large glass coffee percolator recently sent by my wife, and I instructed Cossins in its use. 'And mind, Cossins', I concluded, 'when you bring it in, it must be very hot!'

The meal was appalling in its simplicity, but as an occasion it was fun. None of the French officers could speak English. Charles Blount, of course, could speak French well, and I could speak a little, too. None of the rest of the Englishmen there was willing to be overheard by other Englishmen speaking any language but English – except, perhaps, Hindustani. Pierre Vanlaer, the interpreter, was in Paris trying to recruit a chef. Bobbie la Chaume, the other interpreter, a naval officer, for some reason unknown, placed himself remotely from any of his soldier countrymen, so general conversation was out of the question. Mutual, halting interchanges about the food and the weather was the best that could be done.

Now and then the gayer of the two colonels, clearing his throat noisily to ensure an audience for a prepared sentence in English, announced very slowly some cliché in which he had been coached by Louis Jarvis, and all would cheer and clap. I was glad I was not in Capel's shoes. But Blount, as ever, kept everything near him in a state of animation. In NATO, now, colloquial languages are learned as it were by machine. But then, despite a thousand years of intermittent Anglo-French warfare, we could barely communicate more than our mutual frustration.

At last the time came for the *Pièce de résistance. Le café noir (à l'Anglaise).*

Cossins came in bearing my glass coffee-maker. Belching out steam its glass bowl was half filled with a pale fluid. Round he went to each place, pouring with a trembling hand. Too hot to taste, it was nevertheless certain that coffee had been used. There was silence while everyone sipped. Then the gayer of the two colonels pushed his chair back from the table with a growling sound over the polished oak timbers and there was silence again. Cup in hand, the colonel cleared his throat. He sipped luxuriously, bowed to Blount and declared with emphatic sincerity 'Nobody . . . nobody but zee English . . . know . . . how to make tea!'

This observation was greeted with English cheers and the other visitors took the point when Charles Blount rejoined, *sotto voce*, 'Café Khaki!'

It was on such a slender basis of mutual understanding, and yet on such a basis of goodwill, that our military alliance rested.

Next day Pierre Vanlaer returned with a chef, procured by dint of some private contrivance at a high social level. Things were better after that, but the magic of *sans souci* in the Mess began to evaporate. The picnic was over.

There may have been another reason for that change of feeling in the Mess; it may have been due to the fact that the so-called 'phoney' war was becoming harder to accept humorously and with forbearance.

Many of our own countrymen in England were becoming dismayed and cynical. Disruption caused by the evacuation of families, from London particularly; the black-out, recession of normal trade and business without the compensating excitement of war; restrictions and officialdom, the call-up, the frost, the rationing – all these hardships with nothing but a choice between holocaust or ignominy in prospect, were having ill effects on the people at home. There were no tales of heroism to take precedence over dark stories of intrigue. Consequently, letters from home were infecting 'the boys in France' scattered in chilly billets in villages, or in hutments in frozen woodland, lacking all the sporting interests which at other times keep men in good heart. For static troops not on construction work, the 'phoney' war was bad.

Concert-parties and celebrated music-hall artistes came over to retone falling spirits, and so it happened that Gracie Fields came to Arras. By way of nostalgia over 'Sally' ('Pride of our Alley') and delight about 'The Biggest Aspidistra in the World', she sang the troops into adoration of her, allegiance to all she represented and cheerful acceptance of frustration and deprivation. When other helpers failed, Gracie Fields personified for soldiers a motherlike, or sweetheart-like abiding 'help of the helpless'. The heart of the

British soldier, essentially compassionate, responds fervently to the invocation of kindly light in human affairs.

A tabloid newspaper of the kind most popular with men in the forces had been saying that our soldiers in France were 'love-starved'. On that line of thought it could be said that each of the two thousand men attending every performance held out his heart to Gracie Fields to fill and took it back brimful. Be that as it may, we were happy in the prospect of that most favourite 'Lancashire Lass' coming as a luncheon guest to No 1 Mess in response to our gallant AOC's after-the-show invitation on the opening night. After all, we had acquired a chef!

All doubts about the heart-nationality of that lady were dispelled by the peculiarly English fragrance of her charm when Gracie entered that gaunt château of ours and shared our fare and talk. She was the first Englishwoman we had spoken to for months. She was the only Englishwoman, so far as I am aware, who entered an Officers' Mess of the Air Component of the BEF during the eight months' duration of that force.

When the meal was over and it was time to go back to work our guest seemed to want to stay on awhile, saying that she needed to laze and that there was 'a look of coming spring in that old neglected garden, there'.

I pulled two chairs to the big window, and we sat and talked for an hour; of what, I cannot recall. Certainly we did not discuss stage performances or the popularity of 'stars'. But I recall a generous, kindly nature in a gallant bondwoman to a role. Cheer to the drooping spirits of thousands of weary hearts was the special gift this artiste had to give. How sad if in exchange her heart received their pain.

Mess life in the Air Force in peace-time was in those days a highly variegated experience on a slightly elevated platform of modified monasticism. Generous amenities in the form of buildings, grounds and furnishings were (and still are) provided out of public funds, for recreation. On top of that, the Mess members' monthly subscriptions to Mess funds, plus the bar profits, provided other amenities and amusements – social, sporting, athletic, artistic, intellectual.

Nevertheless, the majority of officers, if they could afford it, spent more of their leisure time out of Mess precincts than in them. Indeed, most of the officers over twenty-one years of age were married or aspiring to be married. That was a recent change. The Mithraic ordinance of military celibacy had been destroyed by official encouragement in the shape of money allowances to marry young. The fact that members of a Mess may, at any time day or night, be in life-and-death action against an enemy in distant skies is incidental. Mess life, which is essentially family life, goes on and there is no distinction between men engaged in the air battle and those with whom, many miles from the scenes of air action, they share their meals and leisure.

Mess life of a squadron on active service needs to be gay, if only to divert the living from death-consciousness – from too much awareness that, day by day, friends without adieu are parted and familiar faces fail to re-appear. But in Château Écoive we had no members of the Mess on operations, so no such state of strain-reaction prevailed in No 1 Mess. We were unworried by our harassments and seemingly ignored by our enemy.

PART II

CHAPTER SEVEN

Night Sorties

Anyone who has watched a reconnaissance bomber taking off on a war mission alone at night knows the feeling. On the occasions when we had gone unofficially and in the middle of the night to one of the night bomber-reconnaissance airfields used by the Blenheims of Wing Commander Grey's wing, Blount and I would just turn up at the dark shelter hangar where the 'duty' Blenheim was. There were eighteen of those half-oval, corrugated-iron, camouflaged shelters scattered around the airfield, each harbouring one erstwhile silver, now black, twin-engined monoplane. Having been given the location at the guard post, we would drive round the airfield till we came to the dimly lighted one containing the Blenheim whose turn it was for that night's sortie. On this particular night Blount and I arrived when the Blenheim's crew was already aboard. So, on foot, we moved off to find our way in the dark to the place to which the Blenheim was about to taxi-out and where it would begin its take-off run. That would be the start of the flare path (so-called), and the take-off would be over the airfield expanse to windward.

There would in fact be no flares to mark the line for take-off; instead, at intervals at two-hundred yards there would be six glowworm points of blue light – glim lamps by name. Rumbling and throbbing the Blenheim would taxi out, invisible to us until, close by, its black silhouette swung dimly into view and the thing halted, head to wind for the final running-up of engines before take-off. Both engines tested and shut down again, there followed a brief period of ticking-over, of final preparation. Then the dark air would begin again to tremble and crescendo to a clatter of explosions. These were accompanied by stabbing flames of blue-white burning gas from the engine ports; brakes off, and the unleashed monster would roar away in a fury of noise which would diminish as the shape receded into invisibility. Then, lifting at last, it would be seen to ride in the sky.

As night smothers the sight and sound of the departing warriors, awe in the mind of the ground observer gives way to a sense of loss; the roar from boosted engines and whirring propellers dwindles as the gaunt silhouette shrinks to no more than a pin-point glow of red exhaust; then to nothing. My eyes, lacking anything to see in the overcast, moonless sky, then fell to the ground where all was black except for a half-a-dozen glim lamps, just visible, aligned for a thousand yards.

The inner hopings and wonderings found no expression in the casual words soon to be exchanged between the watchers. They turned away to walk back and someone with seeming bright unconcern said, 'You would know that that was Peter Watts – always takes off a bit left-wing low.' Blount, absorbed in his own thoughts, said, 'Well, they've got a good night for it. Fairly reasonable cloud cover. Now we must get back.'

It should not be supposed that the feeling of spectators are by any means reflections of the feelings of the crew. At take-off there is a parting of the worlds of ground and air. The crew are busy and concerned with their professional tasks. For them it is a time of concentration on the skills involved in that transition. But when the craft is steadied to its climb each man may, if he so wishes, reckon chances. Perhaps not, perhaps so; some cannot help supposing . . . as though the mounting number of the sorties which a crew has made should alter adversely the prospect of a safe return, and take it below the average of, say, ten-to-one.

Each man would know that as a crew they were in for a desperate game of hide-and-seek, and would hope that the clouds would stay to afford them cover in the nick of time, when needed. For soon, that crew would be expecting to be caught by searchlights guided by listening devices; then they would be dazzled by the piercing glare of light and unsighted from their instruments of flight and from any view of objects on the ground. From then on they would be expecting momentarily at least a shaking by an exploding shell, or fearing, maybe, some shattering somewhere in the structure. They knew, too, that they might become prey to unseen Messerschmitts – unseen even by the rear-gunner in his lonely, freezing turret in the tail. Unseen, but not unheard; for, even above the engine roar and despite the sound-baffling of his helmet earphones, each man in his loneliness would hear the vicious crack-crack-crack of passing bullets or cannon shell, or feel the shock and hear the crash of their detonation in hull or wings – before his whole being, body and soul, would be flung into a swooning sensation of tense, nauseating thrill by the swoop of avoiding-action thrust into that Blenheim by the pilot's hand and foot.

Too often in the past no more had been heard of those Blenheim crews, not even as prisoners-of-war; too often the luckier in the returning sorties, coming back from England next day, would have seen nothing on the ground and had nothing to report upon save the intensity of the enemy's defence. They, the Blenheim squadrons, and we of the management of it all, knew that that reconnaissance was what they and we were in France to perform; we had no higher function than that; it was our primary duty to the Army. We were going through the motions of performing it, painfully, tragically. Reconnaissance means 'getting to know'. What *were* we getting to know?

Blount did not enjoy being confronted by the actuality of the reason for our being in France at all. Nor did I. We could, perhaps, expect to derive some satisfaction from success in overcoming some of our handicaps on the ground; we could have no satisfaction in our fruitless endeavours to overcome the impossibilities of our reconnaissance role in the air. I say 'our endeavours' but I personally could only be a detached observer of air matters; it would have been intolerable that I, as an administrator, should express uninvited opinions about our strategic reconnaissance situation. Charles Blount, and all below him and all above him who were concerned with strategic reconnaissance, knew some of the facts; and they knew that they were unalterable with the equipment we possessed – Blenheims, flares and box cameras. The Germans by nature were too well disciplined and discerning to allow their movements or positions at night to be seen from the air. Our work was based on an almost forlorn hope. But I kept my thoughts to myself. And that was just as well, for there would be an exception to the rule before we were much older.

It was certain, then, that there was nothing happening on the ground which was worth seeing. On the other hand, if the ground was naturally illuminated by moon or stars, so would the flier be and it would almost instantly become impossible for him to remain on a steady course to make steady observation. To remain steady in the air may be a mark of courage or of folly; the certain result of doing so for too long is that you and your crew, or at least, your aeroplane, would be destroyed.

'Too long' was a matter of seconds, even in 1940, when flying in a

Blenheim over the German Army areas, whether by day or night. Even in blinding cloud, when neither fliers, nor searchlights, nor gunners could see what they were out to find, the men on the ground could still hear and triangulate their bearings upon a lone aircraft, then woe betide the pilot who continued on a steady course. Or, I wondered, could the Germans have RDF – radar? Indeed, according to a report that I had had through Wing Commander Winterbotham of the Secret Service a year previously, they could and did have it in a rudimentary form: it said that the Germans had an installation in the Hartz Mountains for that very purpose. But our aircrews had no inkling of that.

What then could the Blenheim observers do to enable them to observe? They could and did drop parachutes from which, as they descended, the flares they carried automatically ignited, and then brilliant illumination sufficient for night photography could be achieved. But this required the aircraft to turn about and traverse again the track of illuminated ground, flying steadily the while for photography. And how confined would be the area illuminated: how unlikely was it to be the area intended, because of the unpredictable drift of the parachutes in the lower streams of air: how unlikely that the chosen area would contain anything worth seeing which had been allowed to remain visible from above.

And what, it may be asked, did they go over Germany to look for? Their mission was for strategic, not tactical information. This meant determining, night by night, the intensity of movement of freight trains on the railways – trains which never carried lights and were themselves as black as night and as black as the railway tracks themselves on a moonless night. Those trains, if there, were virtually invisible to high flying Blenheim crews and to their cameras; they were actually invisible for the much simpler reason that they were not there! Because no reconnaissance aircraft could operate by day, and because Germany held undisputed and indisputable control over her own air-space by day, all important movements for military purposes of a steady kind for a build-up on the Western Front could be made in daylight. There was nothing going on at night, and nothing was going to be done in the way of vast movements while Daladier and Chamberlain talked war and hoped peace.

So, the nightly efforts, self-denials, heroisms and sacrifices of our Blenheim crews were not only vain but futile. At least, that is how it seemed to those who had to provide for it and enforce it, including the handful of men who lived in No 1 Mess, and who, having pointed that out to GHQ, said no more.

The demand for these reconnaissance runs over Germany was French and political. Daladier knew well enough that there was going to be no invasion until Hitler was ready for it in the West. Then there would be two aspects to that readiness – his own to invade and Daladier's to succumb. For Hitler knew the divided state of France, her lack of national integrity, her militarily static dispositions and the weakness of her air power; he knew that France was incapable of withstanding the onslaught of the Wehrmacht and the Luftwaffe combined in blitzkrieg. As soon as the French recognised that their vaunted Maginot Line was not only penetrable but had actually been outflanked, they would no longer persist. And the English, as Hitler called the British, could then be disregarded as a military factor in France.

Meanwhile, Daladier continued to give the fullest possible semblance of sincerity and determination in his declared war against Germany, but only up to the point of actually fighting it. Air reconnaissance, from that point of view, was acceptable and therefore necessary. Bombing of shore, as opposed to shipping, targets was not.* Anyway, the French High Command demanded continuous long-range reconnaissance. And thus, because the French Air Force did not possess the right kind of aircraft for the task, even on paper, the whole of the deep penetration reconnaissance fell to our slow and relatively sightless Blenheims.

As usual, in those days, ground-minded Army commanders could not grasp the essential doctrine of air power, namely that liberty of action over enemy-held territory is not simply to be taken by air power, it has to be *won* by air power; the enemy's power to resist in the air (in the regions where liberty of action is required) must be destroyed; destroyed day-by-day, week-by-week to a degree that gives not immunity but air ascendency in the required regions. There could be, of course, another kind of winning of air ascendency for reconnaissance, a technological winning; that in

---

*Moreover the French were above all reluctant to provoke the Germans into retaliatory bombing of French towns and cities. The most that the British had gained by the time blitzkrieg broke out was a reluctant consent that the British might without further consultation with them strike against the oil refineries and marshalling yards of the Ruhr in the event of German aggression against the Low Countries. The French would have preferred to retain all the bombing strength of the Allies to be employed against a German troop advance.

The entrance to the Number 1 Mess at Château Écoive (*Drawing by Austin Blomfield*)

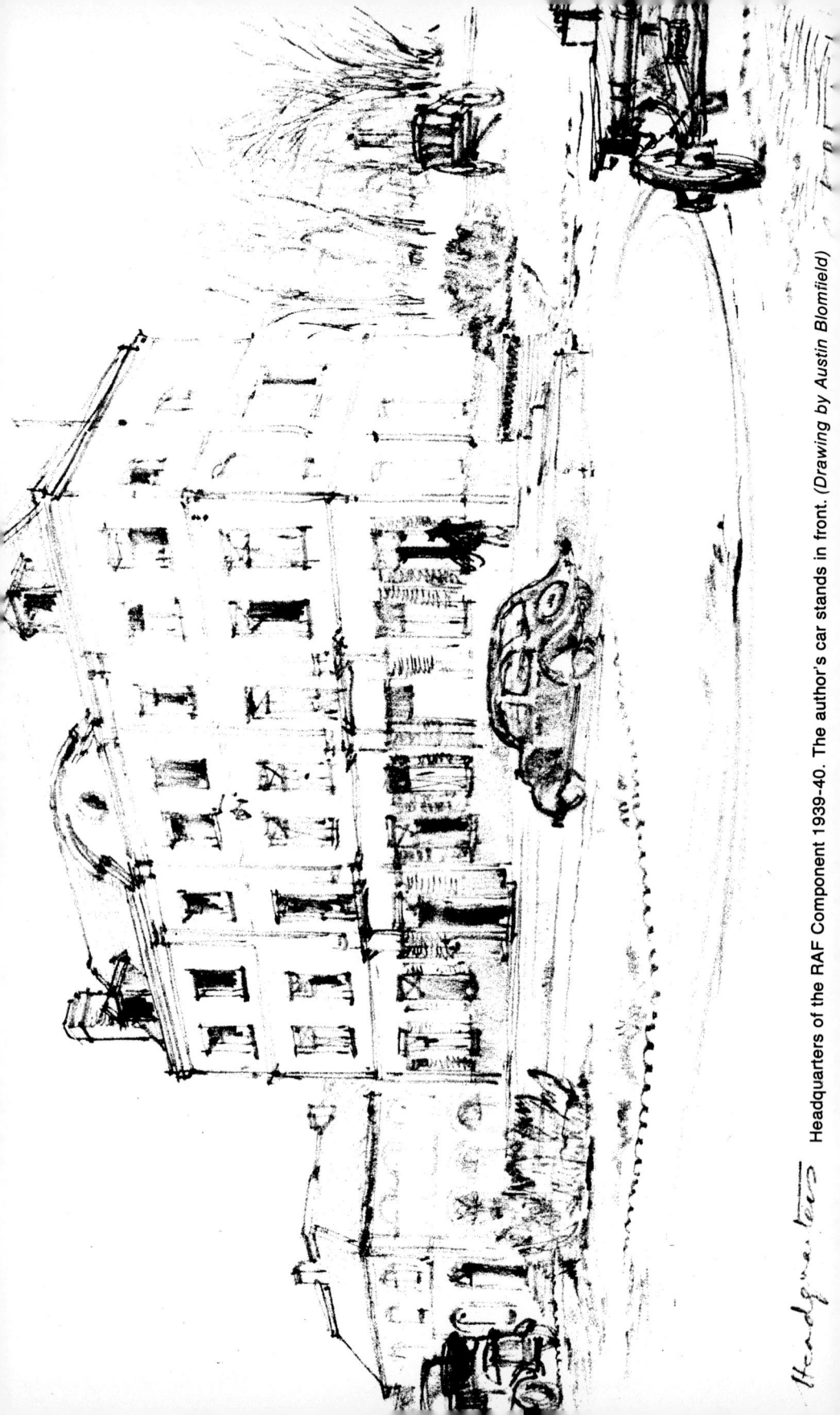

Headquarters of the RAF Component 1939-40. The author's car stands in front. *(Drawing by Austin Blomfield)*

which you fly higher than the defenders can reach with their defending aircraft or guns. The Germans held that kind of air ascendency and did not have to fight to maintain it. They had their high-flying, high-speed, unarmed Dornier 17s – the 'Flying Pencils' as they were called in Britain.

Without any sort of ascendency, our Blenheims had no reasonable hope of success in their missions, but they still did hope and act as though both their hoping and their actions were reasonable.

At the start of this slow destruction of our Blenheim wing, Charles Blount dealt directly, but on behalf of Gort, with the Supreme Commander in the Field, Général Gamelin and his Air Staff. This arrangement did not last long. The French required a British air officer of Commander-in-Chief status to be at the elbow of the Supreme Commander. The reasons for this expensive arrangement were logical. There were already two altogether separate major Royal Air Force formations in France: the Air Striking Force centred on Rheims and the Air Component of the BEF centred on Arras. (And there was later also a possibility of another separate RAF bomber formation in the south, in the hope of frightening Mussolini against coming into the war on the wrong side.)

Even if the British did not want these British air forces to be co-ordinated by one man in France, the French did. But they wanted much more than that. They wanted to make sure that, when the time came, the resources of the whole of Bomber Command and of Fighter Command in England would be at the beck and call of the Supreme Commander in France. Such a need was not likely to be met in full, but if there were a British air chief in France whose sole job it was to win the air war in France, that man was likely to make louder noises in the ears of the Air Ministry as the mouthpiece of Gamelin, than could Lord Gort, Charles Blount or 'Pip' Playfair of the Air Striking Force, each crying for resources to meet only his own particular needs.

So the need for an overall British air chief in France was established, and a new headquarters was formed around the person of Air Chief Marshal Arthur Barratt. He was to command all British air forces in France, and his main headquarters at Coulommiers (where also were situated those of the C-in-C of the French air forces) was referred to by its diminutive, BAFF, rather than by its code-name Eagle. So BAFF it was and baffling were its tasks and its relationships. That it responded to a vital purpose is a matter of history; that it added to the perplexities of our lives was a matter of experience; that it affected the course of events in any appreciable degree is doubtful. Certainly it could do nothing to enhance any value which might be gained from the nightly toll of death and frustration of our Blenheim reconnaissance squadrons.

But what a hierarchy of supervisory commanders and staffs hovered mentally over those who nightly flew.

Despite all failure, there always remained a hope, a chance that some vital sighting of a great military movement at night might give warning of an enemy deployment of the highest significance and urgency. Because of that chance, the slow attrition of Blenheims night by night, had to go on. That fact is the chief reason why life at the château, which I have sought to describe, was never very gay at nights.

Although I was not personally concerned in the orders issued, and never discussed them with Blount, Capel, Desoer, or Claud Pelly, I had a feeling of association. I had had the self-same job as those Blenheim crews, when I was their age. Throughout the six months of the Somme disaster of 1916, our army's one and only night-flying reconnaissance of which I was 'second captain' was a black airship, a blimp – SS 40. We might as well have been shot down on our first excursion for all the good we were. But we never were.

Driving back to Château Écoive with Charles Blount, twenty-four years after that Somme experience of night reconnaissance, I would feel again the blackness, the cold, the menace and the uselessness which I had known when I was nineteen and which I knew those young Blenheim crews must then be experiencing. Thus in silent rumination would end our joyless excursion to take a bystander's share in our Blenheim wing's nightly offering of a lone sortie in the barren dark.

CHAPTER EIGHT

Secret Operations

Except for some unheeded minor though dangerous night-raiding on the ground and night reconnaissance in the air, 'no enemy but winter and rough weather' continued to epitomise the experience of the BEF. For us in the Army's Air Component there was, however, a continuously active day enemy to fight; an insidious, mostly invisible, enemy in the air. Daily he was flying in the high skies over our territory; daily initially and nightly latterly he was gunning at our men high over his territory and deploying his fighters there. Short of our initiating and sustaining a vast bomber offensive, those enemy air activities could by no means be quelled. The total impossibility of such action suited the Allied governments. None was in the mood to do anything which might evoke a counter air offensive. We accepted our impotence; our challenge to the enemy was minimal; air warfare remained a matter of big theory and small execution.

As winter gave way our organisation found shape and order, not to say routine – a staticism as unrelated to the dynamism of violent turbulence that surely and soon must come. Or, we wondered, would the Allied statesmen shirk it after all? – after all their promises to each other, to Hitler, to Poland and to the world at large? Was Chamberlain himself or was it Daladier that was still secretly set on avoiding total conflict; still secretly pursuing escapist hopes through devious neutral channels towards appeasement? We did not know. We suspected but scarcely breathed our fears that we were merely stage soldiers in a play of make-believe.

Major action by the Allies being ruled out and no blast of bombing coming from the east, the only bombers raiding were the British – paper-raiding. In darkness, through the clouds, or from clear skies on moonless nights, leaflets showered down and lay as a pretty scattering on a few German fields and forests – few as the bombers from which they were forlornly flung. Rarely did any fall on towns. The naivety of Chamberlain or Daladier – though what else could either of them do? – made only for cynicism. In most British people's minds it was Chamberlain's 'Peace for our time' that persisted. It found no echo in our warlike hearts. Many of those who did the pamphlet dropping recognised its futility.

For the Germans, on the other hand, our pamphleteering policy served well in many ways; most excellently it helped them in perfecting air-defence techniques. They too – by then, I felt sure of it – had radar of a kind. But our scientists had not only doubted it; they had scouted it, alas. And so, to be shot down in flames while commuting for the scattering of wads of paper was the nightly fate of men more dutiful than fortunate. Glory for valour that much later shone upon 'the few' never illumined the prowess of those bomber crews. But none of that was really our concern, in France.

What we wanted to know was what was the real military situation? Months back we had seen, in our mind's eye – and mine had experienced modern war in Spain – the devastation and total subjection of Poland under blitzkrieg; we had visualised the cataclysmic destruction of Warsaw, in particular. Yet we had not learned, apparently, any lessons: our situation was open, receptive, static and vulnerable. Yet though we had no grounds for hoping we were full of hope for battle – none for peace. And Blount was bent on dominance in the air.

My business, however, was administration on the ground. What had chiefly impressed me in the news that had filtered through from Poland was the total collapse of administrative services and communications in the Polish Air Force, from the start. Theoretically it was for the Air Staff, not the Administrative Staff, to make plans for mobility and communications. Indeed, the Air Staff were planning for the great forward sweep of the Allies into Belgium at the drop of the first bomb. But I felt sure that this would be accompanied by ten thousand others – all on the air forces and the headquarters which controlled them, as in Poland. Then, there would be no forward sweep into Belgium.

We had to have a plan of our own, not the Army's, to avoid total destruction on the ground of all the Army's flying power – i.e. us, its Air Component. The very first stroke of German blitzkrieg must be to demolish enemy air forces on the ground at daybreak. We must have none of that. Somehow, we had to have discernment of when that first stroke was to fall and, the day before or the night before, we must quit our static locations and re-dispose ourselves elsewhere. Even though we had but slender chance of knowing the moment to act; even though we might incur chaos by the action; we must have a plan and rehearse it, secretly, piecemeal.

All that was only common-sense. But it did not seem sensible to our wing commanders and their squadron commanders. To create disorder at the very moment when order and the known system would be of paramount value, seemed to be fantastic. Only recently – April had come – we had moved some of our squadrons to reasonably well-established French Air Force stations, the French units having at last gone to appropriate French Army zones. These airfields, though administratively and operationally more satisfactory, were not tactically well suited to the British Army's plan, nor were they in any way defensively secure – not that any airfield could be made secure against the scale of air power confronting us. The twenty new airfields on which the Air Construction Corps were feverishly preparing concrete runways were to have substantial ground and air defences. But none of these airfields could be ready before the end of May, so none could be included in the plan. Besides their unreadiness, they would be too far back for the fighter and Lysander squadrons to use when the Army front was away to the east, in Belgium.

Security was our purpose. The only possible security against destruction on the ground which could be provided in our dispositions must be of a passive kind; we could effect wide dispersion, we could set up elaborate camouflage cover, or, as I maintained was paramount, we could make a pre-emptive general-post to hitherto unknown, unfinished, unfurnished airfields, immediately before the enemy launched his surprise attack. But how to surprise surprise? There was no technique for that. The cracking of the German most secret code first described in Winterbotham's book *The Ultra Secret* may then have been available to Gort. It was certainly not available to Blount.

Now, in addition to the recently-acquired French airfields and our new airfields then being built, we had somehow managed to prepare about fifteen other grass airfields with scattered shelter-hangars, camouflage netting and minimum facilities. With these secret resources as a basis, we devised our counter surprise plan for the sudden mobility of all our squadrons. Overnight, all would move simultaneously to fields other than those upon which the enemy had surely located them and recorded them as firmly based. With luck, we should be able to operate all squadrons from their new positions next morning . . . with luck!

Air Force commanders of wings and squadrons are not by nature defeatist, they are essentially practical and positive. They can, however, become brassed off like any other man under stress of prolonged frustration. Surely, they had all been aware of what had happened in Poland? But that was not what they wanted to contemplate, then. Poland was Poland. Although they had had time to get over their first negative reactions to the plan, they continued to regard this general upheaval requirement as a nightmare; planted on them as it was, not by the operational Air Staff but by the Administrative Staff.

They foresaw chaos coming to the recently-won order and stability of their business; they urged that it was time that the well-being of their hard-pressed airmen – who at last had got tolerable living and working conditions – should be given priority over other factors. The then state of efficient workability, all so arduously and so painfully achieved through the winter months they held was too precious to relinquish simply because the AOA (that was me) had got the wind up. To go out into the wilds once more, and to try to operate with makeshift facilities and communications untried at the start of the battle was crazy. The thing was anathema to all the commanders – all except one, Charles Blount. He had accepted the plan, and he stuck to his decision.

Unknown to me, I was about to take over Ben Capel's job and become responsible for the sections of the Air Staff called Plans, Intelligence and Operations, and for the Signals Service which was then beginning to include, most secretly, the mysterious thing called RDF – radar. I was, in short, to be Senior Air Staff Officer (SASO) and hold the post to which I had first been appointed but from which, quite reasonably, I had been switched. I had not objected at the time; I had thought it right. But when, six months later, evidently on the brink of blitzkrieg, I was confronted with a whole range of (new to me) Air Staff problems I wished that things weren't so urgent.

My first job, however, would be to hand over my AOA job to my successor Air Commodore Cole-Hamilton. But he was not due till Monday. I was officially ignorant of the plans for the swift advance of the BEF into Belgium. But unofficially I knew. Highly 'secret', though known to the enemy, those plans had been imposed on the Air Staff by GHQ in conformity with the French overall plan. The plan for the Air Component had not even been glimpsed by me and had not been subjected to administrative planning by my 'admin' staff. When, on the following Tuesday, I saw the plan, I was frightened. It certainly could not work, as things then were, at the beginning of April 1940. I was more than frightened: I was appalled.

The plan for the BEF as I then learned, was to race headlong into Belgium at the drop of the first German bomb on French territory, or the first German incursion into Belgium. The Army co-operation squadrons working with army corps and army divisions were at once to occupy unknown airfields on Belgian soil – unknown because of Belgian neutrality. Those airfields, unnamed and unlocated, had been secretly prepared (so our Air Attaché was informed) but the Belgian Government dared not tell us where they were until a German invasion of Belgium actually began. Their reticence was a mystery which persisted until that fateful time of invasion. Then, we discovered its justification. No airfields worthy of the name had been prepared for us. Our Air Attaché in Brussels was virtually incarcerated, his every movement watched. He could not leave the city to investigate on any account. He was told nothing and could find out nothing about Belgium's war plans. So we were quite in the dark about where, when the time came, we were to direct our squadrons to base themselves at the end of the Army's head-long race to the River Dyle. That was to be 'the front' for the BEF, its redoubt and line of defence across mid-Belgium. That river, of course, presented only a minor tactical obstacle to a modern army but it was deemed to be the best that could be hoped for.

By solemn agreement of long standing, our Secret Service neither initiated nor supported any kind of spying activities within the territory of Belgium. Although, unbeknown to the Belgian Government, the clearing house for the British Secret Service was in Rotterdam, no Belgian secrets were housed there. So the Belgians could give no help. Nor could we help ourselves from France: we were forbidden to fly beyond the frontier. In situation of unpreparedness, how, asked Charles Blount, could he possibly go on leave? At any time the balloon might go up and we had no notion of how to order the squadrons to move into Belgium with the Army.

My take-over from Ben Capel had its bleak aspect. Indeed, it seemed to have nothing else. That we could get no information about Belgium, our destined ally, seemed crazy to me. But in fact, the whole territory confronting us was already being mapped by the only possible means – secret, unarmed, high-flying photography. This was a feat which could at that time be performed by no known Service equipment and only by one Australian – an adventurous commercial gentleman with an impatient character, an uninhibited imagination and a most courageous heart. His name was Sidney Cotton. That information I gleaned from Blount under caution of special secrecy. I was not altogether surprised. I had had dealings with Cotton in the past.

Fred Winterbotham, a wing commander RAF in the Secret Service, was a warm-hearted friend of mine who used to arrange special things for me when I was doing Intelligence in the Air Ministry before the war. He had found a curious Australian businessman who was also a most competent pilot. Winterbotham provided him with a new Lockheed to fly about the Continent. This was Cotton. He was the inventor of the first properly functional flying clothing – the Sidcot suit. This enterprising commercial traveller was also a free-lance air adventurer with a camera. He, and one or two others like him, quite independently, had done some excellent clandestine military and economic photography over Germany in peace-time. Cotton had repeatedly done this even while carrying unsuspecting German staff officer friends on joy rides.

For the mapping of enemy and neutral territory, Cotton had stipulated that he must have Spitfires, as a gift, all their eight guns having been taken out. That was like asking for sacks of diamonds. The Air Ministry would not play. There were at that time only a small number of Spitfires and all were vitally needed for Fighter Command. Cotton's need could only be met by stealth with Air Chief Marshal Sir Hugh Dowding's connivance. The Spitfires, gunless, were installed with extra petrol tanks and Cotton's own cameras. The cameras were rigged for taking photographs vertically downwards and, at the same time, obliquely sideways. Cotton himself had had all outer surfaces highly polished for the utmost speed. He and his two colleague pilots flew those Spitfires as the Dorniers were flown, at 40,000 feet or so, under a clear sunny sky, with no under-cloud.

After a few parallel runs over Belgium they would be able to map the whole country. Half-a-dozen sorties should suffice. If it happened that one was shot down, that would be, officially, a case of bad luck on a harmless non-combatant. But none would be shot down over Belgium. The Belgians had nothing to touch the Spitfires at that height and speed. In case of engine failure, so that the pilot had to make a forced landing, it might mean gliding towards the sea and ditching the Spitfire out of Belgium.

Thus the Germans first, with their Dornier 17's, and then the British with their Spitfires inaugurated the technique of 'PR' – not public relations, but unarmed photographic reconnaissance. That was a practice which featured dramatically in international relationships later on between the Americans and Russians, until Sputniks took over the job and super powers from then on watched everything that occurred on land or sea with impunity.

Back in April 1940 one quiet evening, Charles Blount and I went over to our then largest fighter airfield, at Lille-Seclin. We were on the the ground there at dusk when a shining, pale-blue Spitfire came whistling in, literally clandestinely – pale blue for invisibility against a sun-lit sky. It taxied without any change of direction straight under cover. Soon after, there followed a light-blue, twin-engined Lockheed. That was Cotton's private property – the one he had used to serve my purposes in 1938/39. Blount and I followed to the hangar. Cotton, the pilot of the Spitfire, a determined-looking young man of about forty-five, came to meet us. Charles Blount and he had a few words together. Cotton had his self-imposed orders: people did not tell Cotton what to do – he told them what he intended to do, when he knew their needs. We left him at his secret operating base. By then it was dark.

Next morning, as daylight was becoming bright enough for photography – and it happened to be a perfect day for the job – the Spitfire was off over Belgium. Within three days he had mapped the whole of Belgium in quest of airfields which might serve our needs. Meanwhile, under pressure from me and unaware of what was to come, Charles Blount gave in, and flew over to England on a short leave.

The night Blount went, the tragic drama of Western Europe's World War II began in hot earnest: 6th/7th April 1940.

For six long months our Blenheims had persisted, latterly singly, toiling over Germany in their unrewarding, perilous and too often fatal task. Their reports often contained interesting words, but never, hitherto, any which carried intelligence commensurate with the effort and the sacrifice of those who failed to win through.

Soon after five in the morning on that night, 6th/7th April, my bedside telephone rang. It was the Duty Staff Officer. Would I get to Air Headquarters as soon as possible to speak on the scramble telephone there to Group Captain Grey about a reconnaissance report? ('Dolly' Grey was commanding the Blenheim Wing.) I asked the Duty Staff Officer whether Grey had passed anything urgent that he might have received to GHQ, and was assured that he had. You see, these Blenheim reconnaissances were not being made to produce information for air forces but for armies. The Air Component existed solely for army work. So it was primarily for army authorities to receive and make use of their reports. But we of Air Headquarters had responsibility for, and an interest in, the air aspects of the work and the reports. Knowing that Grey would not haul me out of bed at 5 a.m. for nothing, I asked the Duty Staff Officer to send me a car and so was soon at the office.

I got on to Grey. He told me of the report he had had. It related chiefly to the region Hamburg-Kiel. The pilot – alas, no name –had been astonished to find the autobahn lighted all the way by continuous parallel streams, two- and four-abreast, of headlighted, tail-lighted, vehicles. A vast eastwards movement was in progress. Thousands of lorries in lines abreast moving at speed all the length of the wide autobahn on both sides, right into the port of Kiel on the Baltic coast at the eastern end of the Kiel Canal. There, the port and the ships in dock and harbour were 'ablaze with lights'. The pilot who had landed in England could not estimate the number of vehicles with any reliability. All he could say was that the operation was on a colossal scale. What shocked the captain of that Blenheim most, on reflection, was that the port of Kiel and the shipping there – all transports, presumably – were not blacked-out; the port was brilliantly alive.

That was all.

I said, 'What d'you make of that, Dolly?' to which he replied, 'There must be a party on somewhere! I've already told GHQ and, though it's none of his business, I'll tell my corps commander in the morning. Not that he can do anything about it,' he added, 'but he'd like to know that one of his Blenheims has seen something of interest to somebody, at last. No doubt he'll have a crack about it with Gort.' Grey paused; then evidently mystified, he asked. 'Where d'you think they're off to?'

By then I had had time to reflect. This kind of thing was in my old line of interest. German intentions and German movements had been my concern since 1935 up to the outbreak of war.

'Norway', I said, 'by the back way' and I rang off.

I did not go back to my bed in the château. I sat and thought. Perhaps I should have asked Grey to check whether the Intelligence Officer at Leconfield, who had taken the report from the Blenheim captain, had made sure that it had gone straight through to the Air

Ministry. Like the rest of us, he might have said to himself, 'This is not any concern to us.' At best, he might have told his own Bomber Group Headquarters. Would they tell Bomber Command, I wondered? Would Bomber Command tell the Air Ministry? It seemed to be up to me.

I had not been in touch with Archie Boyle since he and I had parted on the stairs of the Air Ministry the day that Germany invaded Poland. He had stayed on there to become, quite recently, Director of Intelligence. After several frustrations, I got Boyle on the line about an hour later. Meanwhile, I had told the Duty Intelligence Staff Officer in the Air Ministry that he might do well to send for the Blenheim captain before he returned to his squadron in France.

'Archie', I said, when Boyle came on the line, 'the balloon's going up at last,' and I read him Grey's report over the scramble telephone.

'What d'you make of it?' he asked.

'Norway,' I said.

'What makes you think that? Why not Poland?'

'What for? That country's done. Norway's the next preliminary.'

'What d'you mean, preliminary?' asked Boyle.

'You remember that map of Nazi expansion we got a year or two ago? – the map I got from a refugee that you didn't think much of – a photostat map which one of Vansittart's protégés brought?'

'Yes. What about it? That was all about eastwards expansion – the Ukraine and all that.'

'Mainly, yes – the eastward countries were all shown black on the map, I know. But there were a lot of countries that were neither black nor white – they were grey-dotted all over.'

'Turkey, for instance, now you remind me.' Boyle was being his cautious, ungullible self, refusing to be rushed into a scare. But I was sure in my mind of what I was putting to him.

'If that map meant anything other than some wild man's fancy, Archie, it meant that the Ukraine was the main objective; but that's hardly on just now. Russia's virtually an ally of Germany, believe it or not. The main objective is in abeyance, don't forget. The Germans have to deal with the West, first.'

'But your report says they're going east!'

'Don't let's argue, Archie. This sudden and vast night movement to a port means nothing if it doesn't mean invasion – somewhere. Well, *where*? Poland was dotted grey on the map and it's already gone black! Denmark and Norway were not dotted grey but I feel that it is their turn next to go black. There's no military sense in seizing Sweden. Hitler daren't grab Lithuania, and what would be the point? So where can it be but Denmark and Norway, or both? "That Man" is going to try to frighten us out of the way by holding all the eastern seaboard of the North Sea. You watch!' (How cocksure I felt! Indeed, I had the sensation of *knowing* I was correct.) 'If they do that and we still don't fight, what *will* we fight for? But surely we shall, and then when properly involved there, it will not be long before we get what we've been waiting for here – blitzkrieg.'

Something seemed to register with the sturdy, stalwart unflappable Boyle. He said that he would get on to the Admiralty and the War Office; it was, he explained politely, 'more their pigeon than ours'. I replied that the only people who could *do* anything about stopping it were all in Bomber Command, and I hoped he'd see that Portal heard the news. Despite his many years in the Air Ministry – or perhaps because of them – Boyle seemed to have no awareness of the immediate potentialities of air power. He said no more.

That ended our conversation. Boyle, with a sceptical, 'You may be right – we'll see!' and a genial farewell, rang off. He had told me to leave it to him and certainly I had to do so. The imminence of invasion of Scandinavia was no part of my business as SASO with the BEF.

I sat ruminating, wishing I had said more and wondering how long it would be before Gort, or the Admiralty, or Portal, or somebody, got the news through to the Prime Minister, and whether, then, the Prime Minister would at last take the offensive. Or, I wondered, would the French still stay our hand?

Then I realised that the opportunity for Bomber Command had passed. The transports would already have sailed and so would no longer be concentrated like sardines, side by side. The art of bombing ships at sea involves techniques which can only be learned by an air force with the full cooperation of its sister service, a navy. The Admiralty had never fostered that cult.

I presumed that Portal (C-in-C, Bomber Command), once he knew what was afoot – how tempted I was to ring through to Bomber Command headquarters to tell him – would lose no time in getting on to Newall, Chief of the Air Staff, to stimulate the Prime Minister. Neither could do more than urge for action; they could not even send out a daylight reconnaissance in force.

Chamberlain would surely not have let us scour the Baltic by way of Denmark, so sensitive was he about being faulted for aggression upon neutral air space.

How telecommunications change manners. Both Nelson and Newall had a blind eye with which to fail to see an unproductive order regarding reconnaissance into the neighbourhood of Copenhagen. No wireless message from a prime minister could then have stopped Nelson, but a telephone message from Chamberlain stopped Newall. No reconnaissance was sent.* What was not permissible to the RAF was standard practice for the German air force. By dawn on the 9th invasion forces had landed both in Denmark and in Norway and troops were pouring over the Danish border. Danish capitulation was quickly secured and its airfields seized as bases for operations against Norway. In Norway itself on the 9th the seizing of airfields by paratroopers secured Oslo, and provided the opening needed for transport aircraft in hundreds to stream in laden with paratroopers and airborne infantry. Then came the bombers, sweeping in in support of the ground troops.

What a crippling handicap a conventionally prejudiced mind can be. I had just been shocked by Boyle's inveterate soldier-mindedness. His thinking that the movement of enemy troopships from a Baltic port was the business of sea and land power and not of air power, was typical of the times – a conditioned reflex. He was an old soldier. But I was not so very much more realistically aware than he was. To bomb the transports as they lay loading in harbour was my own kind of automatic reflex. That this would prove to be impossible in daylight, because of the intense power of German anti-aircraft fire, I would not have conceded, despite all I knew of the magnitude of German air defences.

So I continued to brood on the imagined situation which was still nothing more than imaginary so far as I really knew. All I had to go on was just one Blenheim pilot's brief report of night movements of road transport to a lighted seaport. That was the only basic fact. A safe precaution in Intelligence work – in peace-time, at any rate – is

---

*In fact, however, Bomber Command had rather ineffectually struck against the strong naval force that on the 7th had been spotted leaving Wilhelmshaven and heading north, a force which included the *Scharnhorst* and *Gneisenau*. Unfortunately bad weather on the 8th prevented further accurate reconnaissance and no regard was paid to reports from Copenhagen of a large force in the Kattegat. The enemy intentions were misread, the assumption being made that the naval forces posed no threat to Norway but were heading towards the Atlantic.

to wait for independent confirmation of unusual reports. All the same, I knew that the Kiel report was true. There are times when you not only believe your inner voice: you *know*.

But even so, I only knew half the truth. When the notion of air assault as a preliminary to occupation of Norway flashed into my mind, I appreciated that Denmark was strategically a necessary first objective; that at least one great airfield was necessary as an air staging-base and that all other airfields must be seized, for use or to be neutralised. Recognising this probability, I began to ring back to warn Boyle of it. Then I desisted. It was not my business. Surely, Denmark would tell the world at once if she was being invaded . . . our Air Attaché would ring Boyle at once. Thus, restraint overcame impetuosity. But my impetus, that time, had been right. Alas that I did not let it drive me into action again. For the Germans first of all put all radio and telephones out of action in the region of Copenhagen, and all of Denmark for all that anyone knew to the contrary. So no demand for help could ever have left Denmark.

My being so personally concerned was due to the background of my recent years of European study. It was natural for me to assess this Kiel report as a strategic move to the north-west. That being so, the corollary was that we were in for a longish period of war operations elsewhere and not in France. During that respite, we could be secure in the belief that no western offensive would be launched through Luxembourg and Belgium. At all events, being an optimist, I was certain from that moment of afterthought and reflection on my talk with Boyle, that the German Army on our front would be static until that Kiel labelled job, whatever it was, was completed. The Germans liked to do one thing at a time, and thoroughly. The German High Command surely had an obsessive determination to avoid a war on two fronts. Hitler, in my belief, had an equally obsessive determination to avoid war with England. The Norway idea was consistent with all that.

I rang GHQ. General Mason-Macfarlane, Director of Intelligence, I learned had not been informed of Kiel. He was interested and felt reassured that Kiel was a good sign for us. It gave us more time.

That secret, spectacular, surprise operation by the Germans had quite put out of my mind a secret, spectacular, surprise operation of another kind which I had determined to carry out while Blount was in England. The acceptance of Kiel as 'a good thing for us' allowed the normal to displace the abnormal. It was a relief not to have to confront and be confronted by the fierce realities of war and carnage. It was too easy to turn away from the contemplation of disruption, terror and dishonour in Denmark and Norway. We had our own urgencies to confront.

To those whose responsibilities are of a routine kind, compelled to deal with details, it may seem that men placed in control over much wider fields of activity involving weighty decisions of life and death should not be concerned with the sort of secret operation which I had planned. It was a project concerned with Charles Blount's over-stressed state of mind. It was planned by me before I knew that Ben Capel as SASO was to depart and I was to take on his job. Ben Capel of course had gone. But I was still in charge of administration. My successor would not arrive until the following week.

At 8.30 in the morning the staff would be coming in. It was then 8.15 on the 7th. The building was empty but for the Duty Air Staff Officer, myself and two telephone operators. Or, rather, I had supposed the building to be empty until I became aware of sounds of knocking and rending, upstairs. It was that unusual noise which brought back to my mind my secret – secret, because I knew that what I had decided to do would not only have been vetoed by Charles Blount as impracticable and unnecessary had I consulted him beforehand. It would also have been put aside by the new AOA, my successor, John Cole-Hamilton; it would not be the sort of thing he would want to do as his first act on taking over the administration of the Army's air force. Certainly, with hindsight it was inappropriate, but could not be cancelled because it had already begun in accordance with my orders. The Duty Air Staff Officer had been briefed by Hardman. But I only had a brief two days in which to get the job done. It was a work of demolition and reconstruction, re-decorating and re-furbishing within the premises. It involved pulling down the internal plastered wall of Charles Blount's own office and several others besides, together with all the communications, charts, maps and furniture. This was an operation of hazard and of fascination, a curtain over Denmark and Norway and the charge I had laid on Boyle.

Deciding, then, to cut breakfast I went upstairs to Charles Blount's office, the place he so disliked and which disharmonized his mood. It was a slip-room, miserably proportioned, only about seven feet wide but eighteen feet long. Its window gave no outlook; its feeble-patterned wallpaper, mouldy and coming loose, and the broken linoleum on the floor, provided a poor inlook. The only service that had been performed for that room since our arrival was to fit the window with a plywood board for black-out, which, at the AOC's evening conferences, added a sense of impending suffocation to squalor and compression. It was no fitting place for a commander to foster efficiency.

Charles Blount happened to be a man of space and of taste, properly accustomed to good surroundings; properly able, also, to be cheerful in adversity when strictly necessary. The continuation of this mean incarceration was almost unavoidable; the whole place was unsuited to its role. Squalor had long seemed to me to be less than strictly necessary. The surprise arrival of Brigadier the Duke of Windsor one afternoon on a liaison visit when Blount and Capel were out was the instigating event. I gave him tea in that singularly nasty room, and I noticed him appraising his surroundings with distaste. Maybe it was the wordless comment of our Royal, but I made my mind up then to transform the place.

Having made, with Donald Hardman, a general plan for certain office changes, I had invited Arras builders, decorators, furnishers, upholsterers to come and view the premises and make a plan for a high-speed transformation of the region beside the AOC's office. The new room, when the partition walls had gone, would be 24 feet by 18 feet; excellent proportions for its role.

I had not seen the inside of any shop since leaving England, nor did I need to enter any for this 'operation'; the local merchants came with samples of their wares. In half-an-hour of French and pseudo-French exchange, the plan was made and all the items ordered. How pleasantly unwarlike, to discuss with unwarrior-like Frenchman the shape of vallances, the fullness and hang of curtains, the tint of paints and lampshades and the lay of close-carpeting. There was luxury in the act of conniving at luxuries amid confined austerities too long resented and too drear. There was delight in the kindled happiness of Arras traders, doom-ridden, seeing this whimsy of mine as a revival of their war-killed trading.

During the half-year that had passed, I must have been responsible for spending francs in millions on warlike and consumable necessities: not a sou on good appearances or aesthetic comfort. How much this furbishing of Blount's official milieu might cost in all, I did not count: and nor did anyone. For I knew instinctively – and I guess those tradesmen knew – that we were all indulging fantasy to create a transient little paradise, an oasis for a respite and a change of heart.

The author's bedroom in Château Écoive (*Drawing by Austin Blomfield*)

Christmas Comforts (Drawing by Austin Blomfield)

In fact, the thing in terms of francs cost nothing. Before the bills were written, the buildings where the actors in this little play performed were heaps of rubble and charred wood. Materially, the transaction was merely a transfer of material from doomed warehouses to a doomed headquarters. Spiritually, it proved to be a good deal more than that.

The operation had been planned as a military operation, on a timetable. The partition walls would be down by 9 a.m. on the Sunday morning, the painters and electricians would be through with their work by Monday midday, the carpet would be laid by 2 p.m., then would come furniture, curtains, lamps, telephone and minor fittings. The whole operation had to be finished by 4 p.m. on the Monday afternoon. If Blount came back to a state of chaos, I might wish that I had never begun.

So abandoning my rumination on what I should have said to Archie Boyle about the rape of Denmark and the coming assault on all that lay beyond, I turned, that Sunday morning, to my own particular act of aggression – my minor war emergency. I went up to see what the knocking was and found the wreckers on the job, as planned. The partitions were nearly down. The fact that German wreckers might be engaged upon their particular emergency of violent destruction of national partitions – those between them and Denmark and Norway – was of no concern to me. Hitler would justify all ruthless upheaval in Europe and beyond as the need of 'the master-race' for 'living room'. When, after the event I considered principles and motives of my actions, unwelcome similarities showed me the dubiety of my altruistic act of aggression. But at the time, I was unperturbed.

Charles Blount was not long to remain ignorant of the Scandinavian situation. Having heard the news from the Air Ministry, he cut short his leave and flew back to our Arras landing-ground where I met him soon after four in the afternoon. Back at Maroeuil, I let him go up to his office alone. A moment later, I heard him call my name sharply. I went up. Blount had left his door open. He was fingering the substance of the new curtains. Aware of an observer, he turned and gave me a look as though I might have been his mother, or, perhaps, his fairy godmother. He was in a very human state, transformed with wonder, delight and gratitude; evidently experiencing the feeling that belongs to sudden awareness that someone cares sympathetically, if recklessly, about one's inner well-being. Miraculously, to him, an unspoken wish and need had been fulfilled. The silence was eloquent of all that need not be said when there is mutual understanding.

At heart a sybarite, perforce a stoic, Charles Blount had never ceased, during seven long months of arduous, relentless, ruthless striving, to keep his mind upon essentials; to build an efficient, happy and healthy Air Force ready both for battle and for the Army's aid. One of the essentials was the welfare of everyone in his command; that is to say, everyone but himself.

That building of ours was not much to look at, at any time, but when it fell it had one splendidly-appointed room in it. I remember it now with pleasure and without regrets at its destruction. For a few busy weeks, Charles Blount used it, enjoyed it, showed it off, regained in it his old happiness of manner, and all of us in his immediate staff who met in that room for conference or orders came to a new recognition of the man and a new cohesion in his service. Right framing, as every artist knows, does much for a picture that nothing else can do; especially can this be so for a living masterpiece.

Meanwhile, Denmark and Norway were framed in iron.

CHAPTER NINE

Der Tag

Respite and warning had come to us all, neutrals and Allies alike, with the news of invasion and catastrophe in Denmark and then in Norway. None doubted that the turn of France and probably the Low Countries, too, must come next; not then at once, but soon. How soon depended upon how quickly the Germans could establish mastery of the North Sea's eastern littoral sufficient for their wider strategic purposes; and how long thereafter it would take them to withdraw such necessary spearhead forces as they might need to use again in the next strategic thrust. It might be, of course, that there was no need for redeployment of the recently used airborne assault forces. In that case – and seeing that within the first few days of their gaining an almost unopposed foothold in Norway, capitulation was a foregone conclusion – we in France would be lucky if we could count on as much as a month for final preparation of the launching of our planned swift counter-attack. For we were left to presume that the Germans would, in their own good time, take, as usual, the aggressive initiative.

Anyway, it was clear that the then Allied political leaders had latterly shown no tendency towards forestalling German initiative. And what advantage could there be in a French thrust? If the Maginot Line was, in French eyes, impregnable how much more so was the Siegfried Line in the Ardennes? The French strategy was basically static: '*Ils ne passeront pas!*' – They shall not pass! With such a mental text for action, the last thing in probability was that the French Army could be committed to dynamic self-immolation on the German's impassable Siegfried Line.

There was, of course, no question of a pre-emptive Allied advance through Belgium and Holland. Aggression into Belgium must first be committed by the Germans before we would move east.

Meanwhile British and French forces had actually been withdrawn from the Western Front and hastily committed to a forlorn gesture of support to an already dying Norway. This may have been actuated by the scandal of nil Allied response to Denmark's unspoken need. Unspoken because the Government of Denmark had all its powers of communication with the outside world shattered by the Germans as their first move. The Anglo-French brigades sent to Norway had been gallantly ineffectual, soon to be frustrated and withdrawn. In relative materiel for war they were pedestrian; in manner of assault they were seaborne, in quantity and timing they had been, as usual, 'too little and too late'. The German grip on both those Scandinavian countries, on the other hand, was by control of the air.

That we, British, the pioneers of air power in its own right, founders of the world's first 'independent' air force, evangelists (for a whole generation past) of the ubiquity of bomber striking power – that we, of all people, should have dealt not one effective blow from the air; neither upon the fleeting invading forces nor upon the focal airfields through which, in broad and vulnerable array, the invasions had to pass – this was an appalling realisation of impotence, a mystifying fact, incomprehensible to air-minded observers of that fast-moving sweep of German air ascendency. But, indeed, the situation moved too fast for public thinking to catch up with the fact that air power is not just aeroplanes but that it is the power of established air superiority applied to conquest. So the nation unable to establish air supremacy *over the vital area* must surely fail to frustrate the enemy's major plans, and cannot hope decisively to influence the course of the land battle for territorial hold.

On that morning after the Kiel air report, I need not have wondered whether Boyle had taken effective action. That Blenheim report was soon to be confirmed by our Secret Service. Everyone in authority knew, that morning. Though there must be lying exposed there hundreds of troop-carriers and equipment-transporters, blatantly spread over the landing-ground while they refuelled, reloaded and awaited orders, all in broad daylight we would do nothing. With Chamberlain in his then mood there was no prospect of Bomber Command being unleashed against even one Danish airfield. That situation persisted, day after day.* There, if ever, was a

---

*Several clear signs and warnings on the 8th and earlier had been disregarded or misinterpreted and although after the invasions had taken place Bomber Command was instructed to try to attack the ships on their return passage, again they failed. Not until the 14th were bombing attacks begun on the occupied airfields of Denmark and Norway.

sitting target, the lynch-pin of the enemy array. Even though we could not hope to maintain local superiority so remotely from our air bases in England, surely we could and should have struck, and struck again. Or so I thought. Desperate, yes – but so was any kind of military counter-action desperate; why not then take a little desperate air action? But there was to be no major foiling attempt by Bomber Command.

Chamberlain remained inert, totally resistant to the advice of his Chief of Air Staff, Newall. Learning that fact, that grand-old-man of the Air Force, Trenchard, boomed in on our unhappy appeasement-forlorn Prime Minister while he was conferring with his Cabinet. Trenchard himself tried to induce the Cabinet to order Bomber Command to assail the German air power concentrated in Denmark. He failed. The Government, Chamberlain replied, would not act unless and until Denmark appealed for intervention; then, and then only in concert with the French, would Great Britain act.

So far as I know, the Danish Government had been unable to make any direct cry for help heard across the North Sea. German parachutists and Danish fifth columnists had seen to it that no radio should flash nor any cable carry such a message until the assault was through.

But even had the appeal been heard and responded to by bombers earlier all to no effect in Denmark, there would have been, throughout the free world, then, an effect worth much to British honour. The mortification of another failure would not then have been dark with shame; no cynicism of neutral onlookers about fine promises unmatched by gallantry. But in the aftermath the costing of lives and bombers for a gesture might have negatived the gain.

Though Trenchard failed to get our bombers launched, he did not fail to move the Government. Almost at once, Chamberlain begged him once more to assume supreme control of all the British forces – Navy, Army, Air. Trenchard's reply was, 'What the country needs, Prime Minister, is not an old generalissimo, but a new prime minister!' That was a signal that Chamberlain both heard and understood: it was his final signal to make way for Winston Churchill.

Meanwhile, Germany's strategic shield against outflanking by British air and sea power had been swiftly established to the Arctic Sea. The setting of their stage for the final confrontation of France was then complete. In France, we had no doubt of that. We did not discuss the outcome. Hitler surely had no doubts, and had seen as future facts his armies' broad sweep to the Channel coast. Thereafter would come his vital challenge.

On the showing, up till then, it would be a challenge which Chamberlain would not take up. He had, it seemed, become the embodiment of a Britain deterred. (I knew nothing of the move to oust him, then.) What would he do, or offer? Bargain for isolation with neutrality? Or accept the bomber threat of desolation, relying solely on our power of air defence? But who in the BEF really believed that we should be totally defeated in France? We in Blount's headquarters certainly did not – nor did I ever hear that fear expressed, not even when defeat was manifest. Yet I remembered Lindbergh's warning and knew that 'realists' in America had come to that same line of thought. Defeat was in the air but not –this is no boasting – in the hearts or minds of the men of the BEF. The point is not that the British are mainly wishful-thinkers; not that they are so blind to facts and logic that they can't reason and deduce; the point is that they are faithful and were right then to cling to faith.

That the thrust would come we knew. What none believed was that before rain fell again on the fields of Flanders or into the vineyards of Rheims, the whole Allied array in France would be in ruins and Britain would be virtually beaten.

By the end of April the fires and fury in Norway were dying down, save in the North. On the Western Front the build-up still continued. Over it, and far beyond, our Blenheims reconnoitred in the dark. Yet night by night no movement of the enemy was seen. Once every night, or every other night, we lost another Blenheim with its crew for nothing gained.

Spring had come smiling into France under blue skies when a shining April gave way to an even more brilliant May. The nights were clear and starlit and on the evening of the 9th, before the moon was up, a Blenheim pilot, shaken and dazzled by exploding shells, discerned, he said, a snake-like pattern of gun-flashes and surmised the presence, thirteen thousand feet below, of the raison d'être of all reconnaissance. Diving to get a closer view, and swerving as he lost height, he eluded the anti-aircraft gunners and dropped flares. At last, he saw what many a Blenheim colleague had lived and died to see – a vast military movement in the night.

Quickly enciphering a standardised report he tapped out in morse position co-ordinates and estimates of vehicles – transported armoured vehicles and tankers, lorries, and anti-aircraft guns in action. This was a Panzer force. Stealthily and blackly, snake after snake at intervals, gliding through the night, winding on hilly roads. This deadly menace had, in part, disclosed itself by gunfire. For the rest of his long scanning, after his flares had died, that pilot had to discern and see the virtually invisible. Whether the starlight glinted on painted armour, or the dreadful influences gave psychic vision, I do not know. He made his second (and last) report *en clair*. No more was heard of these two men. Nor have I been able to find their names. The squadron's base was soon to be destroyed and all their records lost. But they were not alone in their gallant anonymity. The price for intruding upon the armour of incipient blitzkrieg time and again was *life* – by most, called death.

Evidently, that column was heading for Luxembourg.

The time thus suddenly came for ruthless, ceaseless, no longer hopeless but increasingly desperate reconnaissance. Already strained near to the limit by slow attrition, the Blenheim Wing was committed by its commander right up to the limit. In Violet we only had to listen and record. The Blenheims were flying, in theory, for Gort and for his corps commanders: for Barker, for Brooke and Adam. In fact, they were flying for the Allied High Command – for GQG and the French.

That one sighting of a Panzer enemy spearhead made every man in the Blenheim squadrons of 70 Wing aware that the day-of-days for them had come. Here at last was the point in time of vital strategy discernment. The riddle their squadrons had to solve confronted them in that report; it was the reason for their being where they were, doing what they were – the vindication of maintaining through many fruitless months their costly, sightless vigil; the justification both for their living and for their dying.

Airmen of course do not think like that; they feel their knowing and content themselves with the comment, 'This is *it*!'

Long-range reconnaissance, from then on, was continuous. As Blenheim casualties mounted so did vital news come in. Not much, but enough to make the situation intelligible and to make the moving picture unfold its own appeal and menace.

At that stage we were still in our above ground headquarters at Maroeuil. We surmised that the time had come for us to man, and operate from our newly-contrived operations room underground, beside GHQ in Arras. We awaited Blount's order to move.

But I wanted to *see* Blount. I impatiently wanted to urge him to do something. The soldiers could do nothing. But surely airmen *could*. Were we at war or not? Were we simply going to sit and watch the whole Panzer Corps come through as though it were a peacetime exercise for ground forces only – as though we had never said or dreamed or planned anything about striking at an incipient attack from the air, or destroying bridges on the route of a column's approach? This seemed to me to be my rightful concern. Such a scene, on such a scale and of such significance, had surely never before presented itself in all history of war; a target so overtly, blatantly and so unambiguously demanding to be struck and impeded from the air.

Meanwhile, Blount and Gort being both off the map so far as I was concerned – out of touch and out of reach – I got through to Bomber Command by scrambler telephone and appealed to Air Commodore Bottomley. He was the SASO, my opposite number. I explained that as we in Violet would be tracking down the Panzer columns we were in the best position to issue the necessary operation orders. No attack on them could be made before they crossed the frontier.* This was madness, we knew. Presumably, the French would blow the bridges on their side and the Panzers would have to throw their own bridges over the river. That was the time to make chaos for them. (I did not then know what was to happen.) Failing that, our attacks should be made as the columns came through their bridgehead bottlenecks, before they fanned out for the tactical battle and spread themselves invulnerably over the French battle areas. As timing was vital to success, I asked Bottomley if he would detach a force of bombers, to be flown immediately I called, to a field which I would nominate.

I thought that I was displaying a modestly bold initiative; organising a practical decentralisation; facilitating flexibility and surprise. It did not trouble me that the GQG and BAFF might regard this as a wild impertinence and right outside the range of the functions of Violet. It was clear to me that everyone else was letting the golden opportunity slip away and would continue to do so – as, indeed, they did. Born of anxiety and subconscious resentment of

---

*At that time of course we did not know in which direction the Panzers would strike, through Luxembourg and Belgium or turn further south. The French were convinced that the Ardennes were impassable and therefore expected a strike further south against the Maginot line.

our long supineness, my thinking *was* presumptuous; it presumed upon theory.

Bottomley, underground at High Wycombe, was, it seemed, of one mind with me – eager for action but held in check by lack of information or lack of direction from BAFF. He needed my unorthodox demand. A wing or two squadrons of twin-engined bombers – thirty-six in all – was ordered that night to fly over on the following morning, land at 0900 and await orders from Violet.

Part of my notion in getting them under Violet control was to ensure their having fighting escort which would clear the air ahead and all around, I thought. This is a basic problem in air warfare, as on the sea. You cannot make a foothold on a fluid: you can't dig in: you can seek to dominate the region that you need to dominate: establish air superiority throughout that zone: deny that region of sky to the enemy air force. That was the prerequisite which we by no means could achieve. Thus, our bombers operating in daylight would need fighter escorts to clear their track to the target and protect them on the return.

The actual situation was adverse for us. It was the Germans not we who would have air superiority over the zone of their forces. For the close support, so-called, of the Allied armies we had the Battles – minor bombers under the AASF. Their role was only to extend the range of land artillery. These ten squadrons of ours were based on fields in the Champagne country: three wings of squadrons under Playfair's command. But they had been placed under French higher direction. If we wanted extra bomber action, we had to ask for it through Barratt's BAFF. But the idea of going through BAFF for quick bomber action seemed altogether too difficult. At first request, Barratt would not have played. At second request, he would have had to get the French Government and the British Government to agree. That simply was not on. It was for that reason that I had decided to go direct to Bottomley of Bomber Command, as I have already said.

So the bomber squadrons were coming over to France the following morning, to land at nine o'clock on a big field that I had told Bottomley about, ten-and-a-half miles north-east of Arras, unprotected, unprovisioned, and which was marked plainly so that the squadrons would know where to land. Also, I had got our signals section to run a land-line with a telephone at the field and in Advanced Violet. The squadrons were to wait there in the field, at most for an hour, in readiness to take off.

Later in the evening Blount came smiling in, a short length of polo-stick snugged under his arm and his white-piped, fore-and-aft blue cap on the side of his handsome head. He looked at the map, listened to the plan that I had hatched with Bottomley, nodded and enquired, 'Does Ugly know?' He referred to Air Marshal Barratt at BAFF.

'I'm afraid he doesn't,' said I. 'I didn't think you would approve of doing it that way.'

Blount made a grimace. 'When did you say they're coming?'

'To·land at nine tomorrow morning, after Jerry has made his routine, morning Dornier sortie.'

'No question of putting a Bofors battery round the field?' he asked, knowing there wasn't.

'The bombers will only be on the ground for an hour at the most,' I said.

Blount looked momentarily troubled and then said, cheerfully, 'Well, let's hope for the best!' He knew the position. He knew that it was a gamble – just a chance that we might strike a blow at the moment the frontier was crossed, wherever that was to be. But none knew the chosen points.

Blount had just come from a vain request for Gort in GHQ and was immediately setting off, he said, to find him at his Command Post in the region of Lille, right at the front.

How that fighting soldier, Gort, craved to be near his infantrymen and their battle. By nature, more a battalion commander than a commander-in-chief, Lord Gort had been the romantic choice of a new war minister, Hore-Belisha, in 1938, to take the post of Chief of the Imperial General Staff in the War Office. It was Gort's choice to relinquish that post, to lead the British Army in France. He was young at fifty, a VC, three times a DSO. Action with men was his magnet – and his magnetism – he was seldom to be found sitting at his desk in GHQ.

Blount, though anxious to go, took another look at the map as one of Pelly's officers moved the middle Panzer column along an inch. Then he looked quizzically at me. 'How long now to *Der Tag*, Victor?' he asked.

'Tomorrow! At nine, or at latest at ten o'clock!' I replied. 'And if they're striking through the Ardennes, as it seems they might be, they'll be across the Meuse in three days.'

'GHQ think *not*. The French still think the Ardennes are impassable, and after such a fantastic drive even the Hun will need rest or so General Georges thinks. Anyway, Pownall [Gort's Chief of Staff] wants us to get out of here and into our burrow, *now*. They were moving into theirs when I left.'

'Glad you remembered to tell me,' said I. 'So we'll all be on the move together!'

Blount looked mystified. 'How d'you mean?' he asked.

'Operation Nightmare,' I replied.

Blount's face fell. 'Oh Lord!' he began, and paused. He looked at his watch. 'Are you really set on that?' he asked, looking at me hard. I nodded. He said, 'We'd better go to my office and talk it over.'

Blount paused as he went into his sunlit room. His mood changed again. 'What a pleasant spot this is! D'you think it's going to be all smashed up tomorrow?'

'More likely than not!' I said.

'I have slept on it for nights and I now don't like your Operation Nightmare!' he said, with disgust. 'Nobody does!' he added.

I had guessed that this would happen. I was expecting to have to fight for it. Had he been in his dismal old slip-room of an office he might have slipped into his tired, autocratic mood. He motioned me to sit in one of the deep armchairs, flipped open his cigarette case, we each took one, lighted it, and then he put himself in the other deep chair and stretched out his long legs.

'Make your case again,' he said.

I reminded him of what we had long ago agreed about it. Despite all opinion to the contrary, he had firmly maintained that we would do it when the time came. In my view the time had come and would, if we were not very quick, too soon be gone. Were the order to be delayed while Blount consulted Gort, it would be too late.

Blount sprang out of his chair and faced me. He began to speak fast and earnestly, reciting all the arguments against the plan. Was it not madness at that juncture of crisis, to cast away all the well-fashioned order, all the well-tried communications, all the well-known systems, routes, place names; deliberately to smash our standing battle order to known and camouflaged dispersion in exchange for the chaos of packing up all our ground-bound array? At that moment of imminent battle to convert our whole force into twenty-five separate Barnum's Circuses and send them trundling off in dark convoys into the night lanes, aiming hopefully for new locations, miles away, must seem more than foolhardy. Rashly thus to deprive our aircraft of all their local ground protection of anti aircraft guns, and fly them by night to vacant, unprotected places where they would find no fuel, no ammunition, no supplies, food or camouflage – nothing until late into the night? Was it really better to take the risk of total ineffectiveness with an intact force, rather than take the risk that the history of Poland and Denmark and Norway would not be repeated in France before the land battle broke the peace? Must we assume that, with our existing dispersion and camouflage to overcome, the Luftwaffe could and actually would destroy our aircraft in their hundreds by low, unseen, unheard attack before our men could get them into the air? . . .

Blount had slowed down. He knew that the German Air Force knew all our positions. He knew their power, their reputation, the history that he was then remembering. He knew that I knew that he agreed with me.

'We may not be able to defeat the Germans in the air,' I said, 'but at least we needn't let them defeat us on the ground. We could give them a major defensive surprise, and live to fight them another day or two. That's more than any other air force in Europe has yet done, except in bits and pieces, in Poland.'

'I'd like to tell Gort before I give the order,' said Blount, hedgingly. 'He has the right to know. So far, he hasn't an inkling that we might put the whole force into a state of haywire at the crucial moment.' He paused. 'I wish to God,' he went on, 'he hadn't got himself off the map again. Pownall is out of touch with him.'

That was no good to me. But I was afraid. I had a long inbred reluctance – more than that, a positive fear – of challenging my own commander.

'What do *you* think, Sir?' I asked. 'Do you really think that these Panzer columns could not break through Luxembourg and the Ardennes – in three days – despite what the GHQ says?'

'Victor, I don't know whether they *could*, but I feel dead certain that they *will!*' Blount smiled wearily. 'Order your Operation Nightmare,' he said, in a gentle voice, 'and God help us if it doesn't work out as it should.'

I got up out of my chair, unelated. I, too, hated the thing. But I told Cole-Hamilton, the new AOA, that Operation Nightmare was to be put into effect immediately.

'I must go,' said Blount. But still he lingered, looking round his room wistfully. He picked up a brass ashtray from a side table and slipped it in his pocket as he turned to leave. 'They shan't have *that*,' he said. He glanced at me – '*Auf Wiedersehn!*' – and left.

Thus it fell to my old friend of Navy and airship days, my successor in the post of AOA – Air Commodore John Cole-Hamilton – to put into effect, that night, the general post of all the combatant units of the air forces directly serving the BEF. Donald Hardman had got the whole thing cut-and-dried; every squadron and formation headquarters had gone through its own move in detail; there was no known reason why anything should go seriously wrong with the actual moves to the new locations. The weather was ideal. But would the squadrons be in all respects efficient fighting units in a network of clearly operative lines of communication by dawn, next morning? That was the gamble.

Anyway, the thing was out of my hands. I had got the decision I wanted. I passed it on to 'Coley'. I was not going to take any interest in the execution of the general decamping; I had to get myself set up with the Air Staff, underground in Arras. Tomorrow we would have our blitzkrieg, and Jerry would blitz emptiness.

It was easy to make the move from Maroeuil to Arras; the plan and the communications had been prepared. For once established in my new billet, which I later discovered to be the Cathedral crypt, I meant to be quite early. Cossins was to wake me at half-an-hour to dawn: 3.30. The Germans had the same idea. As the good Cossins came to me in my camp-bed bearing the familiar little tea-tray, the gloomy air, ill-lit by slung lights, began to roar through a cavernous crescendo and diminuendo, intense with the meaning of low-flying, shattering intention. It was as though one-hundred-thousand horsemen were thundering overhead at the speed of a gale.

That was the day when Blitzkrieg began – 10th May 1940.

CHAPTER TEN

Into the Unknown

The battle was on.

The dawn swoop by the bombers of the Luftwaffe had been heard throughout the vast rear areas of the Dutch, Belgian, French and British armies as intensively as we in Arras had heard it. It reverberated throughout the frontier lands and the major cities of Europe's traditional war-lands. It was experienced as rending catastrophe and terror on the airfields of the Netherlands, Belgian and French Air Forces. Within days they brought destruction to the airfields of the RAF Air Striking Force in the area around Rheims. Within three days, more than half the available bombers had been destroyed while they were attacking the Panzer columns and the bridges which the Panzers needed to use, and with the breakthrough at Sedan and the insweep of the German armies, from this depleted store well over half again were destroyed. Before the Battle of France was seven days old, racked and wrecked squadrons of that force had to grab and load what they could and depart as speedily as they could.

So great and total had been the destruction of all the Allied air forces and their communications that, as in Denmark, no word of it got through. Our new operations room beneath the crypt at Arras was quiet – cryptic, barren of news. Nothing from our own wing headquarters or their squadrons.

At daylight, I went visiting by car, to see how some of the night moves had gone. The squadrons that I found (somewhat disgruntled) were much too busy settling in to talk to visitors. They had no special news. Things were in working order, just about. The morning sorties had gone off. Yes, they heard the morning bombers and the bombs. What had happened? No one knew!

By breakfast-time, when I got back, we knew in Advanced Violet (our new name for the separated air staff) that all our squadrons, except one, were OK and available for action. This was no special cause for self-congratulation, for none of us then knew the fate of all our airmen allies: we did not know that anything had happened to justify the pain, disorder, sleeplessness and deprivation induced by Operation Nightmare.

The air staff in the crypt were busy with their own jobs. It was for the Administrative staff, still at Maroeuil, to cope with the squadrons' needs. Desoer and Pelly, and their little staffs, were dealing with Blenheim reports, assessing the movements of the enemy in the forward areas where the land battle was about to be fought by the French while the British and French on the flanks raced forward to the Dyle and to Antwerp. But of the start of that event I still had no news. Had, or had not yet, the German land attack begun? Was there to be a target that morning for the coming bombers? Would they come?

Naturally optimistic, I was not worried about the fate of Air Component squadrons generally. About one squadron, the Blenheim duty squadron at Condé, I wanted news. For the rest, the German strike, if there had been one, had drawn a blank. If they had bombed our airfields of yesterday, I would be glad to hear of that. But, anyway, our squadrons, all but one, were operating; there was order, no chaos, so far as we yet knew. Operation Nightmare had been completed so far as I could see. It might have served its purpose. If so, it would be nice to know.

It was days before news filtered through that the French *Armée de l'Air* – almost the entire air equipment of the French Air Force backing the armies, north and south – had been destroyed where, in hundreds of aircraft, it lay, lined-up in parade order on its many airfields at dawn. Successive, headlong flights of low-flying German fighters followed by bombers had swept along the closely-shaped lines of aeroplanes, all ostensibly ready for rapid take-off and battle. Actually, they were ready only for the total destruction which they received.* We just were not told and did not discover that that entirely to be expected, standard blitzkrieg pattern thing had actually happened. So we didn't know. And so we did not discuss the question. We did not assume that it had or had not happened. We were busy enough with our own affairs.

In the days to come we learned that, as with all the others, the same, instant and almost total destruction had come to the air forces of the neutral Dutch, and those of the erstwhile neutral Belgians rendered ineffective. Meanwhile news came in from local sources and our own squadrons to show that the Heinkel *Geschwader* –

---

*In fact, this turned out not to be true. But the attacks, severe enough, had the effect of temporarily demoralising the French air forces and paralysing their war effort.

three wings of three squadrons of bombers – designated to attack our squadrons had swept in, that morning, to find the airfields bare save for dummies and empty shelterhangars, Disconcerted, some had in some cases withheld their bombs and in others had blasted dummies or nothing in particular.

Gradually, it dawned on me that Operation Nightmare had not been a wild-goose chase, as many had supposed: it had been well-timed. But by that time everyone was too engrossed for retrospection, so nothing more was said about it – nor ever has been, since, from that day until this. The fact that the Air Component squadrons alone escaped the initial blitz of blitzkrieg passed as an unnoticed bonus. Operation Nightmare was a secret – a secret that has been well kept.

The corollary to all that, unknown to us, was that from the outset, the RAF Air Component of the BEF – our little lot – aided by a few loaned squadrons from Fighter Command was committed to compete almost alone with the German Air Force then supporting the German Army. Our Lysander squadrons, as an organised reconnaissance force, were prey also to the vast anti-aircraft weaponry of the Wehrmacht then cascading over three frontiers on the ground.

Nor was that all. The enemy's hostility to our aircraft was constantly backed by the uninhibited hostility of Allied and British guns and rifles when they were over friendly territory. From the start, I repeat, our aircraft were the targets of the entire anti-aircraft defences of France and Belgium, not excluding the BEF. On the first morning, five British aircraft were shot down by French guns and that rate of toll, too eloquent of ground-minded ignorance and fear, remained normal to the end of the campaign. No one, from our Army commanders downwards, knew the air situation as we in the Air Component gradually came to know it. Had our soldiers known, their attitude to their own air force might have been quite other than it came to be in those days when land defeat loomed ahead.

I said, 'almost alone' was the Air Component committed. They were, however, never more totally committed than the squadrons of the Air Striking Force. But those squadrons were so fatally mauled in the first few days, and thereafter so reduced to an heroic few and then to operating on the run, that that force reached a state of virtual impotence within a week. Its valiant recovery after retreat is another story.

Before that day of doom for Allied air power passed, we of Violet had had much news of victory in the air: combat reports of shootings down teemed in. Even the old Gladiators had put in claims in double figures. Losses there were, too, but few. News of devastation –none that day.

We had no news of the Blenheim squadrons at Condé. That was the 'duty' squadron of the previous night, maintaining night reconnaissances over the advancing Panzer columns. By orders from their own wing headquarters they had stayed where they were, that night, operating against a live and moving enemy.

At dawn there were sixteen black Blenheims on the ground at Condé. Still at dawn, there were six Blenheims on fire and the remaining ten riddled with machine-gun bullets and torn with fragments or bombed. Two had meanwhile failed to return from their Panzer mission.

*

Our underground air operations room in the heart of Arras was a most secret location. It had been built and prepared as part of GHQ under the supervision of Capel and Desoer, before my time as SASO. I knew nothing about it except that it existed close beside a GHQ operations control centre. I knew that it was temporary. The officially planned, not to say 'permanent', GHQ with its Nissen-hutted camp was being built flagrantly in the open a few miles back from Arras. That extraordinary place I certainly had seen. No one could miss it. I was certain that the vast uncamouflaged array of hutments would be target No 1 (or at best No 5 or 6) for D-Day.

It was. It was rent and torn to twisted fragments over five acres of useless administrative preparation during the pre-blitz 'phoney' war. I had prayed that our people would not be put into that place. The enemy knew, as usual, that GHQ was due to be installed there on 1st May. Un-Germanlike, GHQ had not kept to schedule and had not moved in. The place was utterly destroyed by 7 a.m. on 10th May. Its first visitation of bombs was from the Heinkel *Geschwader* that had gone roaring over low as Cossins brought me my tea that morning in the underground place where they had put my camp bed.

That piece of news, however, did reach us in Advanced Violet underground in Arras. It explained why Brassard's and Violet's old buildings had escaped. News depends upon communications remaining intact. A chief object in blitzkrieg is to ensure that they do not. It is good to have underground operations rooms, but most of our lines of communication to it were above ground in the regions most liable to attack. Thanks to the activities of the French fifth column we remained very ignorant. By intuition, however, we were not altogether ignorant of our ignorance and fortunately it did not matter. Indeed, I had entered that very temporary Advanced Violet of ours by an underground passage through an unpretentious building for the first time, the night before. I did not know until that morning that we were actually operating below the crypt of the Arras Cathedral. Wars are fought in a cloud of unknowing.

Parting from winter friends and winter quarters at Château Écoive and the accustomed routine amenities of La Fabrique Maroeuil; exchanging all that for a damp, gloomy dungeon beneath a crypt, not to mention the unwelcome and incongruous facts of the situation and the questioning faces, produced in me a sense of loneliness and nostalgia. Lest that convicts me of admitting self-compassion, let me also admit to knowing that one's own inward fears are the makers of one's miseries. Whatever the cause of culpability, my background state was not one of reaction to the imminence of bloody, blasting war, but a state of accustomed lack of confidence; awareness of lack of experience in the conduct of operations of modern war.

Of course, we were (in military tradition) too busy to entertain personal thoughts. But feelings are not thoughts. One feels, and one is aware of feelings, whatever one is thinking and whatever the harassment or interest of competing urgencies.

Of course, too, we affected – or I did – a certain nonchalance, and even evinced some semblance of *savoir faire*. But underneath, there was a greenish whispering: 'You don't know how to deal with all that's coming now your way!' There, by implication, lies the merit of a team that is knit and practised. Mine lacked experience of me, and I of them, and all of us of blitzkrieg.

By midday on that first morning of blitzkrieg GHQ had, on their operations map, as I had on mine, three main Panzer columns of tanks and supporting forces, snaking through the Ardennes in sinuously parallel streams abreast; secure, unimpeded by anything save the steepness and twistings of those long-prepared strategic routes to historic battlefields of the past and the imminent future.

Those roads were, to us, but thin red ribbons of print on the wall map, wriggling their way through brown-and-purple printed hachures within the higher contours of hill country and mountains. How did they appear then to the helmeted soldiers riding their steel-cased steeds on that divinely sunny spring morning? Each steed was an armoured destroyer with the power of horses by the hundred. Each in succession was clanking through the peaceful, flowered countryside. How were the Panzer men – the Tiger men – taking it? Some must have been through the same ordeal of pre-battle suspense, before forging and slaying into Poland.

Precisely which sector of the French front those columns were aiming at neither we nor, I guess, most of those German soldiers knew, as they rumbled through the mountain valleys. As seen from the air, they were slow, slim, stealthy, articulated snakes moving in undulations of rippling bulge-and-stretch; relentless, unresting, breaking apart, rejoining, oozing and wriggling lengthily through the hills and the tree-concealed glades.

Six, nine and seven miles long, our (soon-to-be-shattered) Blenheims measured those armoured columns to extend. Following remotely behind were other, lesser streams, less definitely defined, evidently of lesser account. Were those three leading columns, then, the total body of the impending attack? I observed as an airman, not as a soldier might. I guessed not. I guessed that they were the ground limbs of the spearheads. I supposed the vast Wehrmacht of ninety modern divisions and more were already disposed and poised along the frontiers of Germany's four western neighbours – including tiny Luxembourg – waiting only for the Panzer Corps to spearhead through.

By mid-afternoon, that mesmerism of snakes was slowly weaving its wandering, peering heads seventy miles nearer to the Maginot Line. Would they attempt to pierce it, or would they swerve to outflank its fixed fortifications and thrust their way through our less formidable, winter-constructed defences on the Belgian frontier?

We few in the Air Staff operations room were fascinated, almost elated, by the silent drama of that awe-inspiring approach. It was not for Claud Pelly, nor for 'Dizzy' Desoer or me to assess the enemy's intentions; that was soldiers' work, it was for G-staff to assess in GHQ. Or, to be strictly accurate, it was properly the task of the *Deuxième Bureau* in the GQG of General Georges' North-Western Group of Armies. But, of course, every one who had the reports and a map concocted his own plan for the enemy to fulfil.

For many hours I had been wistfully contemplating the destruction of that great Panzer force. It was the ground embodiment of blitzkrieg which none in any Nazi-ravaged country had hitherto effectually resisted. Half-a-dozen European countries, all of more venerable standing as nations than the Third Reich, had fallen prostrate under armoured air onslaughts from Germany; Austria, Hungary, Poland, Denmark and Norway, before the coming of blitzkrieg. Of course then conscious only of the menace and the need, it was beyond me to weigh up the possible effectiveness of our resources in relation to the task. Wishful thinking minimised the three decisive aspects: the need for dogged persistence in attack to blunt the Panzer spearheads; secondly, the lethality of the Panzer air defences; thirdly, the probability that the French plan to blow the frontier bridges would be defeated by the treachery of the fifth column then rife in France.

The deadliness of Panzer air defence had to be learned the hard way. Mobile flak artillery in hundreds, so it was later said, moved with those battle-initiating columns, and a thousand, high-angle cannon and machine-guns. Above, the whole area of Panzer movement was guarded, being circled at levels, close, medium and high, by aircraft all in speaking connection direct with unified ground-air control. That Panzer atmosphere was lively with the drone of Henschel, Heinkel and Messerschmitt fighters.

That was the factual, lethal state which our dead Blenheim men had known. We, in Violet, had not experienced it. So we did not know. Nor had the crews of the coming bombers.

Although the bombing of the approaching invaders on the ground was still tabu from the French, the battle in the air was already, though too distantly, joined. The range from our fighter bases was still too long for equal challenge to the hornet hordes over the Panzer columns. Equal challenge? There could be no prospect of that numerically, but in individual combat there could be. At that range, however, our Hurricanes could but stab and go. Then, tail-turned, heading back to base and gunless to the rear, they would be defenceless to the hornets harrying after them. Even so the news from 60 Wing was that our fighters – Gladiators and Hurricanes – were doing well.

My chief concern, however was for the bombers. Barratt urgently needed permission* to unleash the Battle bombers of AASF against

---

*According to the official RAF History, it was not until mid-day that Barratt decided he could wait no longer, took matters into his own hands and ordered the Battles out to strike against the German columns advancing through Luxembourg.

the invading columns. Yet still the French delayed, intent at all costs on avoiding an all-out bombing war. As I shall shortly relate, I was also preoccupied with the necessity of giving orders to the heavy bomber squadrons being flown in by Bomber Command to await our instructions.

Meanwhile, inexorably, invulnerably, through Luxembourg and the Ardennes, the three Panzer columns moved on. By our map they were static until fresh news gave to the coloured pins and tapes a set of new positions.

Two things in particular, that had come my way that morning of the 10th had arrived at the same time. First, a call from Charles Blount, in General Pownall's office, to go over to him in GHQ; a second later the anxiously-awaited ring of the field telephone laid to the airfield where the bombers were to land.

Desoer answered it. Totally dispassionate as ever, the living antithesis of his nickname 'Dizzy', he lifted the receiver and quietly said, 'Good morning! Operations, Advanced Violet, Wing Commander Desoer speaking. Who are you? . . . Group Captain who? . . . Whitfield? . . . Good morning, sir. Good flight? . . . Thirty-six,' he repeated as he listened, ' – and landing now.' He looked at his watch, '0857, good timing, sir! . . . Yes, hold on, I'll get him,' and he beckoned me.

I spoke. I checked on the briefing Whitfield had had from Bottomley, asked his time for take-off readiness, suggested a likely time as 0945 but said the final briefing would be given by Desoer, and would he please ring again at half-past nine?

As agreed, two additional Hurricane squadrons joined us that morning, but my concern was with a wing of bombers – may be a clutch would be a more appropriate name – anyway thirty-six bombers of unknown name each carrying a ton of bombs, four men, two engines, four machine guns on loan from their English bases. They were then in the act of landing in succession and parking in wide dispersal on five hedgeless fields – one airfield – some fourteen miles away. There they would wait blackly glinting in the sunshine. They were night bombers. How long they would wait, I did not know. Not long, I hoped.

This formidable force was to be committed to a daylight attack under orders prepared by Desoer for issue the moment we could give, by reasoned guess, the map co-ordinates of a place where, at a certain time, there would be a major target. The point to be chosen would be at a convergence, a bridge or some feature of topography which might bottleneck a Panzer force (already splayed, I feared) in France or Belgium. But even then, I still did not know.

This was to be the first strike by heavy bombers at the Wehrmacht made by any air force in this war; the first, indeed, since Trenchard wielded his France-based bomber force just twenty-two years back. (He had no more than two such, so-called, heavy bombers, then.)

But these were not just then my conscious thoughts. My AOC was waiting for me. He was with Gort's Chief-of-Staff, General Pownall. I supposed he wanted me about those bombers, maybe to call off the plan because no invaders had yet broken through. Or had they? I just didn't know. The enemy was jamming our frequencies and our 70 Wing telephone was out of action. I checked from our own visual display that five of the six Hurricane reinforcing squadrons, daily flying in from Fighter Command stations in Kent and Sussex, daily returning there at sundown, had landed and were already in action as were our resident squadrons. I then made my way to Pownall's dungeon office.

Pownall was on the telephone when I arrived. He was evidently receiving dire news. It was that the war had begun in earnest. One Panzer force, at least, was through at speed in Belgium. The Dutch and Belgian air forces had been destroyed. Another Panzer force was speeding across Luxembourg and could perhaps be driving towards the northern end of the Maginot Line. 'Just the news I'm waiting for,' said I, and bolted back to tell Desoer to stand by to despatch the bomber squadrons. Having done that, I returned to Pownall's office.

Blount was saying as I returned, 'I suppose that the BEF and the French Seventh Army are already racing forward into Belgium.'

Noting my return, Blount told me that Gort was concerned about fighter aircraft. Ours had in fact been doing marvellously well, operating far afield, to judge from 14 Group's reports. 'Nevertheless,' said Blount, 'the French Ninth Army were reporting continous unopposed air attack. They said that no fighters were to be seen.'

I thought naturally not. The fighters' sky battle-zone would seldom be seen from the region of ground attack. There was no need for me to say that to Blount. What I did say was that our fighters could not help with the protection of the French Ninth Army; we might incidentally help the Seventh or the First Army because they were on our flanks. I did not know then that owing to the dawn attacks and the ensuing chaos we could expect little support from the French air forces.

The BEF so far was ostensibly immune from air-attack – we had had no news of it. They should soon be deploying behind their destination at the River Dyle position. But they were likely to be under frequent bombing and strafing from the air.

I was interested in Gort's demand for more fighters. 'Where is the C-in-C now?' I asked.

'He left his place near Lille at 7 a.m. The answer is I do not know,' said Pownall.

'We could easily,' Blount said, 'employ more fighters and Gort wanted us to put the case to CAS [Air Chief Marshal Newall].'

Blount asked me what I thought. I said, 'CAS will not be willing to increase the numbers of squadrons already commuting across the Channel to more than six. And we are already getting six.'

To that Blount replied, 'Dowding is sure to be as stuffy as ever.'

I spoke again, 'We are not supposed to go to CAS direct, Sir, if we want more than our proper strength in support of the Allies; we are expected to go through BAFF.'

'Well, yes, I know,' said Blount, 'but that is for coordinating Allied needs. This is our own affair – primarily for Gort and for the BEF.'

'Perhaps,' I hazarded, 'CGS would send a signal in the name of Lord Gort to CIGS, and a copy to CAS?'

'I don't mind doing that,' said Pownall. 'And, Charles, you can tell BAFF, if you like. All the same, I think the demand on CAS would come better from you. You're the man to assess the air situation and its needs – and to meet them.'

Blount had already had a great struggle in past weeks to get Dowding's assent to increasing his initial loan of three Hurricane squadrons. One by one, Dowding had put them up to six. Officially, Dowding, as C-in-C, Fighter Command, was interested in only two limited aspects of the air battle in France; first as a means for getting his squadrons experienced in the skills and tactics of air fighting; second, as a means for studying the methods and mentality of the enemy in the air. Dowding's concern was not to win battles in France but to be able to ensure, at all costs elsewhere, the integrity and efficiency of the air defence of Great Britain. It was to provide that deterrent and safeguard that his Fighter Command had been created, and for which he had long trained it, equipped it and was still perfecting it. To Dowding that state of power-in-being was paramount. Indeed, it was his destiny to ensure it.

Blount said, 'You'll have to draft me a signal, Victor. But just tell me the sort of thing you want to say.'

It was no use squealing. The BEF had already got more than twice its agreed quota of fighters and the still scarce Hurricanes of Fighter Command already were being whittled away over the battleground of France. How to appeal to CAS in a way that might also appeal to Dowding? For Newall would hardly over-rule him. I doubted if he could. Newall was, after all, only a staff officer of the Prime Minister. He was not a commander. He could only recommend.

I suggested that the signal to CAS should say that we were in a position to inflict major damage on the Luftwaffe while they were so concentrated on the support of their own army, and that we could operate six more squadrons. General Pownall could convey the gist to CIGS who could, if he liked, put the matter to the Prime Minister.

Blount, Pownall agreeing, said that we would send a message on those lines to CAS and repeat it to BAFF. Pownall could then say whatever he thought Gort would have liked to have said himself to CIGS (Ironside was at that time still in that post).

I drafted the signal there and then, and it was sent to London and to BAFF.

Vitally important though that conversation and that decision were, I had a more pressing urgency on my mind – to make sure that the command of thirty-six bombers got their orders.

I left Pownall's office at once, saying nothing more to Blount. I already knew that he was in haste to get back to Gort. He would be flying in his civil Dominie via Peter Fullard's 14 Group headquarters near Lille.

Group Captain Fullard commanded the Fighter Group. On that man's command, I judged, more depended for the whole Allied strategy than upon any other command in France, so sure was I that air power would dominate the battle from the start. It was Fullard's men, and his men only, so it transpired, who could have any totally modifying effect on the enemy's ten-to-one superiority in the air. During the next few days we were reinforced by five more squadrons, making a total of eleven, loaned (commuting) fighter squadrons added to our own four original (resident) squadrons, two more that arrived on the 10th, and one a few days later.

The skill and prowess of our fighter pilots, Hurricane and Gladiator alike, shook the morale of the airmen of the Luftwaffe from the very start. Often and often those German pilots refused battle. And that was not only because of the devastating fire-power of the eight-gun Hurricanes. Thus before ever they came to face the fury of Fighter Command, the vast Luftwaffe was a shaken force: shaken by No 14 Group, a fighter formation of which scarcely any Englishman at home had ever heard and whose men, alas, the BEF unwittingly reviled.

*

The project for the bombing attack had been neither sponsored nor approved by Barratt's headquarters on behalf of French GQG, but I had been given clearance by G-Staff, in a neighbouring crypt, for the bomber strike. It was for them to advise GQG's liaison officer, for the attack would surely be made within the French Army zone.

Meanwhile the Blenheims of our No 70 Wing would give up to the minute news of the Panzer forces soon to be over the French frontier no doubt. Our 14 Group had been instructed to provide fighter support and escort. Desoer would personally give clear orders by direct field telephone to the bomber force commander on the ground and off they would go. That seemed simple.

The brief signal which Desoer had drafted, embodying a concise operation order, was ready. Desoer showed it to me before going personally to telephone it to Group Captain Whitfield by the landline specially laid overnight. Desoer and I shared unspoken feelings. I scanned the signal pad bearing the operation order, assented and remarked that it was clear. Desoer took it to the telephone.

Men were going to face death, meet death and go through it, because of that order. Men were going to be maimed in body, agonized, crippled, made prisoners of war.

I took a car to our new underground Fighter Control operations room to see how they were doing, and, in particular, to make sure that the fighter cover and escort of the bombers, despite the urgency of all other calls, would be given due priority. It was there that I learned that the bombing order had failed to go through. Today, that very morning, the fifth column had slipped into action, insidiously, ubiquitously. At our Fighter Control operations room, I learned that above-ground telephone lines from several of the vacated airfields had been cut. That was good to hear. But the bombers cut was bad – appalling.

I sped back to Arras. It was noon when I got into the operations room. The order, untransmitted, had soon become out-of-date and useless. Desoer awaited a further air-sighting before trying again. He was still waiting. So were the bombers. Desoer had sent out a liaison officer. I needed at once to advise Bottomley about the delay. I got one of his staff on the telephone at High Wycombe. I told him, first, of the safe arrival of the units which he had sent. Then I told him of the failures. All I could say on the positive side was that we had sent a staff officer to make touch and explain.

None of that gave any comfort. He agreed that those squadrons were there for the task of striking one or other of the formed Panzer forces. If a concentrated, vital target presented itself within the next two hours, well and good. To continue to accept the risk of enemy counter-attack on the bombers after that, would, we agreed, be foolhardy. The operation should be called off at 1600 hours if, by then, it had not been called on for the attack of a vital, hittable target. He added that the bombers would not now be available for the planned night operations, with the rest of Bomber Command. Group Captain Whitfield could be so informed.

The next Blenheim report was received in the early afternoon. Panzer columns had been seen forging through and had splayed into two distinct directions. They were driving along refugee-crowded roads. Dive-bombers and close-reconnaissance planes were seen to be operating ahead of the columns.

Desoer redrafted the operation order.

Our Signals section had repaired the severed land-line and was patrolling it. No time for enciphering and tapping-out by wireless and then deciphering: the order must go *en clair*, in speech, to the liaison officer of Desoer's staff then waiting at the airfield and testing the telephone every fifteen minutes.

Desoer, once again, showed me the order. Then he went to the field telephone, turned the magneto handle and listened. This he did again and again.

The line was dead.

My silent thought was no more lively:

'Oh God! that I could call the whole thing off!' But I couldn't – not that anyone would have gainsaid me if I had.

'Nothing for it but the despatch rider, now,' said Desoer. He spoke with slow deliberation, rehearsing background thoughts. 'Whitfield has put a W/T watch on our frequency and they can receive. Cyphers? No good. Too slow. In half-an-hour the group captain should have this,' he said, looking at the order in his hand.

'He should be able to get his wing airborne by – ' Desoer looked at his wrist watch – 'ten-past-three.' All this he uttered in his quiet way, dwelling in slow emphasis on each word. 'The order provides a second position estimate for attack – the river bridge – in case of unforeseen delay, at 1545 or later.' He looked at me dispassionately. 'Shall I let it go, Sir?'

He was unflappable. The attack was going to go through.

I said no more than, 'Yes, Dizzy, let it go, please. And get the altered timing through to Fighter Ops.'

Before long we knew that the attack was going in. It was no despatch rider who brought the news. Away to the south-south-east, five miles or so at varying height, none more than two thousand feet, we saw black against a calm sky glowing with small, lazy clouds, an array of many black twin-engined bombers. Spread out, they were, in width and in height. All we could see was the take-off struggle of single, climbing, laden bombers; thirty-six individual pilots each leading his own crew and aircraft in pre-ordered disorder, streaming away to the experience for which, thus in daylight, they had been trained, yet to which, in the then accepted policy of Bomber Command, they were hardly destined to be committed. For they were night-bombers.

Were they really, in daylight, going into the attack low and singly, each on his own determining, an unescorted, undefended, skein of anti-aircraft targets? Their night role was to bomb broadly an area of general vulnerability, not precisely to hit an armoured vehicle or break a river-spanning bridge. And yet they were heading into experience for which, all along, and all that day, they had been mentally preparing – for an experience of war in the air accepted in its every consequence, including death.

We stood and watched. Just watched. The wide spread of many droning bombers receded slowly into the semblance of a flock of crows, then to a cluster of gnats; silently they sank in perspective towards the horizon and dissolved into invisibility. There were clouds, there, dark; boding of thunder, static. But there was no fighter escort that I could see.

No one spoke for a long time.

After that, the days must have merged into one, for I remember little more until the order came to quit Arras. The days in between are a blur of ever more alarming news of the pace of the German advance, of rumbling gunfire, and of the heartening news of victories in the air but of heavy losses of Lysanders, Blenheims, Hurricanes and Gladiators.

In Belgium our troops had advanced to the Dyle line, strangely unhindered, but within days were falling south to the Escaut. It was our job in Air Component to protect them, and the job fell chiefly upon the Lysanders of the army co-operation squadrons. They were up against heavy odds in trying to operate from airfields in Belgium.

Lysanders, by intent, were capable of hopping off small airfields, not off the very small Belgian farm fields which in the west of Belgium seemed to be entirely under plough. Lysander squadrons attached to infantry divisions, according to the *Manual of War Operations,* would be expected to settle themselves in convenient airfields so that they could be at the immediate beck-and-call of their divisional artillery and the forward troops in battle. In the event, such airfields did not exist. The air survey of Belgium just received – procured through Sidney Cotton and his secret Spitfires – produced no evidence of the promised 'prepared airfields'; none was to be seen within the British zone.

Pelly's photo-interpreters, however, had detected some wide areas of recently conjoined fields. These, we assumed to be intended for use by us as airfields. Alas, the photograph mosaic showed all these areas to be growing some sort of a crop, probably clover at best – certainly none of these pseudo-airfields had a terrain of firm turf. In all respects they were unpromising; the road approaches mainly primitive, unmetalled farm tracks; no hard-standings; nothing to indicate preparations for servicing squadrons of aircraft; total absence of possible concealment cover by trees and woods. The airfield problem was not going to be solved on the basis of any evidence we could produce of suitability or preparation. It was equally clear that the Lysander squadron commanders must, as indeed they were already doing, solve the problem for themselves. Thus they were driven to use narrow strips of unmown grass between woodlands on hilly ground, or, roadways with wide verges under trees, despite refugees.

We already knew that, although suffering heavy casualties, the two-squadron Blenheim force allotted to the Army as long-range reconnaissance-bombers had not been entirely powerless to see and report the advancing armoured columns of the enemy. We knew, also, that having got to the point of *seeing* the enemy those Blenheims were often shot down before they could report accurate positions. We soon learned, too, that the Battle light-bombers of the Air Striking Force were, as bombers, as powerless as the Blenheims to halt armoured forces with bombs. Whether or not any other bomber effort was being made from Bomber Command against the enemy columns, beside those solitary, pitifully-delayed two-squadron strikes, I did not know. It was not my business to know – it was Barratt's business at one of the various BAFF headquarters to deal with that, and it was part of his business to tell me what, if anything, was going on in the air.

Fortunately, our squadrons were resourceful and the wings to which they were grouped were largely autonomous. Even more fortunate was the fact that Peter Fullard, commanding No 14 (Fighter) Group, was well set up and practised in his role, and had autonomy. His operations controller was continually in touch with Fighter Command at Stanmore.

The long-range reconnaissance (No 70 Wing) headquarters had its own radio links with the several corps headquarters. In the same pattern of decentralization, the Army co-operation squadrons –the Lysanders – each had its own radio tenders with its own divisional commander. And that soldier was expected and required to be mother-and-father to his attached co-operating squadron, though never in command of it. It was incumbent on the Army to produce airfields in the divisional areas on which to locate that division's squadron. The fact that the Belgian airfield promise failed was no exoneration. But since, clearly, their divisional commanders could not be blamed for this, the failure was attributed to Violet who had failed to ensure that the promised fields had really been prepared. That, of course, was true, but could scarcely make the Air Component culpable.

On wheeling back between 16th and 19th May from their eastward-facing Dyle river-line in Belgium to that beside the River Escaut, facing south, the BEF was soon involving in fighting all along their front.

Traditionally, before an infantry attack, the plan of action would provide for artillery fire to disorganise the enemy's defence and help the infantry to seize and hold the ground. But when gunners cannot locate targets with their own eyes, or lack the gun-fire range to reach them, or when no gunners are there to shoot, the Army needs airborne eyes and striking power. Thus, Army co-operation squadrons were primarily the soldiers' extra eyes and, too, as need arose, their substitute artillery. Targets thus found by airmen could, in text book theory, immediately be struck at from the air. This immediacy for striking fleeting targets was – and still is – the crux of army air support. The Germans had developed this facility for blitzkrieg. Our army had not.

Our forward troops and their young commanders were too. perpetually the prey beneath the wheeling Stuka bombers. As in quick succession, they peeled off from their circling to go screaming-down with their one bomb to be released point-blank at their target, our platoons or companies till then on the march, would fling themselves into ditches. The soldier who had the nerve to look up into that crescendo of diving fury would actually see with his own eyes each bomb come loose and fall from the Stuka's belly and make its plunge to the death of him or his comrades. Then as that flying bomb approached, enlarging as it neared, he would see its Stuka-flinger bank over and soar away.

On would come that bomb into its crashing of intolerable violence and the prone soldier would feel, first, the shattering blast, then the scorching heat-wave and the earth convulsion, and maybe, too, a mighty thwack into his body, of metal or of clod; then finally, a hard shower of fragmented earth and stones, All that he would endure, if he remained alive, not once and for all, but again, again, again, in swift succession; a continuing terror of maddening convulsion, injury and din. Dive-bombing is an experience that grounded man perforce goes through subjectively. It takes a man of steel to watch objectively when he himself is in the target zone. But if he is a man of steel he can take a steady aim, and that will be the end of the Stuka.

But most men are not men of steel – or they weren't when the experience was new, as it was then. Then, they experienced an irresistible compulsion to take cover. To do that repeatedly is to know the degeneration that comes to man unmanned. Thereafter, every flying thing becomes anathema. Then, by reaction from his own dismay, the British soldier names the scapegoat. Indeed the 'Raff' became to him an enemy more to be execrated than the GAF. which as every soldier saw was doing its duty by its army, in that army's all-overcoming way.

Nevertheless, despite their contrary experience, our soldiers did receive (without perceiving it) heroic assistance from their own Lysanders – while they lasted. But once the land battle was fully joined, the speed of movement on both sides and the multiplicity of cited targets, the congestion of radio and the disruption of land lines, all combined to frustrate the ordering of priorities. Soon, all the well-practised battle-aiding arts of the Lysanders became of small avail. Then, never could our troops have guessed or known the casualties in those Lysander squadrons, nor how tragic was the experience in the minds of their own flying men when being shot down by frightened friends on the ground, unrecognised as one of their own Lysanders.

Further south the situation was terrifying. On the 13th the Germans crossed the Meuse and on the 14th came news of the breakthrough at Sedan. The German rush to the sea to invest the Channel ports in the rear of the BEF was on.

During the night of the 15th/16th the tattered remnants of the AASF were ordered south. The French First Army on our right on the Dyle line was being outflanked and turned south. The British Army which had advanced at high speed through Belgium was about to be cut off in its rear by the northward swinging prong of the Panzer forces.

It was uncertain at which side of Arras this thrust would be aimed and when, but as no ground forces could be deployed to halt the oncoming breakthrough, the Arras echelon of GHQ – that is to say, the land and air Operational and Intelligence staff then under the cathedral – must get out at once and join up with Gort's command post at some rendezvous yet to be selected.

Things were happening fast. The decision to quit was Pownall's and, of course, I did not question it. I relayed to the Air Staff the order to quit, to load-up and stand by.

Later that afternoon, or maybe early the next morning, Heinkel bombers in low attack struck down the château beside Arras known to me only by the code-name Brassard – Gort's erstwhile GHQ. No one was there.

Within the hour of the order to evacuate we had left Arras and were making slow progress north against a pitiful ebb-tide of laden refugees. We were proceeding independently – Dizzy, Claud Pelly and I, in the Chevrolet – not in a column of vehicles. Hazebrouck was our destination for re-assembling.

CHAPTER ELEVEN

The Breaking of Command

Who is not intrigued by talk of modern technologies – shots at Mars, men on the Moon, or even the isolation of mesons in a cyclotron? Man's ingenuity is limited by techniques – by his methods of moving men, animals, material, down to atoms. In this book we are dealing with armies. It is a feat of astounding methodicity to move a great army into a neighbouring country and maintain it there, in war. The bold statement, 'Hannibal moved his army over the Alps' once arrested my schoolboy attention. I already knew what it was to move myself over. I had known minor mountains and moved over them, carrying stick and sandwiches. I had tried, with other boys on a parade ground, to move a gun-carriage. But to move an *army* – over the roadless Alps! What a performance! My history teacher, I remember, disdainfully explained that Hannibal used elephants, as though that made it easy for Hannibal. The explanation solved no problem for me; it created new ones: how to get elephants – how to make them do the job.

Military movement is a science in itself, involving a wide range of technologies. Basic requirements for military feats of movement are not elephants but time and stability: especially stability of command. Blitzkrieg incursions into the Low Countries and France were, indeed, great feats of planning and command. The military movements which I am now about to refer to are in another category.

In one of the larger histories of the 1940 Flanders campaign, there is a tidy little sentence which reports: 'Gort moved his headquarters from Arras to Hazebrouck'. That remark gives an impression of neatness, like the move which, after careful deliberation, is made by the King's pawn from one square of a chessboard to the next. In fact, the Arras-Hazebrouck event was not like that.

As I remember it, Gort's Operations Staff moved off from the crypt of Arras cathedral at about one hour's notice. While that upheaval was in the act of happening, as I have mentioned earlier, we of the Air Staff learnt of the intention of our soldier colleagues and of their destination and, in the absence of Blount (then due to be with Gort – I did not know where), I decided to comply, and tag on to the Army 'operators'. This was Hobson's choice – we had to move with them, we had no business but theirs to see to. So, we emerged from our crypt in haste and took the road. I made no contact with Cole-Hamilton before departing. He was still at Maroeuil, so far as I knew. We left him there, at the velvet factory, to marshal all the main body of Violet and move them off as best he could in co-ordination with the GHQ administrators. I had been told that they would be going to some place with good communications, well out of the way of the Germans' advancing splay.

One purpose of the German strategy was, in general, to sever and disrupt *all* our communications. That being so, as we were coming to know, the prospect of further cohesion in the British command structure, or cohesion in any other command in Normandy, Picardy and Flanders, was a fading one. Yet I needed to keep – or rather capture from Cole-Hamilton – a few key members of the administrative staff. Particularly, I wanted Hardman, Jarvis, Bird and Rugg, for organization, personnel, technical maintenance and equipment. Without them, we could have no coherence, no operational confidence, no link with all our administrative resources. We had left Arras and I had not told them. Supposedly they would know, and come and find us. Actually, they did. Thus we, as a minor fraction of the 'King's pawn' on an Alice-through-the-Looking-Glass chess-board, were shot off into space in an unexpected direction, or, like a meson might perhaps be flung out from the turmoil of a cyclotron.

Hazebrouck, when we got there, was already virtually a dead town. Its population had fled or was invisible on that bright spring evening. We found our way to the appointed rendezvous at a deserted brick factory, not far outside the town. This became, briefly, Advanced Brassard's new location.

The first thing to be done was to set up wireless communications again. Desoer set about co-ordinating a rudimentary semblance of an operational array and working place, with tallies, registers and maps. As if by miracle, Hardman and Jarvis suddenly appeared. We had our confab about airfields and then I took Hardman, Pelly, Jarvis and Cossins in my car to find a place for us for a Mess and for sleeping-quarters.

We were accustomed to sleeping in beds and having meals at a table, in a château: we were not aspiring to bivouac in a brickyard. It is far less trouble to be quartered in a civilised way, readily, than to rough-it, unreadily. The quartering officer of GHQ was at the Town Hall. We drove there, to learn where we should stay. Fortunately, before we arrived, the dutiful Town Clerk (*Chef de Ville*) still at his post at the Hazebrouck Mairie had made an allocation of houses for '*Monsieur Brassard*', as he said, mysteriously, '*et sa petite Violette!*' – as though the names carried significance other than was strictly military.

We found our appointed quartering in a sedate row of several bourgeois detached houses each in its own uninteresting garden. The front door was locked. So was the side door. No one answered our knocking. We went round to the garden at the back, carefully prized open the French windows of the salon and walked in. Every room announced that the place was either still being lived in by well-to-do but untidy folk, or, that the inhabitants had fled in some state of distraction. Drawers were open, beds unmade, crockery and utensils strewn about, all unwashed.

It was, I suppose, a reasonable confusion of security notions which resulted in thus establishing the nerve-centre of the British Army's command in a warren of kilns in an easy-to-find, easy-to-bomb, out-of-town brick factory, and billeting the staff in a set of the nearest prominent houses in the town. And it was interesting to speculate, mentally (without uttering the thought, of course – too un-English) upon which location of the two was the less likely to attract bombs first. Army calculations upon air security were made, at that time, without recognition of the fact that the fifth column was an integral part of the German invasion machine. The traditional view was that the civil population played almost no part in military/air operations. Spies were, of course, ubiquitous – as everyone was well aware, in theory. But they would be spies who would make reports – not active links in organizing bombing and disruption. Espionage for action and for sabotage however was in the hands of brave, bilingual Germans in disguise, and numerous French traitors – all fifth columnists.

The British line of argument about security was that military headquarters in a town would be expected to be located in buildings of capacity and distinction, therefore, to choose a brickyard would be an excellent disguise – no better camouflage than the unlikely. But such reasoning disregarded the universal infiltration into 'Official France' of the fifth column; it neglected also the fact that, to an airman, a brick factory is an easy target. Also, a row of prominent houses, such as those allotted for our billeting, were easy to locate from the air.

Having seen the place, chosen our rooms, dumped kit and rations, we decided to leave Cossins to do his job of housewife and cook. We would go back to see what was going on among those cavernous brick ovens, in the way of establishing a place and a system for our roving commander, AVM Charles Blount.

We were on the point of departing, when we noticed a happening that would not ordinarily be remarkable. Beyond the front gate, a car pulled in ahead of mine, by the roadside, and stopped. No one got out. A minute or so later we went out by the front door. As we came down the front-door steps, I noticed, but vaguely, for it was dark, a man – presumably from the car – peering through a scraggy bush near the garden gate. I was unconcerned; I supposed that he had come from the Mairie to check-up about the billets, and to see whether we had found the right place. It was still light enough for me to see him take out a notebook, look at the number on the gate and write. I saw nothing abnormal in that, for a civilian billeting officer.

We walked on towards the gate. Then the official, or whatever he was, came fully in sight and we greeted him. He was a youngish man with an anxious look – and no wonder. It must have been wretched to be a French civilian in that part of France, then. But instead of coming to greet us, the man suddenly turned away, hesitated, turned back to give us a quick searching look, turned away again, then he turned his head and looked hard at us again. He was probably curious about the fact that we were wearing smoke-blue uniforms, not khaki. What was his doubt – that we might, after all, be French officers? Dusk though it was, he could have counted our British-looking rank stripes and tumbled to the fact that we were not army but air force officers, for we had come so near to him before he finally turned to make a swift leap into his car.

Certain that the man had heard me call in French 'What do you want?' Hardman's perception was triggered by the stranger's silence and retreat. 'Fifth column!' he exclaimed, with firm deliberation. And Jarvis, or Pelly, chimed with the same thought, muttering darkly, 'That man's a fifth columnist!'

A sudden scurry, all together, we were through the four doors of our saloon in a flash and speeding off in chase of our visitor whose car was already concealed in a cloud of suburban dust.

Descriptive power need not be strained if the reader will now recapture visually what he surely must often have watched on a screen; a Z-car chase – any car chase. He will not have seen anything much more hair-raising than the chase we then made from that suburb into Hazebrouck and through the narrow, stone-set streets of the old part of the town. On the other hand, a viewer of our act would have found it somewhat easier to keep on his seat than did we four somewhat senior and apprehensive pursuers. There was an element of impropriety in what we were doing. We were intent upon something very like murder; preventive manslaughter, at best. Our intended victim was, perhaps, the loyal and devoted member of the Town Clerk's staff. But he was manifestly a fugitive. Perhaps, then, he thought that we were *German* airmen; for they also wore blue-grey uniform, like ours. He might have thought any one of a great variety of thoughts, but we only had one thought about *him* – that he was the kind of Frenchman who should, within the next few minutes, die for his country in a dishonourable way.

We, in our car, clinging to wheel, dashboard and seat-back, did not voice such notions. We did not confer. We pressed on. We just *knew*! When you confront, as we had done before the chase began, an evil eye, you *know* it!

But, how to shoot with a pistol through a side-window? What hope of aiming? Indeed, what to shoot *at* – tyres or man? That was a problem; a hypothetical one, only. For dusk became darkness in those narrow, winding alleys between unlighted shops and warehouses. The fugitive was skilful and knew his way about. We would gain on him along the straights; he would leave us on the turns. He had headlights, ours were masked. So we fired no shot. We lost him.

Afterwards, I wondered if he was as frightened of being shot as we were of shooting him. He would be most terrified of being found out. No doubt, as far as his non-fifth-columnist friends knew, he was a most respected and patriotic local citizen. All his colleague columnists were (afterwards) said to be of that kind, but Fascist at heart. They did not like the idea of France going communist. They preferred the idea of Nazidom. That was understandable.

Just as every man of my railway-minded generation had always wanted to drive – or has wanted to be able to boast that he has driven – a steam locomotive on a railway, so do all of those of the car and cinema era want to make a town-chase of a bandit in a car, and make it in deadly earnest. I am not sure that I really wish to do it again.

With mixed sensations of chagrin and gratification, with warming exhilaration and increasing captiousness about Donald's driving of our Chevrolet, we came to an exhausted halt in the back quarters of that unknown, unlighted town. We needed to calm down and to consider. There was no one in the streets to ask. No lights in the houses. The war had suddenly gone very silent in Hazebrouck. We were aware that the suppression of the fifth column was not our job. We had to get back to our proper business, even although we were, in fact, somewhat lost in every sphere of our thinking and possible action. This perdition was more total than we knew.

'I didn't *like* that man!' said Donald Hardman, reflectively, when it was all over and we were back at our billet. Then he added, 'And I don't like him, now. I give this house of ours a couple of days, at most. The day after tomorrow, not only our place, but all this row of houses will be less than a row of flats – they'll be quite, quite flat.'

And so they were!

The fifth column system of target information worked better in France than it had in Spain, where it originated. The Spanish Civil War, indeed, had been invaluable to the Axis countries in many ways as a practice camp and training school for the development of new techniques in warfare. One of those new techniques was divebombing. Those houses where we then were, were already on the list for the dive-bombers. The art – if one may so call it – demanded very special equipment to stand the strain of the final pull-out. The mastering of that technique for bombing demanded very special courage and steadiness in those at both ends of the job; accurate timing, accurate aim. Both in the air and on the ground, divebombing took a deal of nerve, to deliver and to overcome.

When military pundits talk, nowadays, of *conventional* war in Europe they tend to think of how things were at the end of a campaign of long duration and of profound evolutionary development of new devices. Then tend to forget what went on, e.g. before ever Hannibal moved his army over the Alps, or before Rundstedt launched his Panzer Corps into France, or before Eisenhower gave the word to go back into France in 1944.

Amongst the many things they tend to forget is that conventional war never happens. War is never bound by conventions; certainly not by the same so-called conventions as before; nor is it characterized by the same tactics and weapons as before. Only the same general principles apply. The conventions of war are laid down as law. They are observed to the same general extent as is any law which cannot be enforced. The fifth column was not in breach of law, it was just one aspect of the unconventionality of the war in which we found ourselves in 1940. It is a convention now. Dive-bombing was another unconventionality, it died. A convention which could, but misleadingly, be said to have come out of it is the inter-continental ballistic weapon – that thing of the rocket species which has been so instrumental in keeping major international peace and holding lunar interest.

It was not dive-bombers that finally broke all system of command in Violet; it was the prospect that we should all have been captured if GHQ remained where it was any longer. Those whom we cast off remarked that *Lebensraum* was evidently at a premium for staffs, but what was at a premium was communication. Although we were not then aware of it as fact, and although there were to be further staff conferences and confabulations – based respectively on facts and fancies – the quitting of Arras destroyed the remaining coherence of Violet. We were no longer in touch with Barratt since the Germans cut our communications. Without power to serve, a commander cannot long command. Army command too, was nearing breaking point. Gort could still confer with his corps commanders and with the War Office. He used Blount's own wireless tender for that. But he could no longer handle his army as an army.

The next morning, Desoer, Pelly, Cossins, Pearl (with our wireless tender, its crew and our over-rated ciphers) and I, were about to move yet again with a handful of Gort's operators to a new and 'very secret' location. While we were waiting, one of the Army staff officers remarked to me that it was not likely that 'our lot' would see much more of the war. He seemed somewhat wishful to avoid capture. I heard what he said and disbelieved him – almost, but not quite.

We were standing by our cars in the road, outside that house that was doomed. It was a most lovely mid-May morning. I reflected that the prison camps which I had seen in Spain, not long before, had made no strong appeal to me. For the first time, I was aware that, at heart, I was an escapist. I went back into the house and borrowed some of the owner's apparently abandoned apparel – a pair of fancy socks, a very French neck-tie, and some old, thin trousers. The garments I was wearing were not suitable for the occasions that I vaguely had in view. The conventional rules of war, however, prescribe death for military people found masquerading as civilians.

While slow, dismayed clusters of peasants, and more purposeful parties of dark-clad townsfolk, mainly on foot and pushing barrows, eddied and flowed westwards in France, the armies of four European nations were in violent turbulence in and about Belgium. Two of those armies had known where they were going and had got there fast – the Wehrmacht and the BEF. It was otherwise with the French armies on our left and right. And the Belgian Army, which had begun to be internally frustrated from the start, seemed to me hardly to know whether it was coming or going. I had observed equivalent Belgian units on the same road hastening in opposite directions, but they may have had good reasons for doing so.

That same uncertainty was to become endemic. It seemed that no sooner had the British land forces taken up their positions along the River Dyle than they had to be withdrawn and redeployed at speed, in a desperate endeavour to make a new defence line on the River Escaut, facing south. There they were to make a reunion with the French First Army which, injured and delayed by battle, was soon to fall away in broken wings, its body torn by a Panzer force and a German Army pouring through the breach.

The British movements had been continually watched, ahead and on each flank by Lysanders of our army co-operation squadrons. Their crews, hour by hour, had been monitoring each their own infantry divisions. Far from their airfields in France, they were operating over half the length of Belgium, keeping divisional commanders in mutual touch. Throughout the first days of the main advance, the Lysanders had been deceptively immune from attack. Neither being challenged in the air nor fired at from the ground, they efficiently fulfilled their role unscathed. That this was so generally was then unknown to me. Hearing nothing to the contrary we assumed, correctly, that all was going well.

Gort was said to be at his command post, a spot remote, by name unmentioned but well forward. With him, intermittently, was Charles Blount, when that ubiquitous man was not making flying visits to his squadrons in his Dominie. This separation from my commander put me in a predicament both unrehearsed and unexpected. Commanders isolated from their staffs can hardly expect to be effective for long. Nor should their staffs be expected to read their minds by telepathy. We few of Violet who had been sitting below a gloomy crypt beneath a cathedral were, as has been described, active though hardly effective, uncertain and unsupervised. The same may have been true of Gort's G-staff in neighbouring dug-outs in Arras. But when we quitted our elaborate communications system to scurry away to Hazebrouck we became an embodied ineffectuality in an abandoned brick factory.

Amongst the problems for Desoer, Pelly, Hardman and me to attend to, when we had re-established contact with G staff in the brickyard, the most urgent was to co-ordinate with all concerned a plan of still usable airfields in Belgium.

Hardman, by luck combined with insight had, as I said earlier, run us to ground at Hazebrouck. Still heading the Organization Staff, he belonged to Cole-Hamilton from whom he had departed at Maroeuil. He had to organize supplies to those forward airfields, still unlocated. He was also under orders – and this was stunning news to me – to quit that day with our entire administrative staff including Jarvis and Rugg and that of GHQ. They were to get themselves installed at Calais or Boulogne.

If that, in print, conveys no special thought, in Hardman's words to me it signified administrative chaos. As one small example, I sent an officer post-haste by air to Paris, to buy a hundred pocket Leicas and all the film he could get since I had learnt that our cameras were unwieldy and useless. He took a Moth, flew off to Le Bourget, called Douglas Colyer (our Air Attaché) to his aid, and flew back next day to Hazebrouck, laden with his booty. He found the brick kiln deserted. We had just departed and left no trace of Violet. He was unaware until he found his Moth was bullet-holed, that his return flight had taken him over an area of unfriendly riflemen – a region into which, in fact, the Wehrmacht had been sweeping while he was in Paris.

Easy enough to spend a million francs on German cameras in Paris, but quite another thing to issue them to blinded, lamed Lysander squadrons then in the process of being beleaguered on their airfields. The chief diffculty was not that the airfields were becoming unapproachable by road because of shepherdless flocks of refugees and because of the presence of the German Army itself; it was that the fog of war had enveloped them.

What was even more important than cameras to the Lysanders at that time was petrol tankers for their refuelling. Evidently, they also were blocked on the roads as were all other maintenance supplies.

Nor was it only the Lysanders which were thus deprived of the power of fighting; as the days had worn on, all the squadrons of the Air Component were becoming grounded. If further service for the Army was to come from them it would not be from fields in France and Flanders but from airfields secure and well supplied in England. Within the week, the enemy had all but shattered the Air Component; the time had come for all that could still fly, to fly home. That done, all ground services must get to ports, to Calais, Boulogne, Le Havre, or even to Cherbourg.

After one day at Hazebrouck Donald Hardman and Louis Jarvis departed. They were the last of the administrators with my small Air Staff. They had to go, and we also hastily decamped. They were bound for Calais and England, and we for Lille.

Thus, Violet, a headquarters nearly three-hundred strong with all its ancillaries when the month began, was after but a few days of war, reduced to a total of not more than ten, including Blount, Desoer, Pelly, my batman Cossins, and me; reduced to the state that is most proper to 'air inferiority' in war – a state of futility. Increasing ignominy was unenjoyable to me. But Cossins, whatever may have been his apprehensions, took all vicissitudes with equanimity and without comment.

I did not recognise that our position was one for self-disparagement – perhaps it was – anyway it was deeply ironical. It was experience with which we ought not to have been confronted, as though its lesson was one we had not previously learned; we had known it and preached it in and out of season to all and sundry for years past. Indeed, it was upon the painful acceptance of this very lesson during 1917 that Trenchard, through Smuts, had induced Lloyd George's Government to create the Royal Air Force as a separate service on 1st April 1918, join the RFC to the relatively unemployed RNAS, to achieve thereby a state of overwhelming air superiority over the battlefields of France. In 1917 it became apparent to a few farsighted men in power that while an army might overcome an army by attrition and battle, the modern way was otherwise; first, the enemy's eyes must be put out; the enemy air force must be defeated. Land victory was dependent upon that.

It was ironical that that same lesson should have to be relearned in the same region of geography where the English had so often learned, forgotten and learned again the bitter principles of war. More ironical still, when confronted by the total defeat then close at hand, the general feeling in the Army, and largely among English people, was that the Air Force had let the Army down. It was the English who had let England down, a people who became intelligently strong and warlike only through disaster and the relearning of once known, soon forgotten, facts.

Mercifully for us, the German mentality even more than ours was permanently set upon land-power dominance rather than air-power dominance as a primary requirement for victory. After the defeat first of the Blenheims, then of the Lysanders, then of the whole of the Air Component of the Army, the British Army itself was demolished as a fighting force. Never again (in World War II, at least) was it to be committed to a strategy in Europe without a full assurance of air superiority. That lesson thus was learned again, this time by many more than the few who long had known it.

CHAPTER TWELVE

Candle and Moth

Hazebrouck! That word, long forgotten, comes back to mind loaded with misty uncertainty and the green of spring.

Mention a name of long ago and a vision appears, or a dream enacts itself again. Memory thus roused is often merciful in the reawareness it furnishes of the mood in which past happenings were taken into its store. Or it may be that memory is neutral and its seeming kindness is but one's own self-mercy acting as an inbuilt faculty for filtering out unwanted self-reproach. However that may be, it seems likely that when circumstances and what happens within them are incongruous – as they were at Hazebrouck – the memory-record may be muddled. More certainly must that be so when muddle was the matrix of the mood in which the memory's record was made. Dreams – especially bad dreams – are apt to be like that. Strange Guelphs and Ghibellines persist in entering, fighting, in surroundings that are peaceful and benign.

Irrelevant to the local circumstances of agriculture, coal-mining, in industrial Northern France in spring-time were the intrusions of British and German armies, fighting. The days were halcyon; the happenings in them, drear; present in them together in ceaseless contrast and contradiction, were delight and dread. So Hazebrouck, as I hear the sound of its name in my inner mind, evokes instant pictures in crystal clarity, fair, which then blur into grotesques, fuzzy and fearsome.

It conjures up for me a feeling of dimmed sunshine, a gloom of unawareness, of ignorance, of frustrating inabilities and apprehensions and of confused demand. I hear again the monotonous throbbing booming din of distant guns and the weary drone of death-intentioned flight. Then, as moody thoughts seeped through the mind, a sudden, irrelevant word from a friend would put all gloom to flight and the deluding beauty of the day would flood the consciousness, and make the war unreal.

The distant tom-tom murmur of guns had become a rolling thunder. Whereas yesterday it had come at first from the south, then later from south around to east, on that bright morning at

Hazebrouck the nearer sounds of battle and bombing were coming from a westerly arc of the compass. Arras itself was instantly menaced, and Hazebrouck was not far beyond. The time had come to move again. The place for organising battles is not the battlefield itself.

I was glad, then, when word came from General Pownall – Gort's Chief of Staff – that the operational staffs were once again to quit. Each staff was to split into two once more, the larger portions were to join up with Rear Brassard and Rear Violet in the relative security of the Boulogne-Calais area and quit France. That would leave minimal numbers to go nearer the centre of the BEF 'peninsula'; an area then in the process of becoming an 'island' by encirclement.

How Desoer fared that day, I do not know. We separated; he to go straight to Blount at Gort's latest hideout, while I went in search of our own air commanders – the commanders of the various wings. I found two squadrons, still established where they had been since the start of battle, operating amid strewn wreckage, well aware that their territory was soon to be yielded by the receding tide of French withdrawals. I found another squadron re-establishing itself under trees beside a meadow. I talked with wounded aircrew laid beside a hedge until the ambulance came. I found maintenance units in various states of resourceful resourcelessness. But I found none of the commanders of wings whom I had set out to find.

When that sun-brilliant but war-inglorious day of mine waned through a glowing sunset into dusk, I abandoned my quest for the commanders of the principal subordinate formation of the Army's Air Component; I had to find my own Air Officer (supposedly) Commanding – Charles Blount. To do that, I had to continue the coaxing struggle with my Chevrolet to get it through the still-crowded lanes and highways to a place which corresponded with a ciphered point on my map. My day of tourism had been instructive but not constructive. Gort's latest location, given to me that morning, should surely still be valid and Desoer, so I presumed, would have been there all day, since soon after he and I had parted. Presumably, too, he had done something useful. It was time I got back to the place of decision making.

Although I had gathered little of practical value, I had heard much of topical interest, whether true or not I could not know. For instance, I had been told that our original headquarters building – the place first to be dubbed Violet, the velvet factory at Maroeuil –

had been destroyed soon after Brassard's château went. The despatch-rider carrying that news – an incidental gleaning during his own frustrated mission – also reported that Arras itself was in ruins.

Violent fighting had evidently been going on all day near our erstwhile Brassard/Violet stamping-ground. As I was to learn, later, a British counter-attack was launched on the 21st in defence of Arras to repel an approaching enemy force whose approach had been reported by none other than a Hurricane pilot. That was indeed remarkable. It seemed that Lysander pilots, sick of frustration in their 'slow old crates' had, in some cases, stealthily robbed fighter squadrons of precious Hurricanes, so anxious were they to serve their army masters in aircraft which could at least observe the enemy *and* get back with a record of the facts. So the capture of ruined Arras was staved off for several days.

When I got to the end of my travels that night, I learned, not happily but gratefully, that our quitting of Hazebrouck had been well-timed; both our so-recently vacated places – Arras and Hazebrouck – had been shattered by dive-bombers.

I never afterwards discovered any more about the place of haunting memory where I eventually found Charles Blount that night. The building in which I spent that night was a great and ancient barn whose interior was spacious and darkly high-roofed beyond its spanning beams. The floor of the barn was crudely partitioned, hat-high. Staff officers, soldier-clerks and signallers, visiting generals, all in battle-dress and almost indistinguishable, moved about in purposeful confusion, like ants disturbed, dodging each other and the less easily surmountable obstacles. The floor was encumbered with packing cases. Those stage effects, intended to be unpacked when first dumped, had become writing tables lighted by candles.

A commanders' conference had ended, in some recess unseen. Adam and Brooke, corps commanders both, walked through and out into the night. Then came Blount, wearing his greatcoat with the collar turned up. He greeted me with his usual welcoming gladness, and then immediately was insistent for news and opinions.

Blount was buoyant despite fatigue. Both he and I had too long been making the cardinal mistake of taking Rudyard Kipling's poem for idealists, 'If', as though it were applicable indefinitely –

'If you can force your heart and nerve and sinew
'To serve their turn long after they are gone. . . .'

If you can! For a while, maybe – but not for days and nights on end. Darkness and light had been treated by us too much as though both were daytime.

Charles Blount remained vividly awake that night. He had far more news than I. He knew precisely which squadrons had been ordered out of the battle zone by their own commanders, or were staying put although frustrated by the penalties of insecure airfields, by lack of fuel and ammunition, or because of being crippled by combat and bombs. Naturally, he knew which squadrons he had already sent home – to England – which was more than I did.

All that sort of thing was my business to attend to. Desoer had been seeing to it, quite unperturbed; while I had been elsewhere on a frustrated quest.

I gathered, too, that there had been important visitors at GHQ on the 20th May. The first to arrive had been the CIGS – Field Marshal Ironside.

He had made a flying visit armed with Cabinet instructions requiring Gort to achieve the impossible in some way not then disclosed to me. (It was to take the offensive south-westwards towards Amiens and the enemy, keeping in touch with the French First Army on the right from which we were already hopelessly severed. Gort was to 'attack all enemy forces encountered'. The hope behind the plan was that the Belgian army would fill the gap between the BEF and the coast. Gort persuaded Ironside of the impossibility of this plan and told him of the plan whereby force – Frankforce – would strike southwards in defence of Arras.)

The other visitor was Jack Slessor – Air Commodore, Director of Plans in the Air Ministry. He had been precariously flown out to a nearby field early that morning. His mission, I was told, was for the withdrawal of the whole of the Air Component to England. There, the reconnaissance squadrons were to continue support operations over the BEF should this withdrawal prove necessary. The point was, presumably, that the Air Ministry and Gort were to be the parties to this agreement; the French Army Command (GQG) and the corresponding British Air Command in France (BAFF) were not to be consulted, they were to be informed of the decision and action. And, truly, did it matter?

Bomber Command and BAFF had, apparently, all that day, been endeavouring to co-ordinate a bombing plan to arrest the German drive through the Arras gap. This was direct action in support of the British Army and that, theoretically, was very much Violet's job to co-ordinate. But, of course, we could not do it: nor could BAFF: nor could Bomber Command. No one could. Such things can hardly be achieved in conditions of air inferiority, as we had seen when Violet was in Arras. Even though – as was the case – one hundred and thirty bombers, mainly Blenheims from England, were sent into the battle that day, the effect was virtually nothing but loss to us. At any rate, the tactical results were incommensurate with the hope and heroism behind the effort.

We were in the very kind of war that our government, only a year before, had declared to the French we would not accept; a Continental *army* war. What should have been going on at that time was not what had been happening. There had been, instead, a hazardous, hopeless pecking at fleeting targets of invulnerable German AFV's sweeping through France in conquest. A vastly more powerful RAF would have been needed, capable of striking massively and accurately at fixed national fuel storages – motionless tanks of quite another order of vulnerability – in Germany. It is not matter of hindsight now to declare that there should have been no BEF and therefore no BAFF. What was needed was a paramount Bomber Command over Western Europe, as in the end was over Japan. Terrible, but decisive.

But, that night, we were not bothered about principles of air power, nor about the unknown problems of our principal higher Commander-in-Chief – Barratt. We had to recognise again what we had been forgetting, that the great contest yet to come would be over England. That was where we previously had known it must be, until we got thrust into the wrong war. Our power to win that coming battle was all too slender. Further squandering in France of the Hurricane squadrons of Fighter Command, fighting in a land battle already seeming to be irretrievably lost, could quickly be fatal to all possibility of ultimate victory.

Our forward, close-co-operation squadrons were suffering insupportable casualties; they had been persisting in trying to do the impossible – to fly high enough to use cameras and radio, or even high enough only to see with their own eyes over the trees. Gallantry could be no substitute for tactical power of performance in the air. Then I heard from Blount of the Lysander men who had continued to filch Hurricanes from fighter squadrons. This questionable initiative had been rewarded with startling results. Despite their speed, however, these low-flying, reconnoitring Hurricanes could be shot down by avid machine-gunners and riflemen – enemy, Allied, and British, alike. It was better to lose a land battle, then, than lose only a few more Hurricanes.

The night hours, as they always do when sleep is not in quest, sped too quickly by as we debated in that barn. Decisions about withdrawals had to be made. Instructions to wings and units had to be sent out even though they might miscarry. The Air Ministry and 22 Group had to be informed. It had been decided that *all* the squadrons of the Air Component must be based on English airfields forthwith.* Once safely there, they were to re-fuel and re-arm forthwith in readiness for their next employment under new command based in England. Only a few Lysander army co-operation planes remained by the 22nd.

Thus began the start of a phase known by its ending as Dunkirk. Operation Dynamo, as it was called, had already begun for echelons of the army not required for combat. Meanwhile, the headquarters of the Army Co-operating (Training) Group, at Farnborough, out of which Violet had been wrenched but six months back, had newly been ordered by the Air Ministry to throw off, once again and instantly – this time, as Violet's replacement – a new army co-operation 'skeleton' headquarters staff. Its operational set-up for command communications was to be extemporized at Hawkinge, a disused fighter station, close to Folkestone. The task fell to the new AOC, Ben Capel, to put into effect overnight. This improvised command post was to co-ordinate the future operations of the squadrons then emerging, tattered and shattered, out of the battle but still potentially able to fly and to fight once re-equipped and reinforced with new trained crews.

So, at the dawning end of that night in the barn, our last act was to despatch all but three of the remaining members of the Air Staff, officers and men, to get themselves to Hawkinge. This left with me Desoer (Operations), Pelly (Intelligence), Pearl (Signals), plus three Signals NCO's and airmen, and two batmen – Blount's man, Filtness, and Cossins who was mine.

Soon after the first streaks of dawn, Charles Blount and I set out in

---

*Within two days only one army co-operation squadron was left. In the meantime the remnants of 13 Hurricane squadrons had returned to England, but according to the Official History so rapid was the move that 120 machines which were awaiting repair had to be abandoned. So out of 261 Hurricanes operating at the height of the battle, only 66 remained, after losses, to fight again. We had lost about a quarter of the entire fighter strength of the United Kingdom.

Candle and Moth   161

my car to find the headquarters of the Army Co-operation Wing belonging to the First Army Corps. We had some reason to believe that that command unit was still located in a château about three miles away. It had had one of its squadrons based on a meadow close beside the château. Both these units, like all the rest, had been signalled to quit. The message we had drafted had gone for enciphering at about 2 a.m. As a check of our own questionable power of communication we – Blount and I – wanted to see whether our orders had got through. We also wanted to see how that wing headquarters and its adjacent Lysander squadron were in themselves, and how they were getting on with their moving out.

Blount, I was soon to learn, had another reason for coming with me on that excursion – a reason which he kept to himself just as long as he could.

The roads were no longer in westward spate; they were in a turmoil of eddying congestion, refugees halted, or moving in both directions. A British infantry battalion moved through, concealed in lorries, slowly, on the grass verge and off. Watching them, I could hear no more than the purr of their engines as we halted on the opposite verge to let them by. One would hardly expect to hear much music at dawn, but the impersonality of that column was strange. We met French Army vehicles striving to overtake others of their kind, halted. Refugees with their burdens huddled out of their way.

Blount remained unaware of all this. While I drove, he slept. So we reached the château. Its gated entrance was open and unguarded. What had been a vehicle park in a spinney of young trees beside the drive was empty – but for one derelict. The great door of the château was open. No one was about. I stopped the Chevrolet, we got out, mounted the entrance steps and remained ungreeted. Inside, the litter of unwanted or untaken things bespoke both discretion and haste in that midnight move so swiftly done. Within that packing-up there had evidently been one philosophy; take nothing unnecessary, leave nothing useful. As there would be no shortage of official stationery and forms in England, 'bumph' could be donated to the enemy; but unwanted, useful items of equipment had to be broken. They had been.

Charles Blount and I quitted that devastated château and made our way towards where we supposed the meadow-airfield to be, beyond the nearby tall belt of trees.

As we entered that gloomy glade, stumbling over the rutted and trampled ground between the tree-trunks, we became aware of wreckage in the darkness. Beneath and among the concealing, leafy boughs of beech and oak, we came upon uneven rows and agglomerations of disordered aircraft, many wrecked or part-dismantled, some seemingly whole. In all there must have been about twenty aeroplanes of which half-a-dozen were Gladiators – fighters. Presumably they had force-landed there with battle damage. Mixed in with them was a large number of Lysanders, eight or nine, a couple of Hurricanes, a Blenheim, a six-seater Dominie, and three Tiger Moths.

There, when our eyes had got used to the gloom we beheld a gaunt and sombre sample array of all the flying equipment of our Army's dead Air Component. Some, we could see, had been shot-up, some had been torn by bombs, some wrecked in crashing, some dismantled and in process of repair by cannibalization – as robbing the wrecked for the lacking was called. Some among the wrecks seemed to be undamaged. These aroused our curiosity.

Such a leafy glade would have been dim at any time of day or night, but on that misty early morning – the ground-space on either side of the central clearing being cluttered with gaunt, angular shapes – the spectacle presented to our tired eyes appalled. It materialized the grim reality of our failure. More negatively forceful than the appearance even, was the feeling: a feeling of anxiety and doom.

Here was a stark situation. And yet I felt (as though superimposed on a dull awareness of confirmed disaster) an apprehension of neglect to render unusable the abandoned aircraft which to all appearances, were fit to fly. Or had the fugitives seen to that by gashing petrol-pipes or taking vital parts away? We clambered round to see. Some, yes; a few, apparently, no. But then I found on one of the Gladiators an uncapped petrol-filling hole. The filler neck had been overflowing – with water! So in all probability they were all unflyable.

But, we had not come to inspect demolition work, we had come to see whether, and how, a wing headquarters and one of its squadrons had gone on its hard way to England.

We walked back, Blount and I, without speaking, towards the château and the Chevrolet.

Clear of the wood, Blount touched my arm with his short length of polo-stick. He stopped. I stopped, too.

'Victor', he said, 'I suppose you know it's all up? At any rate as far as our job here in France and Belgium is concerned?' Without waiting for my assent he went on to catalogue factors in the state of our affairs. The armies of the Allies were in retreat everywhere, he said. Our rear airfields were already over-run. Our lines of supply were non-existent, cut from north to south; of the remnants of our squadrons, torn to tatters, all had gone back to England. The only hope of usefulness to the Army lay in our re-organizing – as we had decided during the night, with Gort's prior agreement – our reconnaissance squadrons, in England, as fast as we could.

All that was common knowledge to us both.

Blount jerked his stick towards the empty château. 'This move is all over and done. What next?'

I had sensed what was in his mind. 'Your job is to continue the battle,' I said.

'How d'you mean?' he asked.

I looked back at the spinney. 'We did not check on all those Lysanders,' I said, 'or on any of the Moths. If we can find just one with petrol in its tank and a spark in its engine, you might get to Hawkinge, with luck, in time for breakfast.'

Charles Blount looked at me with the most charming expression, relief and gratitude competing to brighten his tired face. 'Thank God, it's you that have said that,' he said; 'I have been trying to bring myself to the point of telling you to get back to Hawkinge, yourself, feeling that I ought to stay on with Gort to the finish.'

Perhaps Blount hoped that I would reflect in my face some of his gladness that I had chosen or decided for him his course of duty. His relief that he had not had to impose his choice on me, or, worse, to accept that since Gort could not quit, then nor could he, I understood. But the decision gave me no sense of elation. It had not occurred to me until the moment to consider whether either of us could, or should, or would depart . . . escape.

It suddenly struck me that he must, he had to continue the fight, therefore he *must* go. It was common sense. I did not doubt that we could get one of the Moths to fly, and find enough petrol to get it over the forty or so miles of France, and say, the thirty-five miles of sea beyond. What I did doubt was whether the Moth (if any would fly) with Charles Blount in it could possibly escape being shot at all the way until he was killed or crashed. On second thoughts, it seemed more likely that after a while in the air, Blount would be compelled by some defect to come down in the Channel, or that he would just fly into the ground because he had gone to sleep again.

Immediate, certain and desperate danger often give way to the spur-of-the-moment action instantly following decision. But when time gives place to reflection on facts and probabilities, prudence tends to prefer procrastination. Then, that present danger postponed, the remoter prospect of total disaster seems more acceptable, simply because the perennial escapist in man does not accept that prospect as inevitable. I wondered if Blount really would go, then and there – if he *could*. For myself – I recognised, when I came to think of it later – I was not zealous to jump into any of those dejected-looking aeroplanes and fly away, there and then – not, at least, before I had had a nap. But I was primarily considering that point; Blount was going, I was staying; I was vaguely considering Gort's possible requirements of me and Blount's responsibilities that I had to take. But Blount seemed to be questioning his own mind. So I spoke again.

'There's nothing much either of us can do for Gort,' I said. 'But it's clearly for you to get into command again as soon as you can. We can't both go. One of us has to stay with Gort. So let's not mull it over...'

Blount broke in with the thought that was worrying him. 'I suppose you know,' he said, 'you're pretty certain to be captured and see the rest of the war from behind barbed wire.' He said that, without facetiousness. He was meaning just what he said; wanting to show me that he knew what he was letting me in for.

'Let's go and see if we can start one of those aeroplanes,' I replied, and as an afterthought I added, 'I'll get some spanners from the car tool-kit,' which I then did.

We walked round the end of the wood, to the edge of the meadow. The field was clear. That squadron had evidently cared a good deal about concealment while operating there. Not even a pole for a windsock!

We turned to the wood and entered the ghoulish glade between the two belts of trees.

Selecting the Lysander first, in order of good-looks, we found (as we had feared) that the fugitives with loveless consideration for their enemy had watered all the tanks still able to hold fluid. It was the same with a slightly damaged Gladiator. The Dominie had one of its propellers broken.

So we came to the derelict Moths. Blount had never flown a Moth. Did he regard them, then, with some disdain – as not being exactly the kind of aeroplane in which a man of his standing, an

AOC, ought to be seen flying? Those were only *my* thoughts. I had done a lot of Moth flying; and pleasant enough it is if you have warm flying-kit and are not in a hurry. But an open Moth can give you a very draughty ride – certainly not a flagship aeroplane.

Without comment on the obvious and without much remaining hope, we inspected each of those little biplanes in turn. The damages were as incurable as they were obvious. But the very last seemed, miraculously, to have nothing wrong with it at all.

'Here we are, then!' exclaimed Blount. And, a moment later, somewhat shyly, he asked, 'Do you know how these pretty little things work?'

I showed him round the simple controls and reminded him about the 'cheese-cutter' tail-adjustment. Then, in he got. He sat low in the bucket-seat where the parachute should have been and we made ready to start-up, me as mechanic and propeller-swinger. Most obligingly, there were actually chocks already in place. After a little tinkering, the carburetter flooded – and the fluid that spilled-out into my hand was *petrol* . . . . no oily water-drops. I twirled the propeller roundly, sucking-in; heaved a few backward swings on the jerky propeller, and got a good feel of the blade on compression. Then, having cried 'Contact!', I gave a mighty heave and swung myself aside.

That Gypsy engine started like a bird!

Beaming with delight, Blount clambered out, the propeller ticking-over briskly as the engine warmed up. I said, gaily, as I walked away, that I was going to find something to serve as a seat cushion; even, possibly, a parachute pack and harness. Blount yelled for me to come back. Taking off his greatcoat, he wrapped it round his briefcase and shoved the bundle in where the parachute should have been. Then he clambered in again, refusing any further clothing aid from me, and shouting over my warning that he would freeze to death. '*Blistered* to death, you mean!' he said, pointing in the direction of the mounting sun glinting through the trees.

I moved round the front and put the chock-lines ready on the port side as Blount revved-up the engine to see if it would give power enough for take-off. It sounded perfect. Pilot and engine seemed to exult together in their awareness of return of power and at the prospect of flight.

Blount throttled back, waved both hands gaily to signal away the chocks. With their ropes in hand, I jerked them out from under the wheels and trailed them with me as I went to the port-wing outer strut. There I pushed with my free hand while Blount opened-up the engine again. The Moth pivoted round until we had it heading for the meadow – and for the outside world. From there, in the glade under the trees, the run-out to the meadow's length was clear for a no-wind take-off; no need for preliminary taxying into the airfield proper. I moved back behind the port wing, to the side of the cockpit, to satisfy myself that my escaping master had, at least, properly strapped himself in.

There he sat, jubilant, his fair hair flickering in the slip-stream, mounted on his strange saddle, ready to ride, regardless, reckless, determined – a Don Quixote about to assail his windmill. Was he about to be carried over the top to disaster on an ill-chosen wing, I wondered?

My impressions were confused: admiration and wishful thinking at odds with judgement and reasonable fears. Yet the prospect from the glade was truly benign; indeed, it was sweetly enticing. Beneath a sky of scintillating, heavenly blue, the meadow shimmered in its spring green starred with golden yellow; it positively called 'All clear!' Bounded, to our view, only by the bent bow of its own horizon breasting into the sky, the field itself seemed pent and urgent for the flight. No longer could I or any of the parties to this act cast doubts upon the rightness of it.

I stood close by the fuselage, about to say goodbye.

'Any idea which way?' asked Blount. And then, mock-confidentially, leaning close to my ear, he said, 'Don't tell the AOC – No maps! What would be a good course to steer?'

I peered at his compass beyond his knees. 'You're heading north,' I said.

Because of the engine-clatter, we could no longer physically hear the encircling booming of guns, but I at least could hear those guns in my inner awareness. To me, Blount's question was not, 'Which way to England?' but, 'How shall I best steer clear of overattentive aircraft-hating gunners and riflemen of all nationalities?'

I preferred to answer the question actually asked. Gripping the padded edge of the open cockpit to steady myself in the buffeting back-wash, I leant over and said, 'Go straight on as you're pointing. Clamp that on your compass – *Red on red*, mind! You'll soon see the coast, and the lie of another coastline, unless there's a sea-mist over the Channel. If there *is*, and you find you've still got water under you in an hour's time, turn sharp left! – and re-clamp that azimuth-ring, don't forget.' I shouted the last bit.

Charles Blount had heard me. He nodded. He turned his head my way. No goggles in a cold wind can make the eyes water. His were very blue, and brimming over. He was going to say something, but did not speak. He put his left hand on the throttle. Then he looked at me again and said, with a strange smile, a sort of grave gusto mingling compassion, fun and guilt, 'I shall be sending you a parcel every month!' and I replied, 'Good luck, Sir!' having no readiness of wit to counter that promise and threat.

I turned and walked away, out of the glade into the meadow and sunlight. Blount, no doubt, was setting his compass azimuth-ring and making final checks before opening-up for take-off.

Clear of the spinney so that I could see the meadow's boundaries, I waved with both hands a gesture of heave-and-go. There was a crescendo of whirring in the green gloom of the glade as that little biplane got into its run, its box-kite aspect dimly confused with wreckage and trees in the dark background behind. Out to the threshold came the small but expanding biplane; still shadowed it was, as its tail lifted from the furrowed ground. Then, flash! – it was suddenly enchanted into shining silver with a burnished halo ahead as the sunlight took it whole from the gloom. So it passed by where I stood.

Blount had no hand to spare, nor I a cap to salute. He may have seen me wave; all that waved back was his sunlit hair. K.3472, the tail announced. I would have to remember that. 'OK, three and four is seven, twice,' I mused, while up the slope of the meadow sped that cipher, in a flurry of diminishing perspective. Soon the cowering grass showed separation from that Tiger Moth's wheels; they were off!

Over the brow of the meadow they went, no higher than their own height, two fliers, one entity, in instant harmony – Blount and his Moth.

It was not they who sank away from my sight; it was the curve of the meadow's crest that climbed to take them out of my sky and, thus, out of my life.

As I walked back to gather my tools in that dim place of dead hope now re-born, I wondered which of us two then felt the more alone, Charles Blount or I? Not he! I knew it could not be him. He was certainly happy, occupied; not alone. Blount was riding his Tiger Moth; they were in their own element. Blount, to me, was the embodiment of all that could be meant by 'airman'.

It was past breakfast time. The château was deserted. To get any breakfast I must get back to that barn where Cossins would be waiting. The day was warming up. It was Wednesday 22nd May.

PART III

CHAPTER THIRTEEN

Prémesques

22nd May – 25th May

Empty of intention, the purpose of the past hour achieved, I found myself to be alone. My grimy hands reminded me of spanners. I moved towards the wood.

I came to the spot where Blount and I had salvaged that one Tiger Moth from its surrounding dead machines and wreckage. I gathered the tools and quickly made my way out to the château forecourt where we had left the car. The building stood grey, gaping, deserted.

Mentally, as I dodged and threaded my way back to the nameless GHQ barn, wherever it was, I tried to compose a signal. Various people should be given the information, as a matter of form; some would have to act, perhaps. Theoretically, the message should be addressed to Barratt of BAFF. As Commander-in-Chief, British Air Forces in France, he was Blount's immediate Air Force boss. Barratt, I reflected, was a man of endurance, dogged – much loved as 'Ugly' or as 'Barratt of the bull-dog breed'. (Never give up! Never let go! Never say die!) What would Barratt make of Blount's quitting without any by-your-leave? Would he have the imagination to perceive the facts of our situation? – had the CAS (Newall) told Barratt about Hawkinge? Would he recognise the courage and necessity of Blount's act? What good would it do to tell Barratt, anyway? Would it bring him any help or cheer?

I determined to deal direct with the Air Ministry who would already be in charge of the new outfit at Hawkinge. I did not know what to call that set-up at Hawkinge. Musing as I drove, I asked, how then would my signal read?

> Advanced Violet to Air Ministry,
> Repeated BAFF, 22 Group, and Hawkinge.
> For DCAS from Goddard.
> AVM Blount took-off in Moth K 3472 at 0605 compass course north to coast then probably direct to Hawkinge.
> Recommend some leave before resuming command.

I would have to find Gort and tell him personally how it had come about that I had virtually dismissed his Air Officer Commanding and spirited away his principal air adviser, without prior consultation. The prospect did not alarm me at all. Gort was the soul of common sense.

It was mid-morning when I got there. Meanwhile, that GHQ farm – it was much more than an isolated barn, I found, when I saw the place in daylight – was all but deserted. How like a dream life had become! Cossins appeared and seemed pleased to see me but, like Desoer, was a man of few words. Desoer, I learned, had gone on with Pownall's half-dozen officers, to a village called Prémesques. It was said to be near Lille. I found it on my map, close to the Belgian frontier.

Our precious wireless tender was still at the farm, but packed up and ready to move. Already, during Blount's peregrinations with Gort, that unit had been promoted to Gort's personal possession. Now it had become, it seemed, his readiest or only means of communicating with anyone not physically accessible. At Prémesques, there were to be no tell-tale telephones. Such amenities had proved to be the trigger-lines of death-traps. At Prémesques, it was said, no remaining local inhabitant was to be offered visual hints about who or what was there, where Gort was to be: no festooning of the building with wires, no cars parked nearby.

The wireless tender, Pearl had been told, was to be hidden in a nearby wood. Its aerial masts, already dismantled and stowed for the journey as bundles of tubes, announced to me that I need not write out my mentally-composed signal about Blount's departure. If Blount was destined to get through by Moth, he would by then have done so. If not, he would not wish anyone to fret about searching the Channel for him.

I drove across the yard to the farmhouse to collect Cossins and my kit. Both he and my belongings were, as ever, ready and waiting. A glance inside the empty house showed me that the same could not be said about my breakfast. Evidently, in the then new vernacular of flying men, I had 'had it'.

After a further conference with Pearl – Flying Officer (Signals) and his Flight-Sergeant (NCO i/c Wireless Tender) – about the way to Prémesques, we set off together; Cossins was beside me in the front seat of the Chevrolet, Pearl snuggled himself down in the back seat with the kit and was soon asleep, for he also had again been up all night. Filtness (who had now lost his master) rode with the crew of the tender, following.

Although in no doubt about our ability to get to Gort's latest place of command, I did wonder how long this game of hide-and-seek could last. The coil of our encirclement was shrinking and this fact was poignantly evidenced by the turn of the refugee tide. Weary, dejected folk were trudging, laden, back to the homes they had so recently abandoned. I spotted a family I had met before. With a mingling of pleasure at meeting again and grief at their bewildered perplexity and despair, I talked with that pathetic family of five – two old folk and three grandchildren. It was our second brief encounter. I had had a wayside talk with them, when? Five or six days earlier.

'*Les Bosches ont coupé toutes les routes à l'ouest*,' the old man said, this time disgustedly.

I bade him try going north, to reach the coast before again turning west; to which he replied, questioning my sanity ironically: '*À quoi faire?*' Meaning, I supposed, that he had made up his mind to no escape.

As we approached Prémesques along a road of relative tranquillity, a Brassard sentry stopped me. A staff captain of the Provost Corps checked our identities and directed us warily, without pointing. First he told us of the billets in the miners' row. Next he told me where I might hope to find the C-in-C. Last, after a talk on points of technicality, he gave the re-awakened Pearl details of the wood where his radio crew might again set up their masts and aerials. This was servicelike matter-of-fact talk, without any trace of anxiety. Reticence becomes second nature in service relationships on duty.

Entering the street flanked on either side by a row of miners' dwellings, continuous, none detached, reminded me of Z – the 'Shadow Air Ministry' at Garston. Now, after six months, we had come full circle to a similar situation. There we were, the fourth distillation of Brassard-Violet – what might be called the top brass staff – about to muck-in, I thought, with the worried families of Flemish miners all ready to be rounded up together and put into a prisoners' cage. I had forgotten that they would by then have fled. From doorways down the grubby red brick row of double-storied dwellings, soldiers in khaki were going in and out, or putting clothes to air along the fence or hanging out washing on lines. No French folk were visible.

My allocation was to No 4 to share with Desoer and Pearl. To my surprise it was still occupied by a genial quartet of middle aged inhabitants – two miners and their wives. A stalwart foursome, they were; perhaps the toughest of that street community – a community that in peace-time numbered all of two hundred. They had stuck it out till then, for duty's sake or maybe in defiance, while all the others made for western safety, away from the German hordes.

How glad they were to see us! That, too, was a surprising thing.

They were engaged in piling bedding, food and clothes on bicycles and making a final meal before they took the road. Our coming in – me and my batman, Cossins – brought on us a boisterous greeting and fraternal back-slapping. It was as though we had won a noble victory. The rapid, local patois of the women was beyond me; the men I could understand – well, no – I could take in, not understand. They said, 'Bravo! Bravo!'

The arrival of *les Anglais* to relieve these patient folk of their self-imposed duty of minding the mine seemed suddenly to have given them an overwhelming assurance of security; now, they could depart in good conscience; all would be well – *à bas les Bosches*! We drank, *à la victoire*, some flattish *bière* from metal mugs, and I bade them go north and make all speed. But they pointed to their laden bicycles, their laden women and their packs. What could I say? Indeed, I wished them gone. And so, those trusty, over-trusting people trudged away in a mood of generous gratitude, laced with honourable escapism and braced by ill-founded hope.

Leaving Cossins to clear up the débris and prepare a meal, I parked the car. It had to be left invisible, beneath trees, remotely from a certain genteel, isolated bungalow not far away, which I knew to be the command post of the C-in-C.

Unconcealed though that building was, its insignificance was its protection – so long only as anonymity could be preserved. Its only physical protection was a post-and-wire garden fence which enclosed no garden and no trees; only an area of shaggy grass.

Desoer somehow came to greet my arrival at that strange resort. He posed a quiet question, 'Have you seen Blount?' and added, 'The C-in-C's wanting him.'

'Blount,' I said, affecting nonchalance, 'should be back at Hawkinge now, or else asleep in his own bed at Farnborough.'

As Desoer seemed to evince a trace of curiosity in the way he said 'Oh', I satisfied him by mentioning that we had found a Moth which worked, lately belonging to 60 Group. 'Dizzy' Desoer, sticking to the point of his intrusion, said, 'Good! Well then, will *you* come and see the C-in-C?'

He then led me through a gap in the fence at the back of the red-roofed bungalow, up over an open and empty veranda filling the space between the rough-cast walls of the building's two wings at the back. We entered the main room through a glazed back-door. The room contained a half-sized billiard table covered with a large-scale, flagged map. That was on the right as we entered. The front door of the house was straight ahead and there was nothing that caught my eye on the left, except one of the four doors – there was one at each corner – of that spacious, sparsely-furnished room. The door over to the right-front, beyond the map-table, was marked Private. But my immediate glance had been caught by the four officers leaning over the map discussing the movement of forces. They looked up as I came in.

Had it been in England and beside a playing field, instead of in France close by the main road to Lille from Arras, the building might have been adequate for a small-town cricket club. Otherwise, the place had no significance. Probably most of the few who were there to use it already supposed (but certainly had not said) that it might become a place of surrender within a day or two. As I found it, it was a place of calm; rather like an off-day at the village men's club; just a few old regulars there, discussing in a friendly way things of some concern to them but not to others.

The day was grilling hot again. Two of the staff officers at the map were in shirt-sleeves. I recognised Colonel Alfrey whom I had not seen since 1931 on the Plain of Halebja in Kurdistan, Iraq. I was glad to catch his smile of recognition. He was the senior general staff officer, under Pownall, on Gort's staff.

Desoer mentioned interrogatively – should we go in through that door marked Private? As we moved to do so, Alfrey said, 'Hold on a minute. CGS [meaning Pownall] is in with the C-in-C vetting a thing we have to get off urgently. Perhaps you would like to come and have a look at the map?'

We moved to the billiard table and joined Brian Kimmins – Major and GS02 – and the other two staff officers there. The map situation was as ominous as it was confused, with all its probabilities and uncertainties, particularly those of the Belgian Army. Encirclement – the German strategic intention – looked increasingly likely. But whatever might have been in their minds at that time, there was no suggestion in what those officers said to me of the British Army quitting.

The rate of closing-in seemed to be decreasing, our troops were everywhere resisting but news of changing states was sketchy. Much depended upon whether the French Seventh Army could make a westward-facing line with us on that side of the salient, and whether the Belgians could do the same upon the eastward side.

With a shock I learned that Boulogne and Calais were already threatened. The Germans had reached Abbeville. The French Seventh Army's tail-forces in that region having been routed, seemed to have ceased fighting. I wondered how Rear Violet was faring then and whether they were in ships, or battle, or caged behind barbed-wire. However that might be, none of us around that billiard table, looking at that map, supposed that any more supplies or reinforcements would come to BEF from any of those Channel Ports.

It was urgent, Kimmins said, to get certain shipping information about Dunkirk. 'We haven't got a contact there – no one to instruct about priorities – for passing information and arranging matters with Dunkirk naval and civil port authorities. If only someone could *fly* there to get a plan fixed, on the spot!'

At that point, I noted that Claud Pelly had joined the group. He had heard the last part of that somewhat hopeless expression of need. His Air Intelligence work had virtually come to an end; his information sources had dried up, squadrons gone, Rotterdam with all its 'top secret' significance for Pelly's work had been destroyed. He remarked dryly that he thought that, somewhere, he could find something to fly; he said, indeed that he knew that he could find at least a Moth. I knew, too, that if anyone could get through to Dunkirk, Pelly could. But I wondered about the Moth; whether it was the solitary serviceable one that Blount had flown away that morning? Pelly was oblivious to all that.

Shades of King Richard and his need for a horse – to escape the consequences of battle weakness, capture and death. But that was not the state of mind around that table, and Pelly, though he might fly from the battle centre, had no thought of quitting.

If Pelly was to go, it would be for me to send him. He looked at me brightly expectant, and instantly knew the answer.

The door marked 'Private', behind me, opened. As I turned, Pownall was standing there. His background was dark. He held a signal pad in his extended hand. Alfrey stepped a couple of yards and took it, without a word. Seeing me, Pownall motioned me in, saying, 'Charles Blount seems to have disappeared. Have you seen him?'

I said, 'I've come to tell you what he's up to!'

I glanced back at Pelly. That man was nothing if not swiftly resourceful. (He could have been a brilliant fly-half.) I gave him a meaningful nod. I guessed, but did not know, that I should not see him in those precincts, or indeed, in all that long war, again. I learned, long after, that he did find a flyable Moth, at some other abandoned airfield, and flying very low, to give our men and the French the minimum time to have pot shots at him, he got himself, unpunctured, to Dunkirk.

The tide of intention by then had turned. Churchill's new government had taken over on 10th May. The first expansion of Operation Dynamo* was being made in Whitehall. Pelly's task then became the reverse of that for which he was sent to Dunkirk; on behalf of GHQ, he had to see to the getting of men and things in ships *out* of the port of Dunkirk rather than to the getting of things in.

I went through the door. It was dark to me after the glare of the sunlit maproom. The room, I soon saw, was small – only about eight-by-six. Its only window was the green-shuttered, east one, which I had seen through the maproom window a while before. Behind a small desk, and sitting in a wicker chair was General Lord Gort. His hands, folded together, were resting on the bare table. He sat erect, his firm soldier-face relaxed as he looked up while I saluted, letting me see a kindly recognition – a smile of eyes but not of mouth.

Pownall sat himself in a chair to Gort's left, and slightly behind, filling the space between the desk and the darkest corner of that little room. On the floor there, I could just see two gas-masks in their khaki canvas satchels, leaning against the skirting-board. It was an incongruous setting for a GHQ, yet it was vital that that bungalow should not be turned to blackened rubble by diving Stukas as had all but one of the other too briefly secret lairs which Gort had used and quitted. For though by no power of decision could Gort conquer, yet he could still receive the wisdom, could distil a right decision and postpone defeat. And, slender as was his power of command, commanders under him still needed to feel, if not to see, his understanding nod supporting their intentions; and they needed a Chief's discrimination to settle their contrasting claims.

*The named coined by Admiral Ramsay, SNO at Dover, to cover operations to evacuate the non-combatants from Northern France.

After I had saluted and before Gort spoke, I said that I had brought a message from my AOC. Then I told of Blount's departure. Gort said, 'Well done!' and added, 'That's the best thing that Charles could have done – if he gets through!' He paused. Then he said, 'Well, Goddard, I expect Alfrey or Kimmins has put you in the picture' and then he went on to tell me, objectively, of the situation as he saw it. The paramount need, he said, was not the bringing in of supplies by the Dunkirk route but the reduction of consumers of the supplies remaining. Ancillary troops and Ensa people (civilians) all who could not fight, British and French alike, must be got out of the BEF 'peninsula'. He had just sent off a signal to that effect. 'Fighting with what little we have left is the only business, now,' he concluded. No thought of quitting, for him or for the fighting men, seemed then to have entered that man's fighting mind. Maybe he knew that, as C-in-C, he was all but defeated. As Gort, he was not. And he never would be.

Abruptly, Gort changed the subject. 'Can you speak French?' he asked. The question caused in me a flutter of alarm; it might have sinister implications. Had he, instead, asked whether I could make myself understood in French, would not have been so quailing! But I replied that I could 'get along' in French.

Gort then resumed, a little wearily, 'A message has come in, which seems to have come from the Foreign Office not the Air Ministry, about civil transport aircraft. I expect it hasn't got to you. Someone in Whitehall, in his wisdom, has evidently induced the Air Ministry to send out no fewer than five Ensigns. It is about that that I wanted to see Blount.' The news did not register with me and I was further mystified by Gort's next words. 'The arrangement is said to have been made in response to an urgent demand from Paris. I know no more – perhaps you do – except that they are to carry a most extra-ordinary freight. Or do you know this already?' I shook my head. 'Believe it or not,' said Gort, ' – bread! Loaves of white English bread!'

Although the fantastic had by then become the norm, it was unbelievable that starvation or internal unrest in Paris could already exist in a degree sufficient to warrant such an employment of Ensigns. They were the very cynosures of all that was modern in civil passenger airliners, the latest addition to Imperial Airways' fleet. Someone's brain must be cracking.

'The Air Ministry,' Gort continued, 'is anxious to ensure that these Ensigns shall not be shot down by Allied anti-aircraft. This is more in your line than mine!' he said, smiling ruefully. 'Ask Alfrey for a copy of the message. Then perhaps you can persuade the French General of Artillery, whom you may be able to find at his château in the village, to do all he can to restrain French anti-aircraft gunners along the Paris route. He hasn't much to do; he and his headquarters have been cut off from Georges' army – the French First Army – which used to be on our right.'

Pownall suggested doubtfully that the French artillery general might possibly still have some means of broadcasting to the French anti-aircraft *Système Territoriale* – if there was still anything that could be called a system for anti-aircraft – despite the presence of at least a couple of German armies between Prémesques and Paris. 'And what about the Messerschmitts?' he asked as he got up from his chair in the corner, giving me a sympathetic look.

I saluted Gort and as I turned to go, he said quietly, 'Do what you can.'

The glare of the sunlit maproom made me shield my eyes and I realised that I was tired. I was also perplexed. I decided that I should talk better French with the General of French Artillery after a meal and some sleep. It seemed that I had to persuade him to do the impossible about the preposterous in a case that was hopeless from the start. I would have done better, perhaps, to tell the Air Ministry not to be so silly.

I went down to 'Miners' Row', found that Cossins had some tinned baked beans hot in a saucepan. I had them, and afterwards slept till Cossins, with tea and 'the royal cup and saucer', woke me at four.

By the evening I had made the acquaintance of a number of French officers in their beautifully furnished, tapestried Château Prémesques. The place was full of lovely things – more like the Victoria and Albert Museum than a home. To me, it was heavy, too, with its impending fate. Not so, le *Général d'Artillerie* and the three French staff officers whom I met in that château. They were charming; no heaviness about them and there was immediate mutual understanding between us – a mutual wish to serve. Also, there was a tacit agreement to eschew expressions of anxiety or even of sympathy. Once or twice I heard one of them employ, with a slant of ironical fun, a catch phrase – '*C'est la guerre!*' If those officers felt inwardly depressed, outwardly they still evinced the panache of the French Artillery. But I had no confidence that the French or British anti-aircraft gunners would be forewarned of the passage of five great four-engined Imperial Airways monoplanes to Paris on an errand which I had left undefined to the French Artillery General. They were brand-new to Britain and looked like Germans. All I could be sure of was that there was no more I could do about the safety of those Ensigns on their most unbelievable mission.

I had our own anti-aircraft gunners much in mind, too. But that was for Kimmins to deal with.

Was it possible, I wondered, that this was a case of things not being what they seemed? 'Bread' could mean anything. Did not Violet mean us? Who or what was going to be flown into or out of Paris, despite all the dangers? Evidently, if there was in fact a secret, Gort and Pownall were not privy to it. Probably it was to be bread – but I still wonder.

The blue sky that evening, as had recently become usual, had carried an unpatterned weaving of high-flying aircraft, singly and in little shoals. Puzzling they were to identify. I had lived within aviation for twenty-five years; I knew all our own planes, of course... or did I not? Well, perhaps not quite so knowingly as my young sons knew them. They not only knew them at a glance; they knew them by ear. Children knew new things in a way that adults cannot know. But I was supposedly an expert, not only on British types; I knew the appearance of all foreign aircraft... more-or-less. That had been part of my special work for years.

These ruminations had come to mind as I went about Prémesques, that morning. Ostensibly I was looking for anti-aircraft officers, French and British. I was, thus, more than usually aware of the sky and its living content of fliers – unrecognisable by most pedestrians whether armed or not; they could not tell whether those little silver fish so far away were steered by friend or foe. And when they came near, sounding fierce and fast, discernment was at discount, fear would then control decision. But as I walked, looking up, the blue dome above was like a fish bowl containing only tiny minnows, one or two of which – or sometimes a cluster – would be seen to dart swimmingly in a new direction, converging on another fish or little shoal. It, too, would turn... to fight! From there, or from some other part of the sky, a blue-black streaming streak of billowing fluid – not blood but flaming smoke – would, now and then, announce a kill. Those planes when littered around with puffs, black or brown or, often, white, might tell – or seem to tell – of a gunner's kill.

I did not spend long in walking, scanning the sky above

Prémesques and the local country round; perhaps an hour. In those intervals of time I saw three aeroplanes shot down, but not by enemy fighters; presumably – not certainly – they were shot down by British guns. I saw them near enough for me to know with certainty that two were Blenheims, one a Lysander.

The auguries were not good for those five Ensigns.

Among many bad habits, I do not include the habit of thinking when my head is on a pillow. I slept well that night in No 4 Miners' Row.

*

By the morning of the 25th Boulogne and Calais seemed doomed*. Only Dunkirk held a ray of hope. The scene in the map room was the same. Bright sunshine streaming through muslin-covered windows at seven o'clock. Alfrey, Kimmins and two others were again discussing movements. The War Office, I presumed, had approved evacuation of administrative, non-combatant, formations *via* the only port available: Dunkirk. It was not my business to know what, if anything, the War Office had approved and I did not ask.

I had no news of Blount, none of Pelly and none of the five Ensigns. I expected no news of Air Component units and their affairs, nor of all those thousand interests which had been my urgencies for the past half-year. The Air Component of the BEF, mutilated, dismembered, dispersed, was for me as an institution, dead. I knew nothing of Back Violet's formation in Hawkinge; I was only aware of ashes, not of a phoenix rising.

Leonard Pearl – flying officer by rank, cipher officer by appointment – came through the maproom.

'D'you you think the Air Ministry has written Violet off?' I asked him. 'Or just assumes we're all dead?' I added.

Pearl said, 'Sure I don't know, Sir! I've been bung-full of Brassard stuff! The tender's been working several frequencies and may have missed things meant for us. Would you like to have them call the Air Ministry?'

'No, Pearl,' I replied, 'I would like to know a lot of things, but – let it go! You and your little lot have all you can do, to cope for *this* lot!' – I waved a hand to indicate the khaki group in the maproom. 'I have

*Official records suggest that Boulogne was completely in German hands by midday on the 25th, with the main evacuation completed during the night of the 23rd/24th. However it is my clear recollection, and that of a colleague, that it was still holding out by the time I reached England on the morning of the 27th.

become a passenger, with nothing to do and nothing I *can* do, except admire the view!'

'Nice change for you, Sir,' said Pearl and went on his way.

After a while, a Signals captain – working 'opposite-number' to Pearl – went through, scanning a message he was carrying. He opened the door marked Private, looked in, then went in, re-emerged and brought me a carbon copy of a message. 'Just given the top copy of this to the C-in-C,' he said.

A moment later, Pownall came out, shading his eyes, spotted me at my small table by the west window and said, quietly as ever, 'Morning. Would you come in and see the C-in-C?'

I had begun to read the message. I took it with me.

The scene in the small dim room was unchanged. It might still have been the days before. Presumably those men had slept. Maybe there. A pleasant, cool twilight quickly displaced the first feeling of gloom.

Sitting, holding a message, Gort said, 'I see that only two of your Ensigns managed to get through and that they too were damaged.' He saw that I was unaware of this and went on, 'Very sorry about the other three – shot down. Rifle-fire! Flying very low in thunderstorm.... heavy rain. That seems unlikely – rain!' I was looking at my copy of the message. Gort said, 'Oh, I see you have a copy. All three crashed in the outskirts of Paris.'

Apart from the tragedy of it, this was an astonishing message. how could it have come, so detailed, in the time; and why to Gort?

That message was not a deciphering: it was an intercept: intercepted by our wireless tender: transmitted in plain-language morse. It was sent out by the captain of an Ensign – one of the five, presumably, and evidently it had been patched up quickly and was flying back.

'I see it was addressed to Imperial Airways, Croydon,' I said. 'That captain,' I went on, 'seems to have been determined that someone should know the facts before he too was shot down by some frightened Frenchman, or an enemy.' I imagined, but did not say, that if he ever did get home alive he would probably have to answer two charges on breach of security regulations: breaking wireless silence in flight and the non-use of cipher.

He did in fact get back to Croydon. I do not think he was reproached. I have gathered that he did the reproaching. His name was Henry Broad. (Much later, he was killed in a crash in Jamaica.)

Gort said, 'I wonder what *did* happen in Paris.' He turned to

Pownall. 'You had better tell Goddard about the air-lift we have asked for.'

Pownall said, 'C-in-C is asking CIGS personally to have ten thousand rounds of anti-tank ammunition flown out . . . . defence of Lille. If we can get it to the forward troops tomorrow it could be in time; they have almost run out of anti-tank cannon-shell. Unless they get some – and it can only come from England, as things are' – he looked over his right shoulder, nodding his head in the direction of the nearby city – 'Lille will be gone by tomorrow night. Not a bright prospect, either way,' he commented, drily, adding, 'We have to try it: we may be lucky!'

So, looking at me, he said, 'You will have to do again what you did yesterday. This time it should be easier. Tell the Air Ministry that whatever aircraft brings the ammunition, it – or they – *must* land near Lille, preferably near the only ammunition supply park in the Lille area, so that our men can get the stuff distributed forward, right away. So now it's up to you,' he went on, 'to say where it's to be landed and prevent the whole lot being shot down by the the French, on the way. They seem to be scattered all over our area, shooting at everything.'

'Not only the French!' I said, needlessly, and added that I would see about giving warning of the flight to all gunners who could be reached, as though I supposed that good would come of it. The turmoil raging between Lille and the coast would hardly be conducive to attention, even though a cautionary message might, here and there, be heard and borne in mind.

It was agreed that the flight should begin at first light, next day. That should give sufficient time for the various tasks in England: delivery, air-loading, route-briefing.

So it was to give that small task and its co-ordination to me, then, that Pownall had called me in. The Paris Ensign disaster just happened to be co-incidental. I withdrew to see about the job – one that was hardly at the exalted levels of military execution associated with the senior ranks involved. As will transpire, however, it had great strategic consequence. Meanwhile, that Paris happening had alerted those two exalted men to the 'sharp-shooter' hazard; they must have perceived, too, the slenderness of the prospects for success.

Portraits of famed commanders at their famous battles traditionally display a great-booted, blazoned man with sword or baton, against a background of forces battling to victory. But Lord Gort had been cast for a less self-liberating role. The picture I had seen was quite inglorious. There, hidden at Prémesques, in a poky room in semi-darkness, was the frustrated Commander-in-Chief of the entire British Army-in-the-Field, sitting in silence while his rugged Chief-of-Staff discussed with his stand-in air adviser the movement of a few crates of ammunition for a regiment or two of infantry to blaze away in maybe a score of light-weight guns.

As for myself, the air adviser, what could I offer as advice in such a project? Could I have said that in view of the losses of three precious Ensigns over Paris that morning, the game was not worth the candle? It was for them to evaluate crates of ammunition against the Wehrmacht; was it for me to compare their value with that of an Ensign air liner – one of the few remaining, then? I offered no advice and decided that warning AA gunners would be a waste of time.

Out in the dazzle of the maproom, I found Desoer and saddled the airfield task on him. So he went off to settle the little plan and decide which of the local airfields, all deserted then, might best serve the ammunition men, wherever their depleted park might be. He was to return and tell me the airfield chosen. Meanwhile, I would take a morning off. Such brilliant sunshine called for basking out of doors.

CHAPTER FOURTEEN

Lines of Power

26th May

Having no duty to perform I stood by the veranda door watching Desoer as he went to find a car hidden in the trees beyond.

Seeing a lonely deckchair I went to it and sat down, realizing that there was nothing for me to do. I had a sudden sense of holiday. What a glorious spring day! I could hear birdsong, the rustling of the green leaves in the tall group of nearby poplars. Those sounds were real to me – more real than the rumbling tom-tom of percussion murmuring from the southern front, and its accompaniment of pulsating airborne tympani. Sounds of war, however, were rational, acceptable, despite the menace they implied; for they were noises proper to soldiering business; no more to be complained about by soldiers than would be the thud and ring of hammer on metal by men who work in a forge.

Before I had lowered myself, full-length, into the 'hammock' of that canvas chair I had been hearing quite another kind of noise – plaintive sounds of suffering; the moaning of cattle in the byre of the nearby farm, and the howling-barking of a dog, abandoned, chained. The mental torment of that and of all else that was out of tune with spring I wanted to evade. My deckchair seclusion I had hoped would provide that escape. When the sounds of distress abated, it did.

There, I was cut off from the war on three sides by the walls of the bungalow. The forward space, northward, being open only to woodland and the sky, the sounds of battle and farm lament became inaudible. The blue sky above and the carolling of larks, invisible in that blue, became all my consciousness.

I had no distant view, only a square of sky with no horizon but the tree tops to the north. As I have said, there were roof-gutters to east and west, and me in my deck-chair. All within those boundaries was blue – free of any cause for wonder other than its azure clarity. This was pleasure. I had not known the like of it for many months.

A diamond-flash broke through the hard frame-line to my right. The clear blue beside it was swiftly pierced, and pierced again by glinting crosses of silver. High – very high – an aircraft had darted into view, followed by two more – an arrow-head of three, each trailing brilliant white 'rods', as their trails seemed to be. The intelligence officer in me awoke, with his vocabulary of German Air Force names. It was a *Staffel* – that is, a flight, in English – another *Staffel* and another – right and left. I knew that arrowhead of planes to be a bomber squadron – nine Heinkels. All were trailing gleaming narrow blades of white.

Heinkels I had seen before, but never those white ribbons extending in their wake, like rapiers.

Impressions and thoughts came swifter then than can their recording here. Bombing had been my business in the past. Those bombers were carrying bombs to be dropped on their enemies, quite presumably us. My instant anxiety was, *were* they for Gort, personally, and us here – and, if so, had they just dropped them, at that moment? I wondered, fear swiftly mounting in my mind. Bombs, when falling, stay beneath the aircraft, lagging behind but little as they fall. As the bombers pass over their target through its zenith, so, next moment, their bombs strike ground or building, and explode.

Those Heinkels were nearing, then, the bungalow's zenith – or, perhaps not – not quite. The moment of first appearance would have been, I judged, about the moment for release, if this small house was to be their target. But surely, anyway, we could hardly be their target – Heinkel 111s at 20,000 feet would not be aiming at a pin-point target such as this. It was, however, a comfort to detect that their line would not pass through my vertical. Bombs from that formation, *if* they actually had been dropped, would all fall in the wood. No need to move. Indeed, I could not have moved – I was spellbound.

I had continued watching the right-hand eastern sky space to the gutter line. Into it, flight after flight emerged in strict precision, unopposed. No gun was fired from anywhere around.

Here was a startling sight: bombers, remote and swift, in seeming silence, on the war-path – on an invisible sky-way – invisible until formed into a white-lined highway by vortices of the many thousand horsepower of aero-engines; each track in that array of parallels being headed by a silver cross – a bomber; each cross, the hilt of a long, gleaming sword.

A layman, not aware of technicalities, might have assessed that spectacle of trails as being no different from that which he had often seen at Hendon, or in pictures, year-by-year, when, for display, squadrons of the Air Force enhanced the thrill of manoeuvre-in-formation by ejecting from each pattern-weaving aircraft a trail of artificial smoke. But in this war-display that I was watching, there was no artifice for effect – the happening was natural and uncontrived. In my experience it was entirely new, and enigmatic, startling – new to western Europe, anyway, though Warsaw may have seen that striping of the sky – white parallels on blue – before it knew the terror which was then portended. There, in that spread swathe of stripes was a portending. It was phenomenal; I knew no explanation – until I perceived its fortuitousness and the natural vapour-principle involved.

Clear air, when moist enough and cold enough, admits of its being triggered into instant visibility if only traces of dust and water are added. Thus are clouds formed, day by day. So, then, in cold clear air the passage of a plane, omitting dust with water-vapour inherent in its exhaust fumes, aided by the vacuum effect of vortex, may create cloud – a 'vapour-trail', as, later, that phenomenon was named, and now has become a commonplace in the skies of every day.

That spectacle of white (as inadvertent as it must have been unwelcome to the fliers, because of the help it gave to gunners and pursuit) held half my mind in thrall as the other part of my observing counted the numbers. German *Staffel* after *Staffel* – flight after flight – second by second, had pierced my sky-line, expanding the Vee of incandescent crosses into an arrowhead of twenty-seven. Three-times-three-times-three: three Heinkel squadrons: a wing of Heinkel 111s: twin-engined, medium bombers, as we would say. To the Germans they comprised but one *Geschwader* of strategic bombers – a mere twenty seven, drawn from their 'bomber first-line strength' of fifteen hundred.

So they streaked across my erstwhile astral sea of blue, spinning as though by magic their silver strings, making a long-extending harp of chords. Meanwhile, but not till most had come to view, their sonorous roar of power flooded my bay of country air with thunder. Whither were they carrying their fifteen tons of bombs? To Calais or Boulogne, I guessed, for sinking ships. Back Violet and Back Brassard might still be there at one or both of those ports, and likely already to be embarked.

So they sped over to the west-north-west, twenty-seven Heinkels in perfect order, magnificent in luminous array, unchecked; their white lines narrowing in perspective to my horizon of green treetops.

'So that's what a *Geschwader* of Heinkel 111s looks like,' I said to myself, with the kind of satisfaction a birdwatcher might feel on sighting his first great Golden Eagle. For three years I had been dealing, month by month, with paper estimations of the rising German bomber strength. In Germany, in Hungary, even in Czechoslovakia, I had actually seen *Geschwader* of Dornier 17s and Junker 52s showing their paces to military staffs, to politicians and (not least) to the populace at large. And in Spain's agony of Civil War I had experienced war-bombing and witnessed the devastation wrought in the blasting of Madrid and Teruel. But Heinkel squadrons in review order, gleaming at 15,000 feet or so, were new to me; as, too, were then their brilliant 'carpet' of trails. It was an experience that thrilled this jaded deck-chair warrior.

I had not moved. Only my eyes had followed. My head, laid back on my clasped hands, was being used for ruminating. In a way, those bombers seemed to belong to me. So long had I watched their evolution out of surreptitious factories, emerging at first as civil transport planes for a 'League-permitted' Lufthansa civil air fleet. I stayed in my deckchair, remembering. There was nothing else that I could usefully do.

The maproom door onto the veranda opened. I sat up and looked round, to see Brian Kimmins and another officer standing there. One said to me, 'We didn't like all that roaring! I do hope they've all gone away!'

The other said, 'I wonder, where's the Royal Air Force?', echoing the Army's catch-phrase of that time.

'Give me a chance!' I said. 'I can't lay on everything to take place immediately over GHQ just to amuse idle staff officers.' And to Kimmins I added, 'Shades of Camberley! Do you remember?' He had been in the same syndicate with me for a great inter-Services staff exercise, at Camberley. He would remember that I had been allotted the role of Reichsmarschall Goering, as head of a fictitiously *small* air force, pitted against overwhelmingly strong French-British air power, while Kimmins took the part of General Rundstedt, the German Army Group Commander.

Kimmins nodded recognition of that staff college fantasy as I began to say, 'It seems that, after all, the Germans have got quite an air force!'

To which he replied, 'You're telling me – the sky's been lousy with German aircraft every day and everywhere, ever since the balloon went up.'

'Ah,' said I, continuing the backchat, 'but you're talking about army-battling aircraft, and all this local nonsense I've been dragged into with all you brown jobs! What *I* am talking about is real air power. That lot that you heard just now is just a first sample of its kind to pass this way.'

Banter was but a cover, I think, to conceal our sense of awe.

'Your old hobby-horse!' he taunted, in friendly recognition. 'Where d'you think they're laying that carpet to? And why the magic carpet, anyway? – what's *that* for? Dunkirk?'

I said, 'More likely Calais or Boulogne, I think.' But we did not talk about the carpet of trails; it was no time for a theoretical discourse and the phenomenon of sky-trails was new to all of us.

The two at the door went back to their business in the maproom and I resumed my sky-watching, contemplating the broadening and dissolving of the trails above.

Then, once again, as startlingly as before, there pierced through the eastern frame of my sky and into my vision, a second series of 'incandescent' bombers, again in successive Vee formations. The tracks of this second *Geschwader* seemed to lie parallel to those of the first, but more northerly. Otherwise, it was the same precisely: Heinkel 111s: twenty-seven in all: same altitude, say fifteen thousand feet: same speed, not quite two hundred knots I thought. But as their broad band of many trails extended, I could see that their aim was different from that of the first. Perhaps the first *Geschwader*'s target could have been Boulogne. If that was so, this second strike might be on Calais.

My line of thought, speeding on ahead of the bombers to their target, was snapped by a happening in my foreground view. It was a black limousine of an unusually 'Whitehall' appearance coming to a stop by the gap in the wire fence. From leafy cover beside the track, a Provost officer and a sentry quickly emerged to intercept the dismounting, khaki-clad passenger. Instructed by the sentry, the driver backed-down to get under tree cover. No cars might be left in the open. The Provost officer scanned the proffered pass and pointed the brass-hatted visitor to the door on the veranda. The man, despite his khaki, turned out to be an admiral; two rows of gold oak-leaves on the peak of a khaki-covered Navy cap announced that fact. I got to my feet as he came to the veranda steps, saluted as he mounted them, feeling, as he was coming up that 'ladder' onto that 'quarter-deck' that he ought to be piped-aboard. What a place of surprises. Where could this admiral have sprung from and why?

Not tall nor young, but every inch a sailor, the visitor returned my salute and, in that act evidently brought to his hearing for the first time, the diminuendo phase of the Heinkels' roar. He turned his head and with a startled look, saw the white sky-sword pointing west-nor-west. In his limousine, he must have been oblivious of the happening. 'Great Scott! What's *that*?' he asked, by way of greeting me.

'Heinkels, making for Calais, I would guess – Good morning, Sir!' I answered, recognising him. He was a famous national hero.

'Morning,' he said, 'I've come to see Lord Gort. I'm Keyes.'

At that moment, Alfrey opened the half-glazed door. Admiral Roger Keyes went in. His fame came from World War I. He was the leader of the desperate Zeebrugge raid of 1918. Latterly, he had had much notice as an admiral-MP championing the Navy's air needs in the House of Commons. What was he doing here?

I resumed my sky-watching, ruminating while still basking in the sun, waiting for Desoer's return. It was no longer the entrancement of the fading sky-phenomenon that filled my reverie; it was Keyes, and the strangeness of human nature, of tradition, loyalty and prejudice – of admirals and air power as epitomized by Keyes. His saying, 'Great Scott – what's that?' evoked a whirl of feelings. Keyes – inveterate enemy of 'Trenchard and his Air Force' – had persisted in the wake of Beatty and the other anti-airpower pundits, clamouring for the splitting of the Air Force so that the Navy could secure autonomy in meeting its air-ancillary needs. Great Scott! What he had just seen, unknowingly, was strategic air power on the warpath; a line of power proceeding from a reservoir of air power ten times the power of our own. And the admiral asked, 'What's *that*?'

Keyes was a traditionalist. But he had all the true qualities of the hero plus those extra ones that make the English hero. He was a zealot for the Navy. I loved the Navy, too – and could not help loving that good man. But I did wonder what he had come to see Gort about.

Motionless in my chair, relaxed, I watched the dissolution of those vapour trails – no longer dazzling white. They spread themselves into hazy blurs which soon became filmily diaphanous. The sky was of a lighter blue than it had been before.

Too mindful of that peaceful transformation overhead to think about tragedies of bombing I was conscious only of regret that my sky, so deeply blue before the Heinkels passed, had been paled by a man-created covering of translucent film.

Suddenly I was alarmed by a rapid happening in that sky. It was not aeroplanes. Nor was it trails of white vapour. Quite the contrary; it was thin black lines, racing parallel across the sky, one after the other.

I became deeply afraid of coming calamity.

Fear of the unknown assailed me inwardly. I knew dread. It was fear of a scare-mooted 'thing' – the Death Ray. Persistently its existence had continued to be reported, since 1935, as being in Hitler's secret weaponry; persistently I had, as head of European Air Intelligence, continued to deny its possibility, and that, on the authority of the scientist inventor of radar, Dr Watson-Watt. But what was this terrifying, swift sweeping-over of visible black rays?

What was I seeing, racing across my placid, tranquil sky? Thin lines, black-seeming, not cords of white; they were one-hundredth of the width of the space between each successive parallel; they were like lines of longitude on a revolving globe. Totally unlike those trails of white, their sky-sweeping was transverse to the erstwhile Heinkel 'sword'. These diabolical new lines-of-power – 'wires' of near black in a blue-white dome – were racing across my whole span of sky, at lightning speed, one after the other, in parallel. In two seconds or maybe three, each and all successively traversed my view of the pale blue above me. Not quite evenly spaced, were they, yet almost so. One after another they came apace, and went, three or four in the sky at a time – reaching out of France away to the North Sea.

Who, or what, could be generating those swift power-lines, straight as a die – or, were they not slightly bowed? On, on they swept, successively, much faster than I could count. Fifty must have passed in less than ten seconds. Then they ceased . . . but not their mystery.

I lay back, stilled – stiller than I had ever been. Not stunned; simply astounded . . . awed.

Nothing happened. I began to think. What did I *not* know about war – about German air power – about German secret science? Evidently, a lot. I did not know about *this* – and I dreaded the knowing that might soon come.

Still nothing happened. Well, were those lines the rays of enemy-killing power – German-generated? They did not emanate from

Germany. On the contrary, it was *towards* Germany they were sweeping . . . like waves . . . like thin crest-lines of waves, such as I knew at Polzeath, on which surf-riders sport. But their pace was beyond believing as wave-speed. It was of the speed of lightning, or, might it be . . . of *sound*?

Yes, that was it. It was the speed of sound – they must have been the sound-waves of bursting bombs coming from Boulogne.

And then my fear dispersed. I understood. Only a sense of awe remained. The lines which I had thought were black, I then knew must have been dark blue – the deep blue of the sky beyond my man-made film of vapour. That film was no film, in fact, but a shallow cloud-mist; it could but be a few feet thick. That vapour film, then (to call it so), had suffered the passing action of successive pressure-waves. Each fleeting impact of pressure had instantly evaporated the film; in the next instant the film instantly re-formed as vapour. That swiftly moving moment of clarity of air, between two instants at each succeeding point, had given me a fleeting view into the darker abyss of sky beyond.

I knew then – or I thought I knew – what that special power must be and that it was, itself, a neutral, natural power. If so, then each of its wave-crests was a 'news-broadcast' to the world at large of the bursting of a German bomb at Boulogne. If that was really so, proof would come within four minutes or so from Calais. Then would come swiftly to me the dark announcers of the deed being done; I should see again dark, fleeting lines parallel as before, but their orientation canted a little, clockwise.

If ever I have done an act of thinking more coldly calculating than that had been, I am not desirous of recalling it. But it was all due to the fact that the vapour trails left by the formations of Heinkels had formed a shallow mist which I have referred to as a film.

I waited.

What had just been happening was, I felt sure, unprecedented in the world's history – unless in some 'Atlantean' war in a past era, such power-lines had been seen. Having it now in retrospect, I can aver that it was never seen again – not, at least, by English eyes, or we would have heard of it. The sky conditions of that morning at Prémesques must have been unique.

At first, with no humane regard for any fact of life or death attendant on the generation of the coming proof of my deduction, I waited. The proof must surely come. Then waiting still, I surmised but dimly, what this manifestation's cost might be, in death and doom and suffering. And I felt too feebly for effect, I fear, a mood of prayer.

Then, over the sky was flung line after line of slender bow strings, blue – dark blue – parallel and slightly bowed. Those lines – quite fifty in all, there must have been – were lying at right angles to the flight track of the second wing of Heinkels.

Bow strings? That was how I thought of them. In fact they were arcs of circles, like those caused by a stone dropped into a pond. I had been seeing sounds that could not be heard which, too vivid then, have ever since lived in my memory.

When in an arid state of inability, and in circumstances which carry no joy, relief which is relative pleasure can still come from a by-product of bad happening. So it was with me, on converting a nameless fear of nameless forces into a certitude of understanding. Not an acceptance of the deep diabolism of bombing as though it were benign, but an acceptance that there was no deeper diabolism in those once terrifying 'rays' of secret power. So I relaxed once more into my sky-gazing and my waiting for Desoer's return.

Then, for the third time that morning, on came a new *Geschwader*. Heinkels, once more, speeding over the eastern sector of my sky, and they were heading north.

This time, I had no fear of bombs being dropped on us. Indeed, I had expected that there would be this third attack. I had even made a plan to use it. That plan had to be put into action quickly and test my theory. I looked at my watch. It said 11.14 and twenty seconds. Then I looked up again at the skein of bombers.

There was the same arrowhead of Heinkels – so German-like in uniformity – there were twenty-seven; same type, same height, and same formation. Again, they left the same white, brilliant trails. More quickly, this time, those trails spread into a silky vapour-'film'.

Again, no guns challenged. Could that be because they had run out of ammunition? – or had we and the French no guns about? I did not know. Neither did any fighters then attack, but that I understood. Ours had all gone back to English bases; the range-of-action thence of Hurricanes and the new, few Spitfires barely extended beyond Dunkirk.

I looked at my watch. It said, 11.14 and fifty seconds.

Three successive *Geschwader* of strategic bombers had passed over that one little spot and through my small space of sky, all within twenty minutes. But yet it had only absorbed one-twentieth-part of

Germany's strength in bombers. At the rate of three bombers a minute, this could be kept up all day – or could it *not*? As yet, I had seen none return. But such one-track mindedness was hardly to be expected, not even in a German plan of action. They would return another way.

This latest lot were going north, I noted. They must, then, be aiming for Dunkirk. (The time? – 11.15.10.) Dunkirk! I knew that with conviction and got up at once to act. Not to give Dunkirk warning; that was impossible. Nor to call the soldiers out to see the trails; they were already at the windows, watching. I had to make a reckoning quickly, and went to my table for my small-scale map.

'Where's that lot going?' asked a GSO3, as I came in. And I replied, 'Dunkirk, this time, for sure. But I want to check it.'

I had already had (when I first read my watch) a private notion to trade on my new knowledge. I was to astonish the soldiers by predicting to them the coming of, and the precise timing of, a 'secret-weapon' phenomenon in the sky. Those racing, 'darkpower', once-fancied 'death-rays' would surely come once more. The question was, precisely when? Hence the need for measuring, arithmetic, and haste – to get the time of happening fixed, and get the soldiers out to the veranda a minute or two before 'the thing' was due.

I had had my nerve-scare when those 'rays' of dreadful mystery first raced over my sky. Perhaps it might be a distraction for my khaki colleagues to be put through that ordeal, too. At any rate, it would be a test of the stiffness of their upper lips. Of course, the notion was a puerile one: an act, someone might say, of 'fiddling while Rome burns' for my own amusement. But I did not see it like that. The experience might not be exhilarating but the dénouement would be pleasantly relaxing for all concerned. Besides, a lone airman has to keep his own end up somehow. I was unaware of any Neronic aspect, nor was I thinking of the death of friends and hope. Besides – I truly wanted proof of a notion.

The compass direction of Dunkirk on the map tallied with that of this latest Heinkel bomber force. I took the distance off the map, guessed again the speed of the bombers at their guessed height, guessed the speed of sound at that height and did my calculation. When I had finished it and checked it, I had two minutes and ten seconds left before the dark lines would be sweeping overhead.

The third swath of white lines had dissolved into a sky which was still clear blue and faintly hazed. I knew that the magic would work.

Unconcernedly, I strolled out to the veranda and looked up casually. There were no aeroplanes in sight.

I came back into the maproom more purposefully. Alfrey had joined the other three. I said to him, 'Have you noticed how clear of any other kind of aeroplane the sky had been during the progress of those formation raids?'

He hadn't. Indeed, the sky to the south most assuredly had not been. Battle was raging there, as they too well knew.

Undeterred, I said, 'Something extraordinary has been going on to the northward. Do come out and watch. In about half-a-minute I think you'll see something really remarkable. Perhaps it could be the explanation?' (I was trying to make mystery.) 'You've heard talk of the German "death ray"?' Alfrey nodded. 'Well, do come and see what's to be seen.' I spoke loud enough for the others to hear. I looked at my watch. 'Don't delay!' I urged. 'I reckon that the next sky-sweep will be over within a minute from now.'

Those frustrated staff officers had been too long suppressing anxiety, and were somewhat devitalized by fatigue. In their view, I could have been at a low ebb, too. They looked at me; they looked at each other with eyebrows raised, seeming to hint to each other that my unexpected emergence as commander-in-the-field of a nonexistent air force had sent me round the bend.

No one spoke. No one moved toward the veranda door. Was there a sudden atmosphere of fear? Each of us knew the BEF was all but surrounded, that our little piece of geography was likely to be bitten off at any time, that we might soon become helpless observers of chaos and catastrophe. For a moment longer no one moved and I heard again the pitiful moaning-mooing of unmilked cattle, the fretful howling of that chained-up dog. My mind switched back to Alfrey and his little staff of soldiers. Into their state of over-strained fortitude I had thrust a stab of anathema – the devilish notion of the forgotten 'death rays'. I began to feel a touch of shame.

Turning back to the veranda, I murmured, 'Well, never mind! I just thought to let you see a bit of a miracle. It will be over in half-a-minute from now.' Looking at my watch, then looking up, through the doorway, I moved out.

Kimmins and Alfrey followed, then the other two hesitantly came out, too. We all looked up at the sky. It was empty of interest. All was motionless and silent. That interval of nothing happening became a duration of suspense. Kimmins snapped it, saying, 'I don't see much!' Then, hearing the moan of cows again, he said, 'Hadn't we better go and milk those cows?'

'Wait!' I countered, looking at my watch intently, 'In ten seconds it will come. Look to the north!'

Long seconds, they were; but whether more than ten, I do not know.

Suddenly, a thick dark line, then another, another, another, swept out of the tree-tops into the upper sky; then another, another, another and another, showing the slight curve of a bow as they swung over the bungalow; another, another... swoop-swoop-swoop to fifty times and more. The five soldiers on the veranda with me had seen them from the first of that fifty series. They had seen. I knew the feeling that they had experienced – awe; uncomprehending awe, blended with archetypal fear of the unknown.

'What the devil's going on?' asked Kimmins tersely – suddenly angered.

No one else spoke. We all knew that we were observing an unheard-of phenomenon. The racing sequence ceased. After a moment, Alfrey turned my way and said, 'But what *was* it – and how did you *know* that it was to happen – and exactly *then*? Are there more to come? Or is there anything else?' He was apprehensive and mystified, not evidently afraid. 'Do you know about this thing?' he asked, quite calmly.

The others were still looking up and a GSO3 asked 'Who was doing it? The Germans, or us? And what's it for?'

'It's all over, now,' I said, 'There should have been fifty-four of those lines – for fifty-four bombs on Dunkirk.'

Their eyes left the sky and fastened on me.

'Dunkirk? How do you know?' Alfrey asked again.

'Arithmetic, my dear Watson,' I replied, 'I happen to know the speed of sound.' Then I explained that I had seen the same thing, earlier – coming, I guessed, from Boulogne and Calais, and that this third one had proved the theory. 'I only hope,' I concluded, 'that there were less than fifty-four lines. Every reduction by two lines might mean a bomber shot down before bombing.'

'Well, thanks!' said Alfrey, doubtfully, 'I think I feel better for that, and yet worse. Boulogne and Calais – that's bad. And now Dunkirk. There must be a lot of our men there, now – thousands. We want that place.'

Kimmins touched Alfrey's arm, 'What d'you say about a bit of milking?' he enquired, jerking a thumb, 'Shall we go?'

Alfrey immediately reacted. 'Yes, I've been longing to do that, all the morning. Who's coming?'

All but one of the soldiers moved off, together, jumping down from the open end of the veranda, leaping the low, wire fence and racing through the long green grass of the old orchard that lay in the dip between our bungalow and the farm buildings to the west. The odd man out said, when they'd gone, 'I must stay and mind the fort.'

*

Signs in the sky take many forms. Ours was no miracle happening, like the Angels of Mons: just an announcement of the destruction of vital channel ports – an intimation by a means unparalleled before or since in my knowledge of meteorology. When I came to an understanding of it – indeed it may have given me the clue – I recognised the same principle as had operated in a happening when I was eighteen, the juvenile captain of a naval SS airship. I was with Ralph Cochrane in a great hangar near Chatham. Five blimps were bagged-down to the 'deck', their cars ballasted with sandbags. Suddenly they all rose from that concrete floor, together, and, then, all promptly and together, they sat down again. There was no explanation. No sound. The cause was secret – or, rather, it was *made* a secret.

Later, we learned the reason. It was the Silvertown disaster. The pressure-wave from that explosion, when it reached those airships, forty miles away, although it had then lost its power of sound still had its inherent capacity to increase, momentarily, the buoyancy of the gas-bags of those six airships. So they rose to its passing and made its invisibility most startlingly visible to those two young naval officers, Ralph Cochrane and me.

That morning's bomber-happening at Prémesques showed me that the process of quelling fear when love is not in action, greatly depends on understanding. The greater lesson of that morning was taught by a few British soldier friends who found its fulfilment in the act of milking two dozen Normandies and unchaining a hungry, thirsty dog.

Those happenings with soldiers in defeat, with bombers and with milking, gave me new understanding. The strongest human line of power for quelling fear and easing suffering resides behind the soldier's thin red line, which is in fact the soldier's stiff upper lip.

CHAPTER FIFTEEN

A King's Decision

26th May

I was alone again in my deck-chair, letting my thoughts drift among the associations aroused by the events of the past hours. I knew too well why those bomber formations we had been watching would not be defeated by the French Air Force, and that they could hardly be 'seen' by RDF (radar) from England, and so were unopposed. Conviction then began to grow in my mind that the total defeat of the BEF, the French First, Ninth and Seventh armies, together with the Belgian Army, entire, was near at hand.

My thoughts crossed the Channel, not to question whether defeat in France meant defeat in England too – that idea did not occur to me – but mentally to visit my own folk and friends. Were they, I wondered, in a grievous state of anxiety? I did not know how much they had been told: I had not latterly been listening to the BBC. I felt that I knew, and hoped that they at least believed, that England would not be defeated. For that long-held conviction of mine, I had Adolf Hitler and his *Mein Kampf* to thank – not that I thought of thanking him at that moment.

I had been trained to think objectively about power; I had to think of the military effects of destruction of economic resources by bombings. Soldiers always want bridges destroyed or defended. The destruction of defended bridges by bombers (to cite a point of bomber-economics) was always a highly uneconomic enterprise unless surprise could be achieved. So also was the destruction of concrete and steel dock-works. Poorly-defended ships in port, on the other hand, were 'economical' to attack. But to make useful assessments of probable results of any bombing effort, one had to have an array of facts. I had no facts to go on other than what my eyes had seen in the passing of three *Geschwader* of Heinkels and, as it were, heard, through seeing their expanding spheres of sonic pressure, black-lined for me that morning in hundreds of bombs dropped on Allied resources. What could I usefully surmise about physical and psychological results? Of course, I might have pondered upon it in a human way. But to what purpose? To generate a useless resentment?

My ruminations that morning were, I remember, rueful. I would surely have rehearsed to myself the falsities on which the Chamberlain Government's war policy had been based, one of which was the prevalent ground-minded War Office claim that the French Army was not only relatively invincible but also that behind the Maginot Line it was relatively invulnerable. Another falsity was the Government's disregard of the prevalence throughout France of the activities of the French fifth column and its ubiquitous power to aid German invasion. The Chamberlain Government seemed to suppose, also, that Bomber Command had the capability of finding and destroying, by night, economic and war production resources on a scale sufficient to cripple Germany's munition production. Most fatal of all misapprehensions, however, was our military blindness to the absolute necessity in modern war for establishing air superiority in every vital region, from the outset.

The three Service Departments continued to think in terms of independent sea-power, independent land-power and independent air-power, each calling for limited co-operation by the other Departments. The totality and indivisibility of war was well recognised in theory but not in administrative organisation. Britain was, at that time, fighting three wars with separate armed forces having three different doctrines and operated under three separate controls. They were all so arranged by predominantly British democratic preference, uncoordinated by any single powerful body – one existed but had no real power to co-ordinate – responsible to a Prime Minister who had no will to war. Now that Churchill had taken over perhaps something at last might be changed.

The door behind me opened and I heard the voice of General Pownall saying solicitously to someone departing, 'Will you be able to find your car?'

I got up, sensing that Admiral Keyes must be the departing visitor. And so it was.

I knew where his limousine had been parked in the wood, and offered to lead him to it. So he and the general said goodbye, Pownall adding, 'I hope you'll get back all right!' To which the Admiral replied, 'And the same to you!' The idea of getting forward evidently was at a discount.

As we walked down to the wood together, leaving Pownall on the veranda, Keyes asked what I was doing. I replied that I was waiting for one aeroplane to bring one load of anti-tank ammunition. 'That's my entire pre-occupation. It seems that our war, here, now depends upon that one cargo.' Then a notion flashed into my mind, and I added, 'That machine – an Ensign – will be flying straight back to Croydon. Would you like to take a lift?'

The admiral replied that he thought that he would be safer on the ground, and added, that he was going back to where he had come from, the Belgian Commander-in-Chief's Headquarters – in other words, King Leopold.

That reply answered one of my unspoken questions. I did not need to fish for answers to the others. Keyes proceeded to tell me just why he had come to see Gort. He was, he said, not representing His Majesty's Government so much as King George himself; he was personal representative to the King of the Belgians. He had been sent that morning by King Leopold to inform Gort of his (King Leopold's) personal decision to fight to the last. This, said Keyes, was not a decision made *for* the King by the Belgian Government, it was Leopold's own decision, made in his capacity as Commander-in-Chief of all the Belgian Forces. Keyes added that King Leopold had also said that if he were abandoned by the British Army he would have to surrender the Belgian Army; he would have to issue an order to every unit of the Belgian Army to lay down its arms. Every unit would then stand fast where it then was, and allow itself to be captured by the enemy without resistance, without further retreat and without terms.

Here was, in effect, an expectation of imminent unconditional surrender, not by the Belgian Government but by the King and his Army-in-the-Field. The Belgian Government, the Belgian Navy and the Air Force would not be affected by that order; they were to get away to England as best they could. It was the Army that was then fighting bravely as it had been from the start that was inevitably going to die: that would follow immediately if the British quitted.

We continued walking to the wood where Keyes's car was parked. I asked for no explanation and none was given. The admiral surprised me by saying that King George had instructed him to arrange for King Leopold to fly to England but that was certainly not going to happen. 'The King is going to surrender, too!' he said with finality. We walked on a few paces in the wood, dry twigs breaking underfoot and making a crackle with the scuffle of dead leaves. 'King Leopold,' said the little admiral, as though I hadn't heard or as though he were reluctant to believe it, 'is himself going to surrender his army and himself with them.'

No more was said between us before we reached the car. By then – a few seconds later – this dramatic news had become, for me, just another event of that phenomenal morning. The admiral's driver opened the door, Keyes said a kindly farewell and in a moment the car was moved away as I saluted and Keyes put up a hand in benediction.

Both driver and passenger knew what the road problem was going to be. Neither knew what national problems were to result from the information which Admiral Keyes that morning had given to Gort. As the car tyres crackled away through dead brush-wood under the trees, that old hero, smiling as though a spring-time drive in the country was the pleasantest relaxation, waved his hand at the back window. Surely, a king who sees his sovreignty aright becomes imbued with kingliness. This was the truth of King Leopold III's situation. Surrender is by no means abdication; whether inevitable or not it can be the highest manifestation of humility.

I had seen the map. I had no doubt, when Keyes told me of it, that King Leopold had made the right decision to fight on to the last even though he virtually knew that the end was not far away. His army would then have 'to stand and deliver'. I had no occasion to say so: no one asked me what we talked about. Perhaps no one knew that I had gone with Keyes to his car. Anyway, I heard no one on Gort's staff complain. Nor, so far as I know, did Gort. We had all seen the map. Wherever we were when, a little later Prime Minister Churchill made his denunciation of King Leopold's surrender, I hope that those who knew about the prowess of the Belgian army and the wisdom of Leopold boldly declared both. For events that night were vividly to present to me one aspect of the good judgement that that king had used when he sent Keyes to Gort. Later, I appreciated more fully the nature and depth of Leopold III's kingly sacrifice to which I have hitherto seen no tribute paid.

That decision which Leopold III took the very next day was to amount to a total sacrifice of all kingship for him save his inmost own; a deprivation of the joy of living as king and servant of his people; a sacrifice of all power, and almost all hope of real human understanding; it was to become as fatal to his felicity as it was to his kingship. Had King Leopold III then gone to England as bidden by George VI, he might have acquired, when final victory came, a due share of the aura of triumph that illuminated all who came, albeit reluctantly, to England at the time of their defeat. But at that time blame had to be apportioned for failures which were due to our own military blindness. King Leopold III was most unfairly made one of the scapegoats.

To me, it is indisputable that the Belgian King's sending of Keyes to express to Gort his determination to fight on until compelled by a British withdrawal to surrender his Army proved to be vital to the salvation of the British Army.

This is such an unfamiliar view that it may need an explanation of why surrender would inevitably involve days of delay by the German Army in Belgium. I am not suggesting that King Leopold thought of this as inevitable, but he may have.

The German Army was unsurpassed in blitzkrieg. That means 'lightning war'. But to halt from blitzkrieg and accept surrender is quite another matter. First of all, one has to find out the textbook requirements of accepting surrender. No doubt these textbooks were not in the possession of company commanders concerned with blitzkrieg. But all company commanders must study those textbooks. They would surely include checking the lists of weapons, ammunition and perhaps other resources. That would have consumed far more time for the meticulous German Army administrative staffs and company commanders than would have been consumed in continuing victorious blitzkrieg.

So the BEF, although hindered and hampered by dive-bombers of the Luftwaffe, passed slowly through the roads strewn with wreckage of lorries to the sand dunes and beaches of La Panne. There would have been no room for them around the harbour of Dunkirk. The halted German military machine, meanwhile, would have been laboriously going through the procedure of accepting the surrender of hundreds of units of the Belgian Army. The British people should be much more grateful to Leopold III than they are.

My reveries that morning finally ended when Desoer returned from his local excursion. He had been alerting all concerned – more particularly, anti-aircraft artillery authorities – to the imminent passage and landing of that one, highly-important Ensign. So recently brought into service and therefore so unfamiliar as an Imperial Airways craft; so modern-looking (a monoplane) and so Germanic in appearance that it was bound to be in maximum jeopardy from uninstructed gunners throughout its flight. The pilot himself must have been aware of the risk having surely heard of the shooting-down of three Ensigns. He had not been in that ill-fated freighting to Paris.

The landing was to be made at an abandoned French airfield four miles from the ammunition park where an Ordnance Corps unit was to see to the unloading and the distribution to anti-tank gunners athwart the main Brussels and Aachen roads, beyond Lille. That unit was also to provide local defence against intruders on the airfield at the time of landing.

I decided to go and watch this operation. Had not Gort charged me personally with seeing that it did not fail? Anyway, having nothing better to do, I went.

We all knew that an open airfield in our piece of geography would be an unhealthy place to leave a great, gleaming, uncamouflaged air liner scintillating in the midday sun. One well-aimed burst of machine-gun fire from an intruding enemy fighter or reconnaissance aircraft would be enough to end the British usefulness of the air-carrier, and perhaps enough to detonate its cargo. On that cargo, maybe, the British Army's power to hold at a vital point of its 'peninsula' would, before that day was out, depend. This little operation was a crucial one.

Leaving Desoer at Gort's bungalow, I took Pearl with me in the car. He was having time off from his cipher duties while his soldier opposite-numbers took over the load of Whitehall traffic on the Violet mobile radio station. Dutifully, he had his gas-mask shoulder-slung in its satchel, as also had I. Although there had never been the least prospect of the Germans using gas (for the simple reason that the prevailing westerly winds of France could blow the stuff back their way) the carrying of gas-masks was obligatory. But Pearl, forgetting that he might actually have to defend himself, and me, against a *shooting* enemy that morning, was wearing no pistol-and-belt. Rather doubting whether the training of cipher officers included pistol-shooting, I sent him back for his weapon. Then, regulationally accoutred, we set off for the car and for the airfield – a place unknown to either of us.

The roads were surprisingly clear and we got to the airfield fast. We found no Ordnance Corps party about the place, for we still had forty minutes to spare of the pre-arranged time of arrival of the Ensign. What we found there was an atmosphere of desertion and death. Its ingredients might have been pathos, evil and menace in equal parts. Beside the great stretch of the airfield latterly unmown, lay, crumpled, the charred remains of hangars, hutments, the appurtenances of wrecked aircraft strewn around the bomb-poked concrete and earth. The field itself was open, unobstructed and bare. Bomb-craters were plentiful but confined to the servicing and hangar areas. The bombing had been accurate; the work of dive-bombers, no doubt. But there was no impedance to landing.

Half-an-hour soon passed while we tramped about seeing the physical shape of dereliction and sensing the despair which pervaded this erstwhile home of gallant and cheery French aviators. We had left the car in the shade of trees beside a deserted farm. Returning to it to wait for arrivals, ground and air, I became aware of a near and lone aircraft. From the sound of it, it was single-engined; it could not be the Ensign. I located it in the sky, coming through the recent-formed overcast. It was a fighter and it was almost over the airfield. It was a Messerschmitt 109. This identification aroused mixed emotions: first a jerk of fear, then a feeling of minor pride. Like an experienced ornithologist identifying an exotic bird to a tyro, I told Pearl that the visitor was a Messerschmitt 109. Then I had a fearful apprehension. 'Rather strange that it should be alone!' I exclaimed.

Pearl and I continued to walk close to the trees and farm, but more self-consciously, as though caught naked. We were on the airfield perimeter. We stopped. We watched the intruder. That Messerschmitt turned towards the airfield and put its nose down; we had a head-on view of its sleek lines. It was not unlike a Spitfire but not as rare; the Germans had hundreds of 109's.

The German was losing height fast, coming our way. We began walking, again, rather quickly, to get under the cover of an open-sided barn close at hand – the first of the group of farm buildings. We stood on its raised concrete base under its corrugated-iron roof. There, we could see better than we could be seen. Behind the barn was the car. The farm was intact, undamaged. I hoped that the pilot, if he really had seen us, would suppose that the farmer had come back.

My thoughts were cut short by a sudden crack-and-clatter. Bullets! A heart-stopping noise for the uninured. Whether this outburst was meant for the car; whether the pilot, hawk-eyed, actually had seen us from afar, or whether this lethal spraying was simply a routine aggressive overture – a spitting-forth of menace – in case anyone was about, we did not know. We considered the point later. What invaded my mind, at that moment of startling shock, was an intense feeling of the man's animosity, and an equal and opposite reaction against appearing to be moved by it.

That German had opened fire with his two front machine-guns at a few hundred feet above the airfield, swooping as he fired from his dive to level flight, then sweeping overhead in a roar of throttle-wide power to which the iron roof rattlingly responded. Although that spurt of bullets, whose crack-crack we had heard as they passed wide, may only have been a self-protective tactic to discourage onlookers, our visitor must have become interested in our car and, probably, in us too. I do not pretend that I felt flattered.

My spasm of fear was a sudden reflex, internal, physiological. I had not experienced bullets being fired *at* me for ten years. The military man's mental 'conditioning' aims at the rejection of the emotion of fear; or aims, at least, at its concealment. I would not have liked Pearl to think that I was petrified. He, I now suppose, was hoping that I was deceived by his apparent imperturbability under fire. In fact, I was. We each had our own variety of paralysis, no doubt. However that may be, my interest in the situation was acute, and my relief at the intruder's rapid disappearance beyond the trees was distinctly restorative.

Instantly he again flew into view and we saw him climbing away. Speaking deliberately in an artificially-even voice I said that it was a good thing he had timed his visit to miss the arrival of the Ensign. But I wondered – had he? Perhaps he had synchronized his arrival by dint of someone intercepting a signal. Perhaps the much-denied German radio detection organization did really exist and had picked up that Ensign. What had happened to the Ensign? It was getting to be serious.

The Messerschmitt continued climbing away and, pleasantly diminishing in perspective, as also in its prospective menace, it flicked into a steep turn and kited swiftly to the left. It went sweeping steeply round the wood, turning our way again. Down went the nose as the heading lined up with us. Mental stasis seized me as I saw flashes at each wing and instantly heard the crack-crack-crack full twenty times, beside us. Pearl and I had leapt behind barn pillars by then, peeping out, one-eyed. The danger was over in a moment. You can't manoeuvre an aeroplane, and at the same time, keep fixed guns aiming. So, over that German and his thousand Benz horses galloped and thundered, beating the air while our hearts within us went beating on faster than before.

The 109 I felt was going to repeat the operation and come back once more. Third time! We got behind a wall.

Since that morning's vision of mystery, I had been remembering the work my Intelligence staff in the Air Ministry used to do, plotting and identifying the places where German fliers dutifully reported themselves by radio, as they came into the circuit to prepare to land. We had 'watched' the German Air Force flying, day-by-day, and growing week-by-week. We watched them closer than they ever watched themselves, or they would not have given themselves away as they did. I had been imagining that the Ensign could have been similarly tracked. If that cavorting, trigger-happy fighter pilot had come out for big-game in the shape of an air liner he would hardly be wasting ammunition on a couple of harmless individuals cowering in a farm. ('Cowering' – a good farm word: it suited us.) If he had already devoured the Ensign he would have gone back to report his kill.

I could hear him again. He was low, behind the trees. I moved to the open side of the barn. I watched where the wood met the airfield, three hundred yards away. In a moment, banking steeply, his starboard wing-tip almost touching the ground, that madman in his 109 sprang into view, taking off bank as he headed for our barn, flying close beside the wood, his wheels hardly two feet from the grass. This was a breathtaking performance – he, too, must have been holding his breath while he whizzed into that slender alley between wood and barn, resisting the urge to zoom up and clear, holding his course and height rigidly but with scarcely two feet clearance on the three sides of his channel, the maniac! On he came, his port wing-tip barely clearing the line of steel pillars at the side of our barn, behind which Pearl and I stood riveted.

For us, it was like standing on the stone margin of a country station platform, beside the rail-track, as an express locomotive rushes, in widening perspective, to dash thunderously by. For a moment one can read the intent visage of the man looking out at you. So it was then – that Messerschmitt pilot, his eye-level at the level of my eyes, tore past that 'country-platform' and I looked through the domed canopy of that fighter into its fighting man's face. So, we saw each other, as airmen, for a tense long second of time. Then, instantly, in the lightning flash of his passing and the thunder of his power, his port wing-tip near slashing the column where I stood, he turned his head full left, as I did mine, both taking a hard look at each other, face-to-face. He wore the shoulder-badge of *Hauptmann*: he would have been a *Staffel Kommandant:* in our terms a flight lieutenant in rank and, by appointment, a flight commander.

Of course, he had known as I had, from the moment of his impetuous approach that he could not get us two – Pearl and myself – in his line-of-fire, without ramming the barn. To shoot us may have been his first idea, then the pilot in him overtook the soldier: he was satisfying his lust for mastery of his steed when our eyes met. Guns, for him, were secondary, then: they had to be. The look on his clear face – he wore no goggles – was neither venomous nor arrogant, and it was free of fear; it bore a look of nonchalant ferocity, the blending of the airman and the man of war.

Up he zoomed, once more, to clear the trees beyond. For me, the barn's shade had become grey and gloomy. It lightened as instinct told me that that *Hauptmann* would not come again. He had finished, I knew. Why I should know that that was so, I did not know. But it was so.

The spell was broken, but we stayed a moment, where we were, Pearl and I. The rumble of guns returned to my hearing. No Ordnance Corps party had come. I began to think again; I had not been thinking while experiencing. They must come that way. They were late – dangerously late. Without ammunition-lorry, the whole operation would be void.

We had both moved outside to widen our view of the overcast sky. I turned to Pearl. We looked at each other with wry smiles. Release from menace is infinitely pleasing.

'We must get away and find that ammunition lorry and party,' I said, moving towards the car. Then we got in and I drove back down the road by which we had come and I began to reflect on our recent conduct, how passive and unenterprising it had been. We had acted more as though we had been watching a tiger escaped from Whipsnade, than an enemy challenging us to a duel – two fixed machine-guns to two free pistols!

'Why didn't you shoot him down, Pearl?' I asked, with mock reproach, 'you have a perfectly good pistol!'

'Sheer murder, Sir,' he replied, as though he meant it and then, for honesty's sake, he added: 'As a matter of fact, such an idea never occurred to me, I was too scared.'

To which I could only reply, 'And so was I. But what a superb performance he put up!'

'What d'you think he's doing now, Sir?' asked Pearl.

'Conscientiously making reconnaissance notes on his knee-pad: "one airfield, serviceable, unoccupied except by two RAF officers, both very scared".'

'He probably doesn't know,' Pearl suggested, 'that you and I represent about a quarter of the total strength of the effective Allied air forces now based in France and Belgium.'

'That "Hauptmann Schmidt", lucky fellow,' I said, 'seemed to be enjoying his "air superiority".'

We then talked about the difficulty of attacking ground targets from the air with fixed front-guns: of keeping aiming without diving into the ground. Then there was the further difficulty of shooting at someone who was not shooting at *you*. Neither Pearl nor I had ever seriously and persistently tried to kill anyone in a practical and personal way. Pearl was not a professional officer. I was. Such virginity as mine, in one wearing medal ribbons, seemed unsuitable. I had to explain that I had really tried, on one occasion; that I had, in fact, once fired at a man, personally, whose face I could see, with intent to kill him. That was in Kurdistan. I was diving at him in a Wapiti.

Sniping is another thing again, 'Hauptmann Schmidt' had really been sniping, in a way. Its purpose is a simple one – deterrence. That surely is the nutshell *raison d'être* of soldiery and menace –only second in morality to love!

I stopped the car when we came to the main road to wait a while longer in case the missing lorry had overshot the turning. Intuition or impatience soon prompted me to believe that the operation had, like all else in our affairs, already come to frustration. Probably some gunner on the Ensign's flightpath had been its unwitting executioner – executioner, too, of the Ensign's Imperial Airways aircrew. But why had the lorry failed to come.

The battle for Lille, I had come to believe, depended on that cargo; it was worth its weight in diamonds. If it hadn't been shot down, it might yet come; if we were then to depart, sure as fate the Ensign would land soon as we had gone. Then the captain, finding no one, would, with his own crew, unload and hide the cargo. Then what?

After a while, I gave up the vigil. I drove at speed to Prémesques wood. There, we parked, and dismounted to walk to the bungalow, having nothing of arrival at that airfield to report but German bullets.

A column of British artillery had halted along the roadside there, shadowed by the trees. They were thus concealed, or, as used to be said in earlier wars, they were 'taking umbrage' in the shadow.

Gunner-soldiers were resting and loitering there beside guns and vehicles. They were not pleased to see Pearl and me. Their state of mind was one of 'taking umbrage', too. They were giving no salutes to Air Force officers, but showing only derision. One soldier, bolder than the others, called out, 'Where's your bloody Air Force?' Hateful though it was to hear, it was more tolerable than it would have been had he said, 'Where's the bloody Raff?' I much preferred, 'Bloody Air Force'; there was truth in that epithet.

That was not the first time I had heard that expression of English-soldier exasperation, by the roadside to defeat. According to the rules, we should not have uttered, neither soldier nor officer, neither in question nor in repartee. We were all tired and dispirited, victims of provocation. Had I not, myself, in the space of one hour the previous day, seen four of our own aircraft, even a Lysander – essentially the British soldiers' friend – shot down by ignorant, frightened gunners? Though I too, knew what it was to be scared by German aeroplanes, that experience of my own fear did not make me rate fear and dismay as admirable in soldiers. And I had a grim conviction of the reason why the Ensign had not arrived. Therefore, that soldier's question, 'Where's your bloody Air Force?' was the last straw, for me.

'Shot-down by your bloody ack-ack guns,' I retorted, with a resentment as futile as his.

What a terrible training-failure that all was – that our soldiers simply could not distinguish between airman, friend and foe. Speaking generally, the Army at that time – and for that matter, the Navy, too – fired at every aeroplane that came near enough to be shot at. This was pandemic and pathological; it was part of a general phobia – a subconscious resentment of their 'belowness'.

Had our Boy Scouts been distributed throughout Infantry regiments and the Royal Corps of Artillery there might then have been discrimination, and the silhouette charts so profusely issued for identification might have been intelligently correlated to aircraft.

I walked silently with Pearl down the lane to the Command Post bungalow.

'Bloody Air Force' rankled. 'Blooded' they had been to modern war; bloodied they had been, by it.

I came over the veranda heavy-hearted as Desoer came out of the glazed door to meet me. He was, as ever, rubicund but grave. Had he been a poker player, he would have been rich. Desoer's enthusiasms were of the still-water type; they ran so deep that the surface remained darkly unmoved. He was not one of the kind that exaggerated air power. He exaggerated nothing, unless it were the desirability of remaining unperturbed by anything.

'I expect you know,' said Desoer clearly but very quietly, 'that the Ensign was shot down!'

'No, Dizzy, I didn't,' I replied. 'D'you know where?'

'Oh, yes. Quite nearby here! They landed in a potato field. It's quite all right,' he added, soothingly, 'in fact, it couldn't be better!' There was a sparkle in his eyes as he said that, slowly, word by word. Something really good must be coming. 'They didn't know it, of course,' he went on, thoughtfully, 'but the ammunition park is in the barns building of that particular farm – actually beside that very field!'

'Well, thank you, Dizzy. That explains a lot,' I said.

'You must thank our local gunners,' he said, and we went inside.

CHAPTER SIXTEEN

Gort in Reverse

26th May

The news which Desoer had given me had then only just reached him. Neither Gort nor Pownall had yet been informed; they were immersed in the study of a long message from Whitehall. There was really no need to report: their military concern was in regard to many enemy tanks; they could not be concerned about one commercial aircraft. The anti-tank ammunition delivered, the Ensign's mission was completed. The fact that it was sitting riddled with holes in a potato field was not their concern. It *was* my concern.

It had been a long time since breakfast. No doubt, at the billet in Miners' Row, a lunch-concoction *à la mode Cossins* had been sitting on the table since the routine time for that meal. Pearl had gone to dispose of it for us both.

I was not hungry. Glorious though the weather still was, it was too hot for eating – and the news was unappetising. One brief word epitomized all my immediate needs. Within a few minutes I had a steaming cup in hand – far better than the broiling heat of that 'Hitler's summer' afternoon; what need to name it? – tea!

The door marked Private opened and out came Alfrey and Kimmins. Desoer then told them of the landing of the Ensign on the doorstep of the Ordnance Corps. 'Thank God for that!' said Kimmins. 'It may make all the difference in the world to what's about to happen, now!' But neither said what that might be and neither seemed elated by the prospect.

'The C-in-C wants to see you,' said Alfrey, looking at me. 'Swallow your tea and go in, will you? And you might tell him about the anti-tank ammunition. That's a Godsend, if ever there was one.'

I put my cup down on the map-table and went in. The Commander-in-Chief was sitting, just as I had last seen him, in a wicker chair behind a small table in his wooden-shuttered room. It seemed darker than before. My eyes were slower to dilate, perhaps. In the dimness I discerned Pownall. He was sitting, or rather, lying-back in his tipped-up chair on Gort's left and a little further back, in the corner as before. He had his jacket unbuttoned, his legs thrust out, apart, hands in pockets, his general's cap on the back of his head, peak pointing to the ceiling.

His attitude expressed a deal of feeling – not of despair, by any means, nor of anxiety – perhaps he was in a state of silent protest or reluctant acceptance; perhaps of incredulity nearing dismay or, at least, disdain. But those notions come from retrospection; at the time I only noted that Gort's Chief-of-Staff was full of thoughts he did not like. But as my eyes took in the scene and my mind became attuned, I was aware that those men, both, were personally concerned for me. Kindliness shone, if wanly, through their faces for all the grimness that a seasoned soldier naturally evinces. Neither immediately spoke.

I took the opening. 'May I, first, report that the Ensign has delivered her load of anti-tank ammunition? Delivery began an hour ago.'

'Well done!' said Gort, and Pownall said, 'That's quick! Where did it land?'

'Right at the park,' I said, and could not forbear to add, 'The gunners shot it down! No. No one's hurt. The pilot landed with his rudder jammed, making a graceful curve; and nothing broke!'

Gort did not smile. I think he nearly did. He looked at Pownall, and Pownall looked at him. Both said, almost in unison, words that meant 'Thank God for all of that', and Pownall sat upright as though he was newly filled with hope.

'Now, I've got something else I want you to try to do,' said Gort, and I knew from the manner of his saying that, that he had diffidence in coming to the asking. 'I expect you know,' he went on, 'that the Belgians are now, or very soon will be, officially out of the war. The Belgian Army is to be surrendered to the enemy by the King;' he said that without a trace of passion. Looking at me, noting my nod, he continued, 'And you may be aware that so far as fighting is concerned the French armies to the south seem also to be as good as out of the war.' He paused, unclasped his hands resting on the desk, and reclasped them. The silence was seeped into by gun-thunder through the shutters. 'As you can hear, fighting is still going on around this neighbourhood.'

Gort went on to say that I must know that although the French Army was still active in the coastal strip to the north, and although there were 'fluid' areas between the enemy and our east-facing positions in Belgium, the BEF was almost completely surrounded by vastly superior German forces. He spoke quietly and interestedly as though making a presentation at Camberley. 'Very recently, assurances were given to the French Government,' he said, 'that the British Army would not desert them. But it was agreed, at the same time, that non-combatant formations of the BEF should be evacuated through Dunkirk. That process has been going on for the past few days.' Gort, who had been looking straight at me, let his glance fall. He seemed to be contemplating his folded hands on the table.

'The Government now takes the view,' he went on, 'that the French Army has deserted us, and that we are no longer obliged to stay and fight it out to the end.' He paused, looking at Pownall. 'Not that we shall have a great deal left to throw at the Germans in a few days' time – and bayonets are not as long as they used to be.' Lord Gort was an infantry commander at heart. 'In short,' he said, returning his look to me, 'The new Prime Minister, Churchill – or, I should say, the Government – has ordered general withdrawal to England and I have been personally ordered to return, myself, and all my staff, as soon as I can.' He hurried over that part as though it were as unimportant as it was distasteful to him to quit while the fighting continued. He wore the ribbon of the Victoria Cross. His character had not changed since he won it. 'So,' he said, 'we shall be leaving this place tonight and we shall try to make our way by road to Dunkirk. Of course, we may not get there. All movement is held up, especially near the coast where bulldozers are being used to clear the blockages on the roads caused by bombing and by wrecked lorries – in hundreds. The prospects are not very good.'

One has been taught since then, by Americans, to categorize comments such as that last one as 'under statements'. Gort, however, did not pause on that account. He was surely not thinking that he had understated any danger that he might be confronting. His next words showed that he was thinking of another man's danger.

'Had any news of Charles Blount?' he asked abruptly, and I replied that I hadn't but that I supposed that we would have heard if he had not got through. Gort said nothing. Then he began again. 'We'll be going tonight,' he repeated, 'and, of course, you can come with us, if you like. But I think that you may prefer to fly out . . . if you can. What is your idea about that?'

It seemed quite an age since I had waved away my AOC, hatless, in that Moth; glad for him to be going, hopeful about his getting through, but not envious of his doing so in that way. What did I think about going as he had gone? I had just been asked. I hadn't seriously thought of it; I had vaguely supposed that we were staying where we were. I had been in military service for thirty years; I was apt to be a 'yes man' in such matters. But I had to consider Desoer, Cossins, Pearl, Filtness, and some wireless personnel – how they should go. Neither prospect was essentially enticing, by air or by road.

'I think that the ammunition Ensign has only minor damage,' I said, 'and could with luck be flown, lightly loaded, out of its potato field.'

Gort looked quite eager.

The 'yes man' in me operated again – on a false clue. 'Taking you, too, if you like, Sir,' I added, looking first at him and then at Pownall.

'Air travel doesn't seem to be very healthy, just now,' Gort remarked, as quietly as ever, 'and anyway, I must go back by Dunkirk; I must go and see how the embarkation is going. I don't think it's going nearly fast enough and not nearly as fast as it will have to go, from now on. And that brings me to the point – why I sent for you. If you can get out by air, that's what I want you to do. This is not an order, mark you. If you think that you can get an aeroplane that is fit to fly and can reasonably be expected to get it into the air and over the Channel, I would like you to take it. But if it is not reasonable, I do not want you to try it on.'

Gort's manner had changed. The undertone of concealed regret had gone. He spoke clearly, simply; he had begun speaking with emphasis and a new firmness; he had a purpose that was vital to discharge, and I had to play a vital part in it, I sensed.

'You can go back with the rest of us, by road to Dunkirk. But it is a bit doubtful whether we will ever get there, and I am *very* anxious that one of us from here shall get in to the morning meeting of the Chiefs of Staff. That means being there, on the spot, at nine o'clock tomorrow morning.'

I recognised that Gort was wishing to use me, not as an air adviser, but to represent him and his own opinions as a soldier and as Commander-in-Chief. I said that I expected that I could act as his messenger and that I would like to try.

'Right!' he said. 'Now this is the situation. There are, or will soon be, about a hundred thousand men in the region of Dunkirk waiting to cross. Depending on what happens to us and to the French Army, that number could grow to a quarter of a million, or more, not allowing for any Belgians. They are likely to be mixed up with our troops and the state of affairs is not likely to be as orderly as on a parade ground. Bombing is going on whenever ships are embarking. There will be pandemonium.'

'For Operation Dynamo – the evacuation of the non-fighting men,' Gort went on, 'the Admiralty allocated four destroyers, only. The harbour is tidal. They can make two trips a day, while they stay afloat. That's not more than a few thousand a day: how many men a destroyer can take on deck depends on the state of the sea. The message I have had says that Dunkirk harbour can't take ships bigger than destroyers. It also says that the Admiralty can't release more than four destroyers for the job. It isn't a question now of the non-combatant units – it's the whole of the BEF – and they still talk only of bringing off 45,000 men,* before the Germans stop us. A much bigger effort must be made. But that demand will only be seen as marks on a message pad in the War Office. I want you personally to go and impress that necessity on CIGS – not in the War Office, but in the Defence Committee, in the presence of the First Sea Lord. It must be done in the presence of Dudley Pound – he must be there; he certainly will be in the Chiefs-of-Staff daily meeting and he must be confronted with the task. You can't tell the Admiral what he is to do, but you can tell CIGS – Ironside – what I want him to get the Admiral to do. Tell him from me that it must be made imperative on the Navy to produce more destroyers. If the Navy is to fail in this, we had better stay and fight it out here. That would be better than all being bombed to blazes in Dunkirk, and then what is left of us, captured – for that place is indefensible, as things are now.'

Gort paused. I thought he had finished. But quietly, with cold emphasis he spoke again, perhaps to himself as much as to me.

'*Four* destroyers is absurd! The Navy must have forty they could use. It's up to you to get into that meeting. Don't let your own people keep you out. Insist that you are my representative; that you

---

*Plans for a possible full-scale evacuation had been discussed as early as the 20th, and Admiral Ramsay at Dover had been allotted personnel vessels, including cross-channel steamers (these were in use in Boulogne and Calais), Dutch motor coasters called schuyts, and other small ferrying craft, and on the 26th the Admiralty stepped up their effort to gather spare craft for use in Dunkirk harbour. Operation Dynamo was originally intended to rescue only about 20,000 non-combatants: and even when expanded to embrace the evacuation of fighting troops, only the rescue of about 45,000 men was envisaged; it was never planned to rescue over 350,000 men, at least 100,000 of whom were in the sand dunes of La Panne.

have been expressly sent by me. You must talk to them as though you were me, and you may have to go for them if they don't want to listen. But try not to get too excited.'

General Pownall had been showing signs of wanting to prompt his C-in-C. I glanced his way and, in a calm, reflective manner he said, 'Try to find out if you can precisely what ships the Admiralty has to offer *besides* destroyers. The Calais and Boulogne Packets, in so far as they have not already been sunk, are working as hard as they can. There must be some others, not employed, that could be roped in!'

'Well,' said Gort, 'that's the job I have for you. My orders are to get the Army out of France and I have got to make sure there are ships for the task – if I can – at the same time as making certain of getting the men to the port of Dunkirk. Which will be the more difficult, we shall soon know.'

Gort said no more, but looked at Pownall who said, 'But that's not his *only* job. He's got one of his own! More air protection is vital. I gather that Fighter Command can fight as far afield as Dunkirk, but can they cope with the dive-bombers? This is something new. I doubt if anyone in England knows the devastation they have caused. Do try to bring it home to them, somehow. Who would you see, about that?'

To my mind, there was no difference in principle between the interception of a formation of dive-bombers and a formation of high level bombers, except that the dive-bombers had no rear-gun defence.

'DCAS' I said. 'Sholto Douglas. He runs Operational Policy. But CAS himself will be at the Chiefs-of-Staff meeting.'

That was no time for an argument on air tactics. The Army from top to bottom had been dismayed by dive-bombing.

'Well, do what you can, Goddard,' said Gort, 'and good luck with your journey. I presume you won't try it till after dark.' He suddenly looked very weary. Pownall got up, his eyes on me, but he did not speak.

I saluted, turned and left that gallant, undaunted but perplexed man at his desk. His elation, hardly one year back, when Hore-Belisha, as War Minister, assented to Gort's stepping down from the post of CIGS to assume command of the projected BEF had just been finally neutralized by his depression at the prospect of ignominy for that splendid army.

'In case smallest doubt', was the phrase in the message from the

War Office repeating Winston Churchill's order for evacuation. Paraphrased in my mind, that order said that Gort's sole duty, then, as Commander-in-Chief, was to ensure as complete a runaway of the British Army in the face of the enemy, as possible. Hemmed in as that army was, to a long area of the shape of a jig-saw puzzle piece, the task would be difficult until the army got to the sea, where the Navy would take it off . . . if they had enough ships that could get into Dunkirk harbour.

That was not, of course, the wording of the instruction; but that was what it meant; Gort, VC, was to lead his fighting men backwards at full speed. From Gort's point of view, such an operation was certainly 'unexciting', in a Gilbertian sense; certainly more onerous than honourable.

As I withdrew, I knew that Gort had then no great belief in his own ability to impose success upon the existing ruinous failure. I knew that he was going to do all he could to see that none failed for lack of help. I knew, too, that he absolutely relied on others to accomplish the apparently impossible. And I vaguely knew that he very greatly relied upon me somehow to get that Ensign into the air and fly it to England; somehow to carry his most fervent prayer into the head of Ironside, his chief, and into the heart of Pound, the Navy chief. For surely Pound could, if he would, transform the whole structure of SNO, Dover's Operation Dynamo.* That plan, already then in action, had been hastily expanded for the rescue of but forty-five thousand men – one tenth of the number that might demand salvation from the enemy through the harbour of Dunkirk.

I let myself out into the big room and was instantly dazzled by the sunlight. Desoer, who meanwhile had learned of the C-in-C's decision and intentions, produced for me another cup of tea.

Everyone present, then, knew as well as I did that the British Army was now facing unprecedented disaster. They also knew that none of the immediate prospects encouraged much hope of avoiding, at best, eventual capture, for if Lille were invested by the Germans that very evening, as was all too likely, then so far as Gort and we were all concerned, the game would be up; we would be 'in the bag', or fighting a local battle alongside the gunners whom I had met resting up the lane, and goodness knows who else. I was

---

*The Senior Naval Officer, Dover, then was Vice-Admiral Ramsay. It was his naval planning staff which had invented the name Operation Dynamo for the evacuation of non-combatant units of the BEF.

deplorably ignorant about how to fight an infantry battle in daylight, let alone after dark.

Before this special mission was given to me, I had supposed that no one would mind if I attempted to be a fugitive, disguised – if, when the time came, we could not fight a useful battle. Now it was different: I had a job in prospect and must somehow do it.

I heard no mention of GHQ becoming engaged in a rearguard battle. The staff, under Alfrey, were busy organising the job in hand. All but Desoer and I were busy. The Army had to be managed, still. Corps commanders had to be instructed; movement priorities arranged. And the Command Post itself had to get on the move, coherently, before the Germans appeared. Dotted about Prémesques were other small staffs, part of GHQ and essential to command and administration.

About then, someone coming in from the Signals Office announced, 'Winston's coming on the air at six this evening' and added, 'I wonder what he's going to talk about?'

'Keeping white mice, I expect,' said Kimmins, in the middle of writing out a signal message about rearguard troops that had fallen back from Arras.

That torn and battered city – the Arras of our winter sojourn – had passed into enemy hands, after three days of action on 24th May. That was the battle where our 'sappers' had so valiantly fought, though I knew nought of that, then. Nor did I know then of the gallant commander of the counter-attack, General Franklyn, who following the current trend had given his name to his force – Frankforce. Another such was Mason-Macfarlane, Major-General, who until a few days before was Head of Intelligence in GHQ, Claud Pelly's mentor there in fact. He had been sent with Macforce to protect the BEF's rear right. The thought of that transition, from desk to battle, when I heard of it, filled me with sudden recognition of the soldier's role.

I could no more go out and stage the fighting of a battle than I could swim the Channel. But Winston, 'coming on the air' – that I would like to hear, I knew; though none of us then had experienced the magic of his radio orations. Nor did he yet know of that magic, himself.

After a tea-and-talk with Desoer, we had to see about doing what we then decided upon; namely, the transporting of the remains of Violet to England. Indeed, it would be the remains of the Air Staff of the BEF still left in France. The first thing was to get them to the potato-field where the Ensign sat in some state unknown of tatterdom. For, if that aircraft could be got into the air and could continue to fly; if it had petrol and three engines out of four that worked; if it could lift the lot of us – not more than six in all, and maybe three or four of crew . . . . We could not plan without facts, and there were imponderable factors; Pearl with his RAF codes must somehow be sent – he and the other Air Force men – to find the way in daylight; they must go at once, lest the Ensign, lacking orders, should take off as soon as mended. Desoer was to fix all that. In fact, he went himself with all the rest, save Cossins. I had decided I could not lose touch with Gort until I felt sure that I could get an aeroplane to fly from near there, or, at the worst, from Dunkirk. I knew of no possible craft but the Ensign.

If that Ensign would not be fit to fly by midnight, someone was to come back and tell me, otherwise I would set off with Cossins at eight o'clock and find out for myself how things were going. Desoer marked on my map for me the farm where the ammunition park was, and from the lie of the lanes and a stream, we guessed where the Ensign had landed. Agreeing then that we would meet for a meal at the billet at 7.30, he went off to organize the decamping of the remains of Violet,

For a while, I stayed, learning the route from the map. It was only about seven kilometres. Then I must have dozed off. An hour or so later someone kindly brought me back to an awareness that Big Ben was chiming for the six o'clock news in a portable radio set on the map table, and I remembered that we were to hear the new Prime Minister.

But the BBC did not produce that speaker – not then. He was to speak in the House of Commons on the 28th and what he had said was repeated in the News. He announced the surrender of Belgium and declared the decision that Britain would fight on.

The News, that evening of the 26th, though couched in terms of hope and resolution, prepared the nation for a worse disaster than it could yet have apprehended from the battle news. So we knew the kind of thoughts our people would be thinking at that minute. There was not much to comfort us or them in what was said except that the statement added words of gratitude. I think we all felt pleased, a bit, by that – and even felt the echo of it, too, from our own people at home.

Outside the evening was clear and cool. The sky, too, was clear of aircraft, and the sound of battle hardly audible: the breeze was from the north. I walked down the dry grass slope to the lane and to the billet in 'Miners Row'. Cossins would be there. He was. I found him doing something with bully beef and vegetables. He had already heard the news. I asked him what he thought of it. He said it would be 'nice to see the wife again', and I agreed. Whether he knew intuitively that that was to be so, or whether he feared the opposite, I could not know. The understanding that we had between us was that if there was any talking to be done, I would begin it, and normally he would say 'Yes, Sir', or 'No, Sir'. He was a really good man. I told him that the others had gone to the Ensign; that he and the wireless tender's crew were the last airmen – men of the so-called 'other ranks' – of the Air Component still on-the-job as far as I then knew, in the battle zone in France;* he was the last aircraftman. At that, he stirred the stew.

'Aircraftman' was something of a misnomer for Cossins; so was his so-called trade of aircrafthand. He was an AC2. He had another week to go before his first year was up then he would get his 'prop' – the badge of an AC1. Cossins could hardly have seen an aircraft close to, in his life – except the civil Dominie in which he had flown with me to France, at the start. His real job was cutting sandstone into blocks, in Somerset. I suppose that he assumed that he would depart from France as he had come, by air, *de luxe*, with me.

'Supper at seven-thirty, as usual, Cossins, please,' I said, affecting an air of normality, adding, 'I hope that Wing Commander Desoer will be here, by then. We leave at eight – he, you and me – in the Chevrolet. I will bring it to the door so that you can put in all our kit. Then,' I admonished, 'put everything back as we found it when we moved in. We must leave the place tidy.'

I left that humble, willingly-serving but quite unsubservient man to his job. He had a job that he could do; I had none then, only one in prospect that perhaps I might be able to do. I did not much want to go and say goodbye all round. It was not as though I was leaving old friends. Those men of Gort's were men I deeply respected but, because of my belated transfer to the Air Staff, and their being away from Arras from the first day of the fighting war, with Gort in-the-blue, none of them, save Alfrey and Kimmins had known me other than by sight until a few days before. Then, having no useful work

*I did not then know that the remnant of squadrons, some of the Air Striking Force and some of the Air Component, were still in action in France but to the south and west, under the AOA as AOC commanding, Air Commodore Cole-Hamilton.

Gort in Reverse

to do for them, I had gained no feeling of being in their team, a colleague. It was, then, I felt, rather as an intruder that I became a witness of their mounting anguish, bravely concealed. Winston Churchill's hope that the Army might successfully – was that the word? – penetrate backwards through the narrow coastal breach and make its exit from a theatre of defeat, was not a hope that carried balm.

Many millions of our countrymen had, in that hour, been brought to acceptance of the fact of our defeat; to the contemplation of irretrievable and bitter loss and to a recognition of ignominy. What were they offered in exchange? – a hope of a new Gallipoli, across the Channel. But, this time, not unopposed; not planned weeks before in secrecy, deliberately; not to be carried through within a single night and no shot fired until the bonfires on the beaches blazed the news that the escape was safely over. That was Gallipoli: defeat converted to a negative triumph. This time, there was, for our enemies, that rarest opportunity of all the opportunities for deadly annihilation that can be offered to a conqueror – daylight retreat through a defile flanked on both sides by guns and armour, and overset by bombers in continuous relays. The prospect then, so we all supposed, could not be one of ordered embarkation and departure but of carnage, disorder, fire and destruction, Allied confusion, civil chaos, bloody rearguard action, pain and agony while waiting in hunger of body and mind. Who could expect to come through it unwounded, uncaptured, or unditched from a sinking ship? This would not be a nightmare of one night; it looked like being an ordeal of endurance day-and-night for days and nights to come.

But at that time, although we knew about the Belgian Army's imminent surrender, we did not know that the effect of that surrender was to make the German army in Belgium halt for several days and so put an end to blitzkrieg.

Before supper, I did, in fact, go over that veranda once again and in at the back door, as though to collect some thing. The real purpose was to ask for news: had there been a breakthrough on to Lille? No! On the contrary – attacks had been beaten off . . . some German tanks destroyed. Fighting had died down, it seemed.

'It looks as though our chaps have got something to *hit* the tank with, then,' I said.

'I hope so. Their time for withdrawing now may be of our choosing – not of "Jerry's" – and not till daylight, I trust,' said a staff-captain whom I did not know. He was alone.

'If anyone wants to know, you might tell them that Desoer and I mean to leave our billet at twenty-hundred hours; that is, if the Ensign is going to be able to get off. But, anyway, we shall go and see, I expect.'

'Well, good journey! I do hope you get home before we do. Could be quicker on foot, you know,' said the soldier.

I met Kimmins at the door. I said goodbye to him and wished that he were coming with me. He said, 'Fly in that lash-up? – no fear! Nothing like a sea trip for jaded nerves, you know. See you next week.' So we parted, and he called after me as I was going out, 'If you can't get off, hurry back here. We shall be gone by midnight. So long!'

I showed my pass to the guard for the last time and wished him a good ride to the seaside and home. He said, 'I don't see much wrong with this place, except that it's noisy.'

I took the car to the billet. Things there had been nicely tidied up. Cossins brought out our kit and put it in the back. It included a bulgy sack. Leica cameras. They might yet come in handy, I thought – for barter, if we got shot down. Packing a car for a trip is a mood-changing act. We were going home. This was a happy affair. Everyone I had spoken to that evening had seemed happy, sanguine, confident. My thoughts about anguish, anxiety, apprehension must have been out of place, morbid. Things were going to be all right.

The car was loaded when Desoer arrived. He said that he had been in a staff car, out to the Ensign, that it was going to be fit to fly, that it would be dark by ten o'clock and that the pilot would like to take off then. He also said that the French and Belgian armies rather than the Germans seemed to have invaded the British Zone in force and were moving in opposite directions, east and west, mainly. The British Army was moving north, and traffic control was not happening; he had taken an hour to come eight kilometres.

The car, we decided, could stay outside the billet while we had a meal. It would be a waste of bombs, if the Germans strafed the place next day. So we went in to supper.

As we were finishing the meal, the back door opened and in came, wearily, the two big miners whom we had speeded on their way to escape a few days before. Their wives came crowding in behind. All were still laden, as when we last saw them. Embarrassed themselves but heedless of our feelings, they struggled off their loads as we rose to give them greeting. Then they seemed glad, through their weariness – glad to see *us*. More likely, though, it was an automatic glad reaction to the feeling of 'home-again' after anxious travel. The sight of a meal on the table must have been welcoming, too.

Diffidently yet hungrily, they accepted the gestured invitation as Desoer and I moved away from the table. The little room had grown dim and one of the women struck a light and put it to the wick of the wall-lamp. Cossins, having fed already, was packing up the unconsumed rations into a box. He put in the last few tins of stuff and, after opening the front door, picked up the box to go out to the car, visible at the gate with its rear door and boot, both revealingly opened.

The miner nearest to the door moved quickly to bar the way, growling the French equivalent of 'No you don't!' as I bade Cossins put the box down again. The change of atmosphere from amiability to menace was instantaneous. All knew in that moment that we were quitting. Fear, horror, resentment and antagonism fought in the distorted features of those grimy faces, and the anger they displayed was accentuated by the flickering of the flame in the lamp – itself struggling between life and death.

After a stream of confused, patois imprecations there was silence in the room, and stillness, but for the leaping, lamp-cast shadows, and the rumble of guns that came in through the open door. The man nearest to it moved away, jerking his head in a gesture which said, '*Allez-en!*' – which in our idiom would be, 'As you are going, git!'

They were not only disillusioned Frenchmen, they were communists. They knew what the coming Gestapo had in store for them; they knew about forced labour in the mines where each miner stayed below until he had done his double stint, or he and his family starved. They had believed we were there to fight the Nazis, not to quit. They felt about us in the way the French for centuries had been taught to think: perfidious . . . Albion, meaning white and therefore bloodless, cold, unfeeling.

I turned to the women and gestured to the things on the table and in the box as theirs. '*Helas! – il faut partir.*' – 'We *have* to go!' I said, '*Bonne chance!* . . . . *et, au revoir!*' putting out my hand.

The woman sitting at the table raised one hand towards mine, the other to her eyes; but her head bowed with her body and that shielding hand onto the table, limp. I heard the sound of a gasping sob as the hand she would have proffered me fell by her side and touched the floor. I turned to the men, my hand still extended. The two miners shook hands with each of us; and then the women, both weeping. Desoer said to each, quite quietly, 'Goodbye', meaning to him, *'Adieu'*. But communists, then, could have no Dieu. Cossins, most naturally, said, 'So long!' Then we three went out by the open door. The Frenchmen went out to the back to unload their bicycles.

The light in the lamp had survived. As I pulled the left-hand driver's door to slam shut, one woman, hand outstretched to the lamp-wick screw, raised the yellow flame to a fuller brilliance and turned her face towards us. So also, did her sister – for sisters they clearly were. And both seemed freed from rancour then.

When I think of war in France, my mind goes back to that little dwelling and that epitome of suffering acceptance. I suppose, then, that I understand. I suppose, too, that those deserted acceptors also understand, whether still at Prémesques or dead.

Next day, or the next, at any rate before the end of May, the German tide would have flooded into that almost-deserted creek which we had briefly known as Miners Row.

CHAPTER SEVENTEEN

En Panne – À la Panne

26th/27th May

So we moved off in the evening light, out of that street of miners' dwellings into the dim lane where the gunners, since departed, had taunted Pearl and me. There, we passed other miners and their wives stoopingly trudging and trundling back home. Then, Desoer prompting from his map, we turned into a main road with lorries full of troops moving in both directions in the twilight. Whether they were French or Belgian, I did not know; none of them should have been there or moving then, according to the plan. But nothing on the Allied side of the war was going in accordance, then, with any plan of which I knew, except the car-load being given its course so calmly by the miscalled 'Dizzy' and steered somewhat adventurously by me. Cossins contrived to keep our properties steady in the back as I negotiated lorries and took the verge in preference to roadway when that diversion suited movement better than the road.

After a turbulent period of eddying-through, we came to the region of the main road which we had to cross. My navigator warned me that it was a roundabout. Before we finally reached it, however, we were once again in a queue of lorries, stopped. Taking the lumpy verge once more and creeping, caterpillar-wise, over successive mounds and dips of débris and ditches, we clambered through to the main-road junction.

Twilight had almost gone and there was no moon. We were confronted by an indiscernible state of immobilized mobility. I stopped and got out to see better what was there. A concourse of great canvas-covered troop-carrier lorries, none British, had assembled in confusion and were interlocked, heading all ways oblivious of the notion of a roundabout. The scene was motionless, dehumanized, petrified, yet throbbing with leaderless power, frustrated. I felt cold and weary. Cossins gave me my greatcoat. I took the torch, put on the screened sidelights lest we might lose the Chevrolet, and, with Desoer, reconnoitred a tortuous way by which to begin a penetration through the tangle. In the car again, with Desoer on foot, ahead, guiding me, we inched our way, back and forth, into the middle of that stilled melée. There we confronted, nose on, two lorries already nose to nose. Neither would respond to Desoer's torch gesturings to back a yard to let us through. I got out.

'You drive,' I said to Desoer, 'and let me try my French on these Froggies!'

He got in and I, taking the torch, began to bellow to the high-perched soldier driver to get back *'Un metre en arrière'*. I shone my torch on that man's impassive face. He could not hear above the engine noise; or else, he would not. I went back to the car and said to Cossins, handing him my fore-and-aft, peakless cap, 'Give me my brass-hat' which he did, ' – and my pistol, please.'

At that point Desoer said earnestly, 'I hope you are not going to start a shooting war, here – it's bad enough as it is.'

But I had other tactics to try.

Climbing on the step by the lorry-driver's door, I opened it, meanwhile holding on with my torch-hand so that my face and my cap's gilded peak were illuminated. With my pistol, in my free right hand, I touched the driver's hand and commanded, *'Un metre, en arrière!'*, adding, with deliberately limited politeness, *'S'il te plait!'* Then, moving my pistol point so that it touched his tunic, I thus indicated the direction of desired motion.

Without taking his eyes off mine and with no great change of expression – for the sight of my face or my golden peak had caused him surprise, if not alarm – that speechless soldier did precisely as I asked. It may be that he thought I was a German. Why not? I did not know if he was French or Belgian.

The driver of the other lorry, facing the lorry that had backed, seeing what had occurred and my approaching his door, my torch shining intermittently first on the Chevrolet's bonnet and then on mine, did what was required, unasked; he backed a yard. Likewise, his neighbouring driver, beyond. He, I could see, was certainly a Belgian. Surely, this jumbling of a crossroads could not be their passive method of obeying their King's command to 'stand and deliver'? But again, Why not? It worked – and painlessly. They were standing and delivering – confusion. So, what a great mercy if that process of dumb tangle and delay was already going on all over 'Belgian' Belgium. But it was not a mercy for us, nor would it be for the great retreat of the BEF if what was happening then and there were to go on happening all over the British 'peninsula' of isolation. Such a state of impedance as would then have been added to those of bombing would have fouled our army into a final fury of

Hurricane Is of No 73 Squadron, over France.

Lysander I, as used in 1939-40 in Army Co-operation Squadrons, Air Component.

Heinkel 111

frustration. In fact, it did not occur.

The first cause of many a hold-up like the one from which we had just emerged, soon became evident to us by fantastic wayside silhouettes. Lorry after lorry – British, our torches showed – lay on its side, wrecked, pushed sideways, jumbled, toppled on top of another. Initially the work of Stukas, these wrecked lorries; later they had been stacked aside by British bulldozers into a long roadside monument to terror.

Desoer knew when to turn off to the left, not for the farm itself but for the field beside it. So, we came to the final halt in a narrow lane. There, at Desoer's bidding, we got out. He had reconnoitred the spot earlier. Following him, we climbed through a gap in the hedge and walked cautiously up parallel furrows between the withered vegetation of an unlifted crop, watching the torch light-up the parched and stony soil.

When again I looked up there had risen into view from our ground-darkness a silhouette of straight symmetry against the sky: the wings of the Ensign. Startlingly challenged, then, by an English "alt! – oogozair!' I automatically answered 'Friend!'. I knew no password for that night but we satisfied the sentry and moved on to the force-landed aircraft. Shot down, out of control for steering, the expression 'forced-landing' really had its truest significance there. In France the expression is *la panne*. It has a flatness that is eloquent. The Ensign had made *une panne de ferme* – had force-landed at a farm.

We met the pilot and congratulated him on having brought off such a well-executed feat of airmanship and of direct delivery. He said that the work was going well; it might be finished in an hour; all engines should be 'serviceable' by then, and all controls. He could easily take the six of us, and our kit. His worry was not about his take-off; the field was long enough; four-hundred yards should do with full boost on all engines – if they would take it. The lane beyond, being slightly sunk, would make no obstacle; its hedges were low, thin and negligible; the field beyond the lane was flat for another hundred yards. He had enough petrol for five hours flying but the snag was, he said, that he had no radio password for re-entry over the English coast. Perhaps we could talk our way through, he wondered. But radio-silence, except for giving the password, was a rule not to be broken. One thing, however, he said he really needed for the take-off – because of the overcast and the moonless, starless darkness – was a guiding light at the lane-boundary, right ahead.

I offered to set my Chevrolet across the lane at mid-width of the field, its headlights shining down the field. We agreed on my doing this later, while the engines were being warmed-up – whenever that much-desired event might be.

Eleven-thirty came and passed. With it passed the 'point of no return'. Gort would be on the road by midnight. And when that hour came to us, the engineer and the co-pilot were still at work with tools and torches. On further counselling together we postponed our time for take-off until 1 a.m.; the testing of engines to begin at half-past-twelve. Meanwhile, there was now activity at the farm. Their stocks exhausted and their last job done, the Ammunition Park received their orders to move to the Dunkirk area. The night was dragging, and so were doubts and anxieties. My mission was in jeopardy and so, increasingly, were we, at that deserted farm.

At ten-past-twelve the engineer reported the Ensign fit for flight. Was it wise, then, to wait longer? Who could tell? We stuck to our decision for testing at half-past-twelve and tramped the field again while Cossins gave the workers Thermos tea.

All engines started. Each at the first attempt sprang to life in a sudden clatter. Each was run-up with thunderous eager roaring into the night, obliterating the persistent, intermittent rumble of night-gunnery from east and west. Satisfied that the Ensign's power plants were in healthy state, Desoer and I went off to the Chevrolet, to instal it as a runway-terminal light. As we walked into the distance, the engine and propeller throbbing gave us new trepidation – of intervention by intruders roused to action. We reached the end of the field, climbed through the hedge and down into the lane, found the car and manoeuvred it back and forth until it was broadside-on to the lane and its headlights shining straight towards the Ensign. They were just high enough for the full beams of light to clear the road bank in a place where there was no hedge. I left the key on the floor of the car, hoping that the vehicle which had served me so well would fall into good hands but not before we had used its lights for the take-off.

The act of abandoning an excellent car in the middle of the road with its lights full on, leaving it for anyone to purloin, gave me feelings near horror.

We went through the gap in the hedge, by the light of the headlamps and walked beside the twin beams. Desoer lamented the desertion of the car and asked whence I had got it. 'It belonged,' I said, 'to Pierre Vanlaer; we commandeered it from him and I doubt if he has ever had his money.'

'Well, we must tell him where he can find it, if we ever meet again,' Desoer replied, blending heartfelt hope and doubts.

The loudest roaring of the open-throttle power test of each engine successively and one by one had died down before we reached mid-field and the Ensign's gaunt silhouette changed shape as she swung, taxiing away in response to torch directions, to the field's northern extremity. When we arrived, all but Pearl were aboard. Lacking any gangway ladder, we three were hauled up through the doorway, and the door was closed. The soldiers of the Park had gone. The Ensign at last stood ready, loaded and alone; four engines ticking over sweetly.

The captain, guiding us by his torch, took Desoer and me forward with him, to watch the take-off. The light shone on the 'tally' on the cockpit door: Captain Horsey. So that was his name. Strange that I had not asked. I must have been preoccupied.

All I could see on first entering the cockpit was two points of light, together, right ahead. Between us and them there was a patch of black – a quarter-mile of space for getting the structure airborne, ten aboard. But that was no serious worry; the lights were a pleasure to see. The aircraft was not heavy-laden; she carried no seating, no carpets, no provisions, none of the furbishings for passengers and only half the normal fuel-load.

I stood behind the co-pilot on the starboard side. Desoer stood behind Captain Horsey's seat. The latter looked up at me putting the usual wordless question and holding his right fist high for me to see its thumb extended upwards and, when I nodded, holding my left hand with its thumb erect near his, he dropped his hand spreading it over the knobs of four throttle levers and pushed them forward, opening the roaring on both sides. I gripped the sides of the seat-back as Horsey pushed all four throttles 'through the gate' and the take-off run had inexorably begun – a shuddering, jolting and cushioned undulation of pulling acceleration amid shattering roar of engine power.

The points of light ahead turned into tiny discs and expanded into round dazzling suns, widening apart, while the trembling jolting of the wheels below affirmed that the air, though shrieking by, had not yet won the battle over ground and gravity. The pointer on the speed dial was trembling over 60 knots; the cockpit-ceiling filled with the light of headlights; we needed 65 to come 'unstuck' and here was the blazing Chevrolet charging our underside, head-on. Horsey, looking ahead, his face full lighted in the glare, carried the expression of sensitive expectancy that every natural pilot wears at the moment when tense attention turns to action; his hands, right laid on left, moved back three inches firmly, and instantly eased forward, two inches. My feet and knees reported 'lift' and 'off'. Within a second the haloed round nose of the Ensign quenched the twin lights below which already had shed their dazzle, and we surged steeply into blackness.

For the moment, before eye-pupils dilated, there was no horizon. Then it appeared; black undulating, nobbled with trees, above the eye-level, showing the rising ground. This is the crucial moment of a take-off – getting the speed, uncambering the wings for still more speed for climb, with engines all near bursting-point of power and heating-up towards the risk of seizure while throttles remain beyond the danger 'gate'.

But we were passing through a 'danger gate' of another kind – forgotten, not foreseen. Bang! – another bang! Bang! again, and yet another – at intervals of half-a-second. Horsey sharply turned his head to port. Through his window, low, I saw flash and flash again, in concert with successive sonic bangs of passing shell, invisible. A cannon gun was firing – at us, and missing, seemingly above, or else astern, but not by much. At such a stage in the initial climb, to manoeuvre would invite a fatal stall. But ours was not a normal take-off, heavy laden; we had a lightness that could then be used. We reeled into a banked turn towards the flashing gun; the Ensign engulfed it beneath its belly out of our sight and, too, perhaps beyond the highest elevation of the cannon gun whose firing ceased. Horsey next, using night-vision and a skill beyond my seeing and almost beyond my power of holding-on against sideways accelerations unsighted the gunner by losing much of the little height which he had so far gained and thus put some tree-tops between us and the gunner.

After a while . . . after a whirl of steep-banked low-flying in the dark, better for bats than for a battered monoplane, Horsey put himself and his Ensign into a steady climb. He headed north. He and his plane were one flying entity. Soon, but none too soon for me or for his four tormented engines in full torrent of power, his left hand drew back the quadruple levers through the throttle-quadrant's gate, and the tornado-din was quelled to a tolerable roar.

Calm, by comparison, this soaring out from crisis filled me with sudden delight. My heart settled, with the engines, to a quieter pace. Then, though no words were spoken in the dim-lit cockpit, there was an eloquence of gratitude, relief and pleasure in our exchange of smiles. All was going well.

It needed no saying that the prospect of all continuing well would improve when the overcast above our heads had been put below our feet. The countryside below lost its gloomy, swaying hurrying features in a velvet black, unpricked by any point of light. The cockpit wide windows of dark grey showed the neutrality of the sky's covering, but gave no sign of life and very little light. Life was in the flying, and light flowed from a hundred pale, radiant-green numerals circled around pointers (moving and not moving) saying, in all their different significances, that we were flying well and truly, heading home, from and through a long infinity of dark. It was lighter to the north.

At seven thousand feet the scarcely discernible black earth finally disappeared and we were in the overcast. Then, in a moment, we emerged into a new range of consciousness; beneath us lay a silver firmament; above, a million scintillations piercing the depths of deepest blue – the universe of the heavens. The dimly shining, faintly wavy floor beneath us sank away until we ceased to climb. Then, with economy of speed, our wings levelled to the black and white horizon – the airman's all-round altar – held in quietened suspense, in motionless infinitude and in seeming peace. The war had gone, and all memory of it. Had I not been aware of fatigue, I would have continued to stand and revel in the glory of night flight into the stars.

Signing good-night to Desoer, Horsey and his co-pilot, I went aft into the dim tunnel-space for passengers. Stripped of its seating and carpet, the bare, plywood deck was scattered with belongings cast about by the violence of our gun-shy bucketings at take-off. The dark scene of disorder seemed to be unheeded by the passengers still clinging to hand-rails on the concave walls, for they were gazing through round windows at the stars, gossiping in pairs together, mouth to ear.

Waving goodnight in the darkness to the others, I lay on the deck in my greatcoat, my head on two gas-mask packs, and soon became unconscious of any quest or purpose. That oblivion, however, did not last for long, Cold, or the banking of the plane, or the 'heterodyning' crescendo-diminuendo throbbing of engines desynchronized, returned me to our own shockingly chilly din. I got up.

I and other wakened sleepers, went to windows. I felt – and they did too – extraneous shocks or shudders superimposed upon the engine-pulsing. I looked below, the overcast had gone and there were scattered points of light, no longer star-high and many, but low on the port side – and very bright. We were still over land; that I could discern. The lights were searchlights, trained on us. When the brilliance of one of them dimmed momentarily losing its aim, I saw its beam. Two other brilliant lights flashed, intermittently. Then came the shock again; again, again! Two stars, man-made – no, three or four – died behind a small, swelling blot of black. Horsey had turned to port and was swinging back to starboard as that blot of an explosion's smoke swung with the stars around it, over my window-outlook. So, we were under fire again. Consequently, instinctively, Horsey was climbing, altering course, cork-screwing to evade – inducing in me a giddiness near to nausea.

The red light on the port wing-tip was flashing. That told me that green at the other tip, and white at the tail must also be flashing, too; probably white landing-lights as well – all declaring innocence and appealing for clemency. Sickened as much by manoeuvre as by fear, I went forward to the cockpit and, with an affectation of calmness, said close to Horsey's microphone-covered ear, 'What about the *inside* lighting, to show them we are an air-liner?'

Easing the stick to central, pushing aside his earphone and looking up at me, I heard him counter 'or troop-carrier with parachutists about to jump!' He was a man of quick reaction and common sense. 'Still, we can give it a try. It can't make things any worse.' He called for the engineer to 'make' the cabin circuits and switch on all lights. Meanwhile the flashes on the ground had ceased, as though in response to our unspoken prayer, or else untriggered by telepathy, or chance, whichever you prefer.

Soon after that unsteady spasm, we resumed our course through darkness, carrying no lights, the engines out-of-phase, making their undulating throb; though that itself, in its manifest seeking to confuse the sound-locators, could have falsely declared us to be an enemy.

Looking out of the window towards the post-quarter, I saw, successively, the appearance of delicately-shaped curves of pale light, resembling paths of steeply-aimed rockets. Up! . . . up! . . . and over, they went! Then the slim trace ceased in an instantaneous reddish star. Graceful, they were to the eyes; benign to the mind, and quite unmenacing. Perhaps fatigue had slowed my reactions and blunted my receptivity, for they were tracer, anti-aircraft shells. The tail-end star was a lethal burst. Could that firing be from a British battery? Or French? Or German? I did not know, nor care. But though not aimed at us, those toy-like trajectories were aimed at folk *like* us, flying little more than a mile away from us, within the narrow perimeter of the British 'peninsula'. Not Belgian or French, certainly; not British, either – too far afield for fighters from England, too far to the west for a British night bombing raid. Then what was that battery's target? Could it be a German night-fighter in quest of a quarry? It could – or else night-bombers – but whose? German, and none other. Only a few moments ago we had had all our lights full on, like a 'gin-palace' in the sky. I was glad that we had re-assumed our dark incognito. Looking for us now, would be like looking for a black needle in a charred haystack.

Many a young man, then, of any bomber crew, experienced in drear, dangerous nights over Germany, might have said of this account, 'Line! – We've been through worse, *much* worse!' My telling of the Ensign's homebound flight on that night of minor, misplaced, misaimed gun-opposition, may serve to give a measure of the unknowing, save by experience, of penetration through unseen 'forests' of lethal trajectories thrown up by guns in hundreds; of the blinding surprise in flight of fiery streams of cannon-gun explosive bullets from an unseen enemy fighter; of the ordeals endured by airman crews repetitively in every sortie, be it their third, or thirtieth or hundredth. Only the experienced knew the tense drive of attack-determination and its essential blended skills, pitted against the tense counter-drives of defence-determination and their blending of counter-skills. They would know, too (but not write about) the likely-to-happen worsting in the battle, the return in a crippled craft with dead on board, bloody. Or there might be the grim prospect of crash-landing engulfed in flames or perhaps a plunging through the leaden and craggy crust of a dark and deserted sea.

Fortunately for them and for all concerned with their work, most men who fly are not of the sort who think like that, in the abstract. But in the experience itself they all *feel*. Entry into ordeal is a challenge; it evokes a response which excludes dismay. Emergence from ordeal brings that kind of relief, like being 'born anew', like the ecstasy of emergence through the dark turbulence of clouds into sunny, celestial blue. As, too, when a thunderstorm has passed, both mood and air have altogether changed and no boding of storm-to-come remains; so when, in flying, a danger has passed suddenly – it is *gone!* – lost in the turbulence of the wake; the air ahead is clear and calm and so is the kindly forgetful consciousness.

A dark but clear horizon to the north, sky meeting land, had begun to separate, admitting a discernible, thin strip of silver sea; thereafter quickly the land gave way to a widening of that welcome sea.

On the port-bow – left-front, that is to say – and on the coastline, there was a speck of red which, as it drew nearer, grew and was doubled by its own reflection on a plume of black. Fire below! That was the first night, and our first sight of the blazing fires of Dunkirk. Fourteen hours back, my morning sky had declared to me by fleeting 'power-lines', the first branding of that seaport town. The conflagration then ignited was to continue there for yet seven days and nights. In its fierce glow by night and beside its drifting black column and pall by day, another exodus was to be conducted through ordeal. That fire which we were passing over then was symbol of a mighty, spreading fire-of-bombs which burned through Europe for five years until its last embers died with all the hopes of this initiation at the Channel ports. For the hope that Hitler then held was that, by those bombings, the British Army's exit would be blocked and all our fighting power thus brought to an ignominious end.

Below us then were the sand-dunes of La Panne. That was Gort's destination although he had supposed that he would be heading for Dunkirk when he spoke to me at Prémesques. He and my recent soldier colleagues were to be there where most of his army were that morning. In a few days all around them there were the open dunes and on the tidal sands, fragmented formations of the British and French armies – none of Belgium's, thanks to Leopold – would gather and grow. That almost forlorn assemblage was to go on mounting in numbers up to three hundred thousand British soldiers and fifty thousand French, all waiting under daily torment their chancy turn for sea-escape. Yet the Admiralty seemed to be thinking only in terms of evacuation from the harbour.

The foreshore, defined in the starlight by curving parallels of white on black, reminded me of the previous morning's dark lines on blue – and then, as they passed beneath us, they recalled seaside holidays. Although I had then, no awareness of the salvation that was to be achieved there in the days immediately ahead, I was aware of the magnitude of the problem with which my mission to Whitehall was concerned; and I was aware, too, of the privilege that had come to me, and all of us on board, as our Ensign altered course north-west for Manston, on the toe of Kent, leaving beneath us and behind, battlefields and dreadful defeat.

CHAPTER EIGHTEEN

Ad Astra

27th May

Dunkirk's red infernos, its black coastline and its dim outer-harbour extended between two slender arms canted into a dim sea, had all slipped beneath our port wing and were gone. For a few minutes only I had contemplated the state of that burning place not knowing that the graceful curves of tracer shells which I had been watching only a short while before had been directed at night bombers which had been continuing the havoc-making of the morning. Peering into the harbour's darkness, I could see no ship of course, none of the four destroyers of which Gort had spoken.

I had been thinking military thoughts; I had given no thought to the tormented populace. I had thought of one man, momentarily only – Claud Pelly – and his setting-off for Dunkirk.

Was he there, or not? Was he alive or not? Who could say? What use even to wonder? And yet, as we looked down on fire below, questions arose. What about the others – all the men of Violet – in Calais? Or were they at Boulogne? Or had they got out before the shipping there was bombed by the glinting *Geschwader* that I had seen? Were they at that moment fighting infernos of flame?

So, for a while, I continued to think regretful thoughts about ignorances, democracy and war. Then I was aware that Horsey was looking at his watch. He beckoned to me and said in my ear, 'No daylight for an hour or more yet; we shall have to loiter about over the sea,' and he added, mockingly, 'unless you want to see whether our own chaps can shoot us down quicker than we can land at Manston.'

'You please yourself,' I said, 'I'm only a passenger and I'm now going aft to have a sleep. But don't suppose,' I added, 'that you're not being closely watched. At your height, I suppose we can be detected from North Foreland.'

Thoughts about radio-detection (Radar), in those days, were still almost too top-secret even to think. Presumably, an Ensign captain would be 'in the know'. Being only a passenger I did not think it right to say that we would be safer if he brought her down to just above the sea. Horsey, however, showed that he knew my thoughts. He said, 'Now that we are clear of Dunkirk's gunners, I'm going to take her down.' He throttled back on all four engines, and down we went in relative tranquillity, in a whistling glide to find the nearly invisible sea.

When I woke we were flying low over a silvery Pegwell Bay. The still-dim coastline ahead revealed the Manston hangars not far beyond. Soon we heard the rumbling of our own wheels on turf; soon we were were walking on English tarmac. It was 4.30 when we reached the Officers' Mess, the black-out screens still in their night positions keeping out the light of dawn on 27th May.

Strugnell met us there. A group captain in rank, he was the Station Commander and an old friend of mine. He said he was usually up about at that time of day; the dawn-breakfasting of off-course bomber crews who had made voluntary landings there, he told me, had recently become a fairly usual thing, at Manston. They would have had trouble; injuries to men, damage to engines, fuel tanks or structure.

It was good to be in a 'peacetime' Air Force Mess again, geared for war though it was. Strugnell, in the past ever buoyant and gay, seemed, like the dining room, shut in and only artificially lighted – 4.30 in the morning is the time for feeling low. He had no news for me of Blount; he had supposed that he was still in France. Saying, 'Let's hope he got through to Hawkinge,' he fell to other questionings and I knew he was in state of anxiety quite unwonted for the Strugnell, sometime commander of a night-bomber wing, when he and I had both been in No 3 Bomber Group, whom I used to know. And then it occurred to me that he had realized at last, we were at war and alone, against Germany.

I, too, had my own anxieties about my mission. Strugnell, of course, suggested lending me his car, but the Ensign had to fly on to Blackbush and it was only a slight dog-leg to put us down at Hendon, on the way. So by six we were in the air again.

The Thames accompanied us, waveringly and shrinkingly to London, dwindling to a ribbon as Kent became submerged under patterns of street and roofs; under factories, parks, gardens and rows and rows of houses.

Meanwhile, West Malling had passed beneath us; Biggin Hill to the left on the highlands of London's southern fringe, and Hornchurch on the north Thames-side beyond the industrial East End and Dagenham; three airfields nearing their ordeal of bombing while successive squadrons of fighters, old and new, were based upon them. German Plan Yellow for the conquest of France, then coming to its crushing end, was in transition to Plan Red, for the subjection of England.

Heedless for a time of the man-made mass of London – then expanding in my view to cover with its multicoloured pattern all that was visible to us of England – my mind and eyes were set to pick out the little house which had been my home, not far from Biggin Hill. There it was, in tiny insignificance to anyone on board but me.

The Biggin Hill airfield itself was not particularly significant to my mind, then. Still unpocked with filled-in bomb holes, still unroaded with a straight long runway and perimeter taxi-tracks in concrete, white – for at that time, concrete by the million ton was going to make roadside pill-boxes and road stumbling-blocks. So the airfield of Biggin Hill merely lay as a bigger-than-normal field of bronzed green, seemingly empty and inert. Yet in and around it, well-concealed, lay Hurricanes, old Gladiators and Spitfires, then brand-new – fifty and more in all – carrying among their three squadrons, nearly four hundred flying machine-guns and seventy young men, some likely to be in battle that very morning over the place from which we had just come – the Dover Straits, the harbour of Dunkirk, the dunes and sands of La Panne.

The sight of Hornchurch airfield on the starboard bow put me in mind again of General Wenninger and my taking him, with a mission of three German generals, there: Stumpf, Udet and Milch. They were three of the four men then at the head of the Luftwaffe, Göring's air chiefs. As we passed, that autumn morning of 1937, through the East End's unregenerate slumland, in a limousine – it being well understood by all that I could not speak German – I heard Milch, a Nazi civilian protégé of Hitler's, dressed as an air force general, say to the professional airman-soldier chiefs with anticipatory relish, *'Was für ein Ziel!'* meaning 'What a bombing target!' and I detected in the faces of those men, embarrassment and horror. Embarrassment, because they were expected to share in that Nazi jest with its tincture of sadistic glee; horror, because the notion of war of that kind was repugnant to their traditional view of war. Or, more probably, they felt both those emotions because they feared I might not be as ignorant of German as Wenninger had said.

Mercifully, or unhappily – I cannot say which – they saw no eight-gun fighter, then, at Hornchurch. For, in 1937, the original, two-gun Hurricane and Spitfire prototypes had been rejected from development; the 'fighter' men demanded, almost above all else, power of manoeuvre. That quality was then the *sine qua non* of aerial fighting, embodied at its best in lightly-loaded, chubby biplanes. The 'dog-fight' mentality in fighter pundits preferred the Gladiators which we then had, to the swifter monoplanes. Thus pioneers become encastered through backward-looking, and tradition becomes a substitute for thought. Thanks chiefly, however, to a certain Squadron Leader Ralph Sorley – filling the sole appointment then allowed to the Air Staff by the Treasury for the study and policy of operational equipment – the RAF was equipped, despite the pundits, with Hurricanes and Spitfires, not two-gun fighters as first ordered but, at Sorley's insistence, aided and abetted by the then Deputy Chief of the Air Staff, Ludlow-Hewitt, they were equipped to carry an unprecedented battery of eight machine guns each.

My thoughts of Hornchurch and fighters flowed into the foreground of my view as on we flew – the City, St Pauls, and then, Whitehall, where I was due to be by half-past eight.

Soon after seven we landed on Hendon's famous flying-for-the-fun-of-it arena, latterly world-famed for air displays. While Cossins and others mustered kit, I was being solemnly advised by the station commander of the gravity of the state of things in Europe, as though Hendon itself was in some other continent.

The firing of a green ball of fire from a signal pistol announced, as it curved up and over the airfield, permission for another landing. Looking up, we saw, silent in circling glide, a biplane Argosy.

'Must be the one that's coming from Boulogne,' said the station commander. 'Forty passengers with kit, is all we know. Might be bringing anybody. We shall have to give them breakfast and arrange accommodation, I expect. Yesterday we had to commandeer the Hendon Hall for Violet – whatever that may mean.' He said that with an indication of mistrust; our pseudonym seemed not to be well-known in England. It gave me the clue – to tell Cossins where to put my kit.

So this Argosy then landing was coming from Boulogne. If so, the forty men on board could be a batch of our rear-echelon, or perhaps of GHQ. This was exciting. Although I had perforce to wait for transport anyway, nostalgia, I feared, would overcome the urgency of Whitehall duty until I had seen and met the home-comers . . . or were they to be exiles from France – Frenchmen?

The Argosy came grumbling to the tarmac; its four staggered

engines ceased to pant; propellers came out of their filmy transparency each to a jerky and gaunt halt. Chocks were quickly placed – air liners' wheels even then still lacked brakes. Then the side door opened and, helped by airmen below, there being no gangway ladder handy, down scrambled a man in blue. And that was Rugg – Violet's senior equipment officer. Next came Griffiths, chief accountant. So the forty aboard must surely all be Violet men; had there been any Brassard or French officers, there, they would have been given the courtesy of disembarking first.

Soon came Louis Jarvis, and – adding surprise to mounting delight – there emerged two Frenchmen, after all – Bobbie la Chaume and Pierre Vanlaer.

Before imparting any news to me, all wanted news – especially of Blount. But I had little to say and they were reticent about the bombings and other trials they had experienced. The great formation of German bombers which I had seen in passage had, in fact, they said, bombed the docks in both Boulogne and Calais. None of our people had been hurt; some ships were damaged.

Cole-Hamilton had been given command of the remnants of both Army's Air Component and Bomber Command's gallant and battered off-shoot – The Air Striking Force. Of them, none of the Violet men had news.

The two Frenchmen diffidently asked if I could pay the bills still owing on their cars. It was for that, they said, they had flown over, against their orders. After refuelling, the Argosy was flying back and they were going with it. They had no money; they had lost track of their families; they could, they thought, escape the coming capture of Boulogne without themselves being captured, and join up with the remnants of the Air Component in the western areas.

Regretfully, I had no money and could give them nothing, nor any hope of payment then. I had to be in Whitehall within the hour. I was sorry. I refrained from suggesting where one of the cars might then be found; its battery quite dead. With gaiety not noticeably damped, they thanked me 'for all that I had done' – just that – and for 'all the good times we had had'. *'Bonne chance et au revoir'* said Bobbie as we shook hands. 'Good luck – be seeing you!' said Pierre. Then we parted.

How glad I was not to have been a Frenchman, then. How sad I have since felt at every remembrance of our nonpayment of those gay and loyal young men; so typical of the 'reasonable' heartlessness of red-taped delays; so pitifully needless in the circumstances; for almost at my elbow stood Griffiths with a bag containing in paper ninety thousand francs. They could have had the lot, for all the value those francs were ever to be to the British Treasury – or that is how I might have decided then, had I but known, and risked the consequences of the inevitable Court of Inquiry. By the time that would have been completed, ninety thousand francs would hardly have been worth ninety shillings.

Gladdened by the Argosy's home-coming human freight; saddened by the background burden of dismay and war, and after a brief exchange of views with Jarvis, I set off in a car for Whitehall and began to think what I might do to get into the meeting of the Chiefs-of-Staff; and what I might say when in the presence of the assembled masters of our fighting Services. Had I decided then to regard myself as Gort's representative and gone at once to the War Office, I might have been sent to the Air Ministry, then in Kingsway. Everyone knew that the Air Ministry was in Kingsway, few knew that the Air Staff, where I wanted to be, and the Chiefs-of-Staffs were in a Whitehall building. I therefore decided that I was sure to find a friend in the Air Staff place in Whitehall which, six months ago, I had left.

I was fully aware that an entry into the presence of the most secret and most guarded pinnacle of executive strategic direction was by no means to be forced. Nor could I hope to 'talk' myself through the successive filtering portals where a particular pass would have to be produced. I knew the ropes, but they were not for my grasping, then. Indeed, I could not even get into the Air Staff place without personal identification and higher authority. I no longer possessed the necessary pass. So what expectation could I have of walking from that building into the underground War Plans Department and finally into the conference room of the Chiefs-of-Staff, deeper still beneath concrete.

To the man of action and one sure of his case, well-briefed with the facts of the situation, clear-headed and unfatigued; to a man thoroughly competent in his own job and about to do it in the regular way, appearing before the Chiefs-of-Staff to advise on a special matter as a specialist, should not be daunting. Generally speaking, I know that it is daunting. It may be that, to their mothers, the Chiefs-of-Staff seem quite mild. But their mildness is not the characteristic which their official appointments honour. Nor do they evince that quality when their judgement is challenged by subordinates. General Lord Gort may have told me that I was to be not only his representative but also to be him without a doubt. But when the time comes, it seems different.

I had to speak, I thought, to Ironside. That would have been fairly easy. I knew him. But my words had to have their effect on Admiral of the Fleet Sir Dudley Pound whom I did not know. That was the problem.

The WAAF driver said, as we sped over the hill and into Finchley Avenue, that we should be in Whitehall in less than twenty-five minutes. I had not spoken to an Englishwoman since I bade farewell to Gracie Fields on the steps of Château Écoive. It was quite time that I did. At least a question or two might be asked or answered to show awareness of the human situation and the fact that the car was not an automaton. But my problem nagged: I was desperately tired and somewhat dispirited. That girl could have handled the problem of getting an audience better than I. How extremely nice an English girl can look! I noticed that, but said nothing.

Perhaps Gort had signalled Ironside about my coming? I clutched at that straw. But, as a supporting thought, it was no more than straw. Ironside was not to know. Ostensibly, but only ostensibly, I had been sent by Gort to speak to Ironside. Had Gort actually wanted me to influence Ironside, the place for that would have been the War Office, not the Defence Committee offices. But the man whom Gort wanted me to influence was Pound. Pound was my quarry: Admiral-of-the-Fleet and First-Sea-Lord, Sir Dudley Pound, Knight Grand Cross of this-and-that, Chief of the Naval Staff, his forearms smothered in daunting bands of gold ... he was the man who was to be surprised into a sudden confrontation with a smoke-blue clad intruder acting the role of corsair-diplomat; he was the man who looked out from a place of firm authority from under heavy black eyebrows, whose eyes mine had then never met; he would be flanked by his own exalted naval colleagues and by the heads of the Army and the Air Force.

Newall, my own Service Chief, I knew quite well: he, though surprised and shocked, perhaps would be glad to see me.

Ironside, I also knew. He had once stayed a week in my quarters at Mosul. Before he arrived there I had got the blacksmith and fabric workers to modify a bed and bedding to a length of seven-foot-six. He would be glad to see me, too. Until Gort reminded me, I had forgotten that Ironside had become CIGS – the Army's Chief of Staff. But would he play Gort's game, instinctively, and back-up

Blenheim at Condé in 1940

French airfield scene with damaged Lysander and two Hurricanes.

The little ships at La Panne

Requiem for a Hurricane: a scene on Dunkirk beach, June 1940.

this battlefield waif in blue, lacking credentials and any Service right to interfere, let alone the right to attempt to shame the CNS into a change of mind?

Well, what would I do to get in? Go and tell Newall in his office? Short of a row, I should not get in to see *him*, even – not while he was being urgently and finally briefed by his Planners for the COS meeting. This day, of all days, was not one for admitting intruders. But suppose I did get in to see him, I mused, to myself, and told him my mission; and suppose that he then urbanely said, 'That's all right, Victor, you can leave it to me. I can probably handle it better than you. It simply won't do for you to try to beard Ironside in our meeting, you know. Besides we shall be reviewing Dunkirk plans, anyway. CNS will certainly do all he can, and I don't see how you can help. It isn't as though you had come from Dunkirk and knew the situation there. If you had some actual facts that we here have not got, it would be different: I could then send for you to advise us all. All you have got is a notion to be helpful in what is not your business. I'm afraid it won't do, Victor. You go and get a shave and come and see me after the meeting.' What would I do if he said something like that? Would I say, 'Yes, Sir – thank you. All the same, Lord Gort has said that I must go to the meeting myself, and so I must!' Would Newall then smile and say, 'By all means . . . if you can!' What then should I do to get in? Perhaps Peirse, the Vice-Chief of the Air Staff would fix it?

Air Marshal Peirse was a charming man; I had been in his staff for a year or so before going to France. But I knew that he would not do as I had just hoped. He would be going to the meeting himself; he would stick to Air Staff business; he would not get involved in problems of ships, ex-Master in the Merchant Navy though he was. Indeed, for that very reason, he would steer clear of Navy decision matters.

But I was forgetting. I had told Gort that I would get Sholto Douglas to see me through. He was the proper man to see. He had really been Blount's 'master' in the Air Ministry.

Air Marshal Sholto Douglas was then Deputy Chief of Air Staff, highly intelligent, forceful and uninhibited by custom or red-tape. But I didn't know him. Strangely, we had never met. Would he be there, in his office, at 8 a.m. – he had probably been up half the night? Air Operations were his job. Bomber Command was operating at night. Dammit, I thought to myself, I'm going to get in – but I don't know just how. I felt better for that thought. 'Sholto' was the right man with whom to start.

So we arrived in Whitehall. A glimpse of Big Ben showed me only the top of the clock, before it slipped behind New Scotland Yard. My watch said 8.10. We turned right, beyond the three-flagged Cenotaph. Then, going under the arch, we were in King Charles Street, slowing up by the Air Ministry's main door. And I had gleaned no news or views from the WAAF driver.

I got out, thanked the driver and acted as though I were a daily commuter. With unconcern I walked past the first sentry, past the bomb-blast screen, and into the vestibule I knew so well. There, I found my way barred. I produced my Violet pass. It would not do. I was then on the steps leading to the main gallery-passage. I would have to fill up forms, the guardians said, and wait.

At that moment a familiar figure passed. 'Archie!' I cried. He stopped. He was wearing the uniform of an Air Commodore. Since I had departed, he had been commissioned in the RAF Volunteer Reserve – the idea of his wearing a Royal Scots tunic and kilt was too much – and he had become (as I mentioned earlier) Director of Intelligence. That included responsibility for his old civilian post of DDI – Security!

'Victor?' he answered, rather questioningly, 'By God, it is! – I thought I'd seen a ghost! What are you doing here? You look as though you ought to be in bed!'

'Please let me in,' I said, ' – and lend me a razor!'

Boyle – for he it was; the last man I had spoken to in that same building when the war began – said what was necessary to the chief porter and the guard NCO and in I went. Boyle had been sleeping there and had the kit I needed. I had forgotten Boyle's potential. Newall loved him like an elder brother. Boyle would get me in!

'Have you heard where Charles Blount's got to, Archie?' I asked, as we walked to the stairs.

'No,' said Boyle. 'Should I?'

So he didn't know.

CHAPTER NINETEEN

The Little Ships

Compelled by prejudice, I had to have a shave. My most vital need was for immediate cooperation by senior officers, the main one of whom was unknown to me. There would be an innate reluctance to give audience to an unwelcome intruder. It would be folly, I thought, to give the impression of an undisciplined mind by presenting an unshaven face. I was remembering what Trenchard himself had said to me when he was GOC of the Royal Flying Corps in France, 1916. It was the first day of the Battle of the Somme. He had sent for me to give personal instructions about the job I had come over to do. It was not one which depended upon appearances; it was to drop agents – spies – on the other side of the German lines from a small airship by night. 'Young man,' he said, on my being presented to him by Brook-Popham, 'you want your hair cut.' So I was not going to appear before the Chiefs-of-Staff with a stubbled chin.

I told Boyle that I had little time for explanations and instructions; that I had to get into the COS meeting not on Air Force business but on Army/Navy business; to represent Gort to Pound via CIGS. I added that I had no letter from Gort, no pass that would let me in; I needed help. My mandate would be too delicate to mention beforehand; too specious, too unservicelike; my only claim to entry was Gort's wish that I should enter; Lord Gort, as he knew, was CIGS before Ironside.

Boyle interrupted: 'Don't be surprised if Ironside isn't there. Rumour has it that Churchill wants Dill, the Vice CIGS, to take over at once.' 'So much the better,' I rejoined. 'Dill was a corps commander under Gort in France until recently, and came to see Gort only a day or two ago to see the situation first-hand. He knows me and knows the need.' But Boyle warned that he didn't know for certain that there had been any change.

'It seems to me that my entry, if it is to be achieved, must be desired by CAS – by Newall,' I said. 'Would you, Archie, tackle Newall? He regards you as pure gold – those were his own words to me.'

Then I reminded Boyle that I wanted his shaving tackle.

'Ring Newall,' I said, as he handed over his shaving things, 'in five or ten minutes' time, not in his office but where he would surely be then – down in the Chiefs-of-Staff place – just before the meeting. And would you, anyway, please ensure that Newall knew that I was coming. Privately, would you tell him what my purpose is? And would you also, in the meantime – and this is most important – would you get someone in CIGS's office in the War Office, to warn Ironside or Dill that I have been sent by Gort to see him specifically within the COS meeting.'

Boyle, massively tolerant up to a point, was looking increasingly surprised at this somewhat breathless spate of strange requests.

'It's no good,' I went on, 'trying to do the thing through the usual channels, Archie. To attempt to do so would defeat Gort's deliberate device, which was one of guile. The result would only be that I should be forced to wait until the meeting was over. So although you are now my senior officer, Sir,' (I said that with mock humility) 'please don't argue; do as you are told! Now I will use your shaving things while you do some staff work, for your beloved army,' I concluded.

Boyle smiled in his seraphic way, all over his broad face. He was the embodiment of straightforward dealing. He might have been wishing that I had not said 'guile', but instead had said 'wisdom'. Whatever he thought or intended then to do, he kept it to himself.

'Here you are,' he said, handing me a towel. 'Take your time and don't gash yourself.'

In a very few minutes I was superficially clean, and my self-respect was restored.

As I came back through the door labelled D of I, I was admitted by Baring, Boyle's PA. Boyle was at his desk. He again looked startled. He had looked startled when he first identified me by my voice in the main passage. 'That looks a bit better' he said, 'but you could do with a little rouge!' He pushed his chair back from his desk, stood up and came towards me emanating genial goodwill. 'I'm not going to do what you want,' he said abruptly, but smiling. 'I'm taking you straight to DCAS – Sholto – he says he'll see you through if you've got a good case. Let's go along, now.'

Boyle led the way out into the passage, along to the offices of the Deputy Chief of the Air Staff. With a recognising sign of assent from the personal staff in the outer office, we walked through the open door beyond.

'Good God!' said Sholto-Douglas, looking up from his desk as we entered. He had meant to say 'Good morning,' but had contracted the intended greeting into an exclamation of concern. Evidently my appearance had altered since we had last seen each other. We did not know each other, except by sight. He was not at all thin.

'You'd better sit down!' he said, and when I had done so, he asked urbanely, 'Now, what can I do for you?' – as though he did not already know.

'Before we talk about my business, Sir,' I said, 'can you please give me news of my AOC?'

'Charles Blount?' queried Sholto Douglas, unconcerned. 'News? Nothing special, so far as I know. Oh, you don't know about Back Violet. He's there. Hawkinge.'

'He flew out in a Moth,' I said, and as I heard my own words I know that to a seasoned chair marshal that act would seem to be nothing special. Blount would, of course, have said nothing about it to DCAS. How different things can seem – before and after.

'Oh, yes?' said DCAS, mildly, still unconcerned. And then, politely, 'And how did you come out?' he asked.

'By Ensign,' I said.

'One of the last surviving Ensigns,' he commented with an equanimity which must have been forced. He closed the topic with the playfully serious remark, 'It's safer by Moth!' and, looking up at me, repeated his first question, 'Now, what can I do for you?' It was a testing question. He wanted to see, I suppose, whether I was capable of expressing myself coherently.

I explained that I had two things to do for Gort. One was to put CNS 'on the spot' about shipping at Dunkirk, and to do so in the presence of CIGS and CNS. The other was to press CAS for a bigger allocation of fighter effort over the Dunkirk area.

'Well, if Gort wants you to see CIGS in a Chiefs of Staff meeting, and nowhere else, he is entitled to ask you to do that for him, and I will see what I can do to get you in. It will be up to you to get yourself a hearing. But on Gort's other point, the allocation of fighter effort, that happens to be my business and you will do best to talk to me, not CAS, about that.' He said that last sentence with finality. Then, quickly glancing at his wrist-watch, he turned to Boyle and said, 'The meeting will have just begun. I'll ring "the Vice" in the meeting and ask him to come out and get Victor through the security barrier. It would be no use my talking to the security people. That's your business, Archie. Now, would you take Victor down and identify him at the various barriers on the way?'

I was secretly pleased by the fact that this formidable, 'high-up' stranger had used my first name at our first meeting. To do so was, and for our sort still is, almost a pledge of friendship and trust. But I was sorry that Boyle had not warned CAS and CIGS about me.

However, I felt a surge of re-assurance mingled with gratitude at Sholto Douglas's co-operation; his unwinking connivance at Gort's unprincipled ploy. The First Sea Lord had to be confronted by the Chief of the Imperial General Staff (triggered by me) with the fact that his responsibility was to provide for the removal of at least a quarter-of-a-million men within one week; a point which was as unthought of when Operation Dynamo was planned – as it was still unperceived that day.

Gort knew two things; first, the Admiralty was going to do 'all that was in its power'. The other thing that Gort knew was that the Admiralty had already decided that they could not release more than a very few destroyers for the task. But those contradictory thoughts were the whole of my reason for being there. For all I knew to the contrary, Gort might already have been captured or killed in the region of Prémesques. When Gort gave me my mission, he was doing so in part because he did not fully rely upon getting through to Dunkirk himself.

My task was no less than to ensure that Gort's responsibility for the extraction from Dunkirk of his quarter-of-a-million of British men, was firmly placed on the Navy in substitution for the Operation Dynamo's figure of about 45,000. My head was full of that thought, and of memories of thunder – thunder of guns, of bombs, of *Geschwader*, and of four Ensign engines through the night. Those sounds in Whitehall, then, were unfamiliar.

Whether or not I was fit, I felt charged with urgency and destiny. Winston Churchill, by the way, was not then a legendary magician in power. He had only recently ceased to be a voice crying in the wilderness. The last thing I had seen from him, only the previous day, was an intimation that Calais, although surrounded, had not yet fallen and could, or might, even then be re-secured if Gort would send a column to relieve it. Shades of Mafeking.

Boyle and I were immediately on our way to underground territory: the complex of the Central War Direction; the nation's bomb-proofed citadel; the vortex of British war power; in short, 'the basement in Storey's Gate'. I still had no notion of how I should discharge my task.

From the Air Ministry's third floor in that great block of an Edwardian government office building, to the Defence Committee's lower basement in that same building's western end, involved quite a long walk including passing through two security barriers and two descents by lift.

At last, we reached the ferro-concrete depths of the British war-control centre. With Boyle's aid, we were admitted and passed through steel-armoured doors to an inner, *Chiefs of Staff only*, guarded barrier.

Boyle, showing his War-Room pass, explained to the Naval lieutenant-commander in charge that he was accompanying me, to see me through. He said that the Chief of the Air Staff – CAS – would be expecting me: had he sent out to have me admitted?

He had not.

'Then,' asked Boyle of that Naval officer, 'would you kindly go in and represent to CAS from D of I – Air Commodore Boyle – that Group Captain Goddard, with an urgent message for CIGS from Lord Gort, is waiting outside?' The lieutenant-commander thought a moment and said, 'No, Sir. I can't do that! But I can telephone for someone to come out.' And that, by direct line, he did. He put down the receiver and nodded to Boyle without speaking.

There was a pause. No one spoke. There was a silence such as I had not experienced, memorably, before. No one moved. There was no rumble of guns, no thunder of engines, no hum of traffic, no clatter of footfalls and shutting doors. The silence was not sepulchral, it was brilliant; as unreal as the silence of a waxworks show, after hours. There was visual evidence of uniformed service, of order-in-being; no evidence of war as actuality. There was no suggestion of consciousness of catastrophe, of defeat, bombs, tragedy and death. Nor should there have been. For this was but a precinct of a place reserved entirely for calm deliberation.

No one came.

I had no plan of action or of speech. I broke the silence. 'Please ask again,' I said to the Naval officer, 'or shall *I* speak to someone – the Air Force Planner, perhaps? Who would that be, now?' I asked, for I had been out-of-touch so long. He would be at the meeting? I did not know. I had never before been in a meeting of the Chiefs of Staff. Had anyone told CAS or CIGS? I did not know and must find out. No voice that I was hearing whispered: 'Patience!'

The door beyond the barrier opened – it was opened by someone who did not emerge. A voice beyond was speaking with emphasis, deliberately – recognisably a 'naval' voice. The light from beyond was then darkened by a tall man approaching and coming through. it was Peirse – Sir Richard Peirse, lately elevated from the post of DCAS to the new post of Vice-CAS.

Peirce approaching me, smiled. The door behind him closed. He said he was glad to see that I had got back. He said that DCAS had telephoned, and that I might come in, later, he thought; not then. Would I sit down and wait, or would I go up to his office and wait there? He was most courteously considerate.

'My C-in-C,' I began, 'General Gort, that is, told me to insist upon taking his message direct to CIGS and specifically to do so actually in the Chiefs of Staff's meeting, as soon as I possibly could. Would you please ask CIGS if I can come in *now*!'

I said all that with a truculence which surprised us both.

'*Insist?*' echoed Peirse, 'I hardly think that you can do that. You sit down, and wait a bit!' That was an order and meant to be observed as such.

He turned towards the door, went to it, looked back at me still standing, went through, and the door was closed again, shutting out once more the naval voice still speaking.

'Better sit down,' said Boyle, soothingly, 'and don't fret. You'll get in. I'll let DCAS know that you've seen "the Vice". Now I must leave you to him. Good luck to you, and keep calm.' With that and a 'Thank you' from me, he departed.

Half-a-minute later, the door marked *Chiefs of Staff only* opened again and Peirse, standing there, beckoned to me. The lieutenant-commander, seeing the sign, made way. The same naval voice came through the opening, '. . . not nearly enough to go round, for all they're being called on to do. I'm afraid you'll have to tell Gort we're stretched to the limit for destroyers!'

The room was large, rectangular, without windows, of course. The Admiral who was speaking, ceased as I appeared. That must be – without guessing, I could see it was – Sir Dudley Pound, Admiral of the Fleet, First Sea Lord; colloquially, CNS. He was seated near the middle of the far side of an open-square of wide dark-blue, baize-covered, paper-strewn tables. The tables were connected as though all four were one hollow-square table, peopled on the outer sides, revealing in the middle, an empty square of carpeted space. On Pound's left sat a soldier, a general – not Ironside – not quite so large. That must have been General Dill's first appearance there as CIGS: his appointment was confirmed that evening. Then, on the other side, was Newall. He was looking pleasantly at me. He lowered and lifted his left eyelid in characteristic, undemonstrative welcome. That probably served to reduce an oppressive sense of awe and self-consciousness. In the moment of polite silence I had time to see where I was and 'hear' again, with all its significance, what I had just heard.

'Sit there and wait,' whispered Peirse in my ear, motioning me to a chair at the unoccupied, fourth side of the square. He left me and went round to his own chair beside Newall.

I had arrived in the nick of time! The argument about destroyers for Dunkirk was on. There would surely be a come-back from CIGS – from Dill. He recognised me.

There was another general sitting beside Dill whom I took to be Vice-CIGS. And another general whom I did not recognise was sitting separately. I now know that it was General Ismay, representing the new Prime Minister.

Sitting at a side table was a naval captain. I took him to be Captain Andrews – the senior Naval planner. He seemed to catch my eye from his place at the far side. He smiled and lifted his pencil in greeting. I began to feel that I was among friends. Andrews had been on the same Naval staff course with me, at Greenwich, six years back. A friendly, urbanely humorous man. In fact, it was not Andrews, but the illusion served to fortify my nerves. Apparently there were no planners there.

Admiral Pound began speaking again. He remarked on the difficulties of approach and the limitations of Dunkirk harbour, the lack of depth at the quays except at high water, the need to employ destroyers elsewhere, the reasons that not more than six destroyers could be, or should be, spared for the task, since only four could get in at the same time and in view of the lengthiness of the embarkation procedure; this however would be speeded up by the arrival of a supply of harbour rowing boats and motor boats. Although there was a limited number of Channel steamers – or did he say 'Channel Packets'? – already fully employed shuttling they had been suffering casualties, as had the hospital boats and other small loading craft. Besides the difficulty of harbour-room, there was another serious disadvantage to stepping up the numbers of smaller craft, said Pound: those cross-Channel boats had inadequate self-defence; they had some anti-submarine armament, no anti-aircraft guns. And the smaller craft had no defence at all. He did not like the idea of thousands of men being crowded aboard ships totally undefended against air attack.

Swift visions from twenty-five years back flashed into my mind: a succession of pictures of thousands of soldiers' faces, upturned at me, as I flew in my SS – my 'submarine-searcher' airship – over Channel steamers of 1915, tight-packed with troops for France. I was a midshipman, then. No need for AA weapons I thought – for I supposed that all the troops on a cross-Channel steamer would have their rifles.

The moment of nostalgia passed. I was where I was for a desperate purpose. Pound had ceased speaking. There was silence. All I knew, then, was what I had heard being said. And all I could picture to myself then was a lurid configuration of aerial doom in and around Dunkirk and on the shores of La Panne; raging fires and bombers diving, bombing and machine-gunning.

Hardly did I reflect upon my orders from Gort to make a plea to CIGS for more destroyers, nor did I see much sense in pressing Pownall's additional suggestion about more cross-Channel packets. Those two classes of vessels had been disposed of already. CNS had said what was to be said about them. CIGS had not demurred. The Naval measures had been presented and explained. They were the best the Navy could do and that must be accepted by CIGS. If CIGS had nothing further to say, that would be, it seemed, the end of that item on the agenda: 'Operation Dynamo – Naval aspect', presumably.

I had no agenda. My opportunity to give a message from Gort to CIGS for the purpose of a dynamic 'confrontation' between him and Pound clearly had gone. I ought to have been there to speak when the Dunkirk/Navy item came up, before anyone else spoke.

Pound himself was the Chairman. He put the question 'Any more on that?' and looked at his colleagues on either side, collecting glances implying 'nothing further on that item' from those along his side of the table – the Chiefs and the Vice-Chiefs. he gave a brief look at the naval captain whom I had supposed to be Andrews; then, laying his brief for that item aside, he moved to pick up the next.

Dill had but recently given up the command of an Army Corps in France. He was a greatly-loved commander. Perhaps he had had no message to expect me. He just could not know that I was there entirely to entreat him on that topic for Gort and his Army. I looked at him interrogatively, hoping he would realise that I had come from France – direct from Gort. He smiled, in recognition; no more.

Should I utter, then?

Two seconds had elapsed since Pound had asked, 'Any more on that?' 'Well then,' he said, 'We'll go on to the next item.'

But even though Dill had a duty to trust the considered judgement of CNS I had no such duty. I was nobody's agent but Gort's. What Gort wanted was that CNS should be confronted on behalf of three hundred and fifty thousand living men – living then, but how much longer? How many, in one week's time from then? Six destroyers! – at how many men at a time – five hundred? How many weeks? How many ships sunk – men drowned?

There were two other generals there. Would either of them speak? They neither of them did. So I did.

'I have been sent by Lord Gort to say to CIGS on General Gort's behalf as his staff officer that the provision made is not nearly enough for the new task. To begin with, he will need more destroyers. It doesn't greatly matter that Channel steamers have no anti-aircraft. When two thousand men with rifles are on deck and firing, that should be enough protection against low fliers.'

I was aware that all eyes were on me and that a Service enormity was being perpetrated by me. Peirse, bolt upright, aghast, pushed his chair back.

'You must send not only Channel packets,' I went on, 'but pleasure steamers, coasters, fishing-boats, life-boats, yachts, motor-boats, everything that can cross the Channel. And they will find the BEF *not* in Dunkirk Harbour but on the dunes and beaches of La Panne.'

Peirse had got up from his seat and was walking behind the Service Chiefs. I knew what was coming and repeated, as fast as I could, 'Everything that can cross the Channel must be sent; not to the harbour inferno, but to the *beaches* where the troops will be ... *everything* ... even rowing-boats!' I finished, desperately, still looking straight at Pound but knowing that Peirse was looking even harder at me, as he approached.

With cool composure concealing, perhaps, outraged feelings, Peirse leant down to me and said, 'You are a bit overwrought. You must get up and leave here, now.' And I knew that I must. He could not have done it more discreetly – though all could see, none but I had heard. I rose. My ejection was manifest. None demurred. Peirse spoke quietly, again. 'Go up and have a talk with DCAS,' he said, as I made a slight bow to the Chairman, turned and left the then silent room. Whether my composure concealed my shame from others, I do not know. Peirse had, I knew, to do what he did. He did it very considerately. I did not know how otherwise I could have acted.

My immediate reaction to my own action was dejection at failure; failure to win any kind of sympathy or response, or any understanding of the fact that extraordinary measures of an extraordinary nature, but simple in kind, were needed to meet this extraordinarily terrible situation of land-power, sea-power nemesis and the coming sacrifice of, at least, two hundred thousand warriors, dumbfounded me.

My second reaction, as, leaving the lift, I moved slowly up flight after flight of stairs, was one of astonishment that I had said what I had said. I had had no prior intention of doing as I had done. I had had no intention of making a plea for little motor-boats and rowing-boats to be sent. Certainly, I had meant to go beyond my instructions; when I had heard CNS's final remarks I had decided to ask for paddle-steamers, like the *Margate Belle* and *Brighton Queen*. But fishing boats, yachts, and the rest – all that was unpremeditated. They came to me, as I spoke. That is probably truer than I know. But however that may be, at the fifth flight of stairs it struck me as funny. The idea of an airman telling an Admiral of the Fleet in the presence of several generals, *et al*, to send rowing-boats to rescue the army; and the airman then being sent out of the room for doing so. This projected me back into my own childhood when the comicalness of some tragedies made one laugh despite one's agony of tears.

Sholto Douglas saw me at once when I got back to his office. I did not have to explain. He was mercifully incurious about how I had got on, down below. He surely had great problems. Mine was not one of them. There was no longer an Air Force 'overall' Commander-in-Chief of the Air Defence of Great Britain, as there used to be, a few years back. We had been so suddenly expanded as a Service that we simply could not provide the trained staffs to man a great, central co-ordinating command. Maybe, too, the Government was dubious about extending the authority of a single air commander, however logical, if he were not confined within the Whitehall government machine. Sholto-Douglas and his Operations Staff had virtually to *be* that non-existent Air Commander.

He was aware that I was going to talk about the devastating effect of the Stuka dive-bombers. That had become, in England, the leading scare-topic: the papers were headlining deadly hell-divers mercilessly decimating our troops, 'unopposed'. He opened the way by asking whether I, personally, had been under dive-bomber attack.

'No,' I said, 'I haven't. But I've seen them at work in the distance. They come peeling down like plummets. The troops can't face them. Terribly accurate, I'm told. After dropping their bombs, point-blank, they go screaming away at nought feet, so that no light ack-ack can look at them,' I rambled on, anxiously. 'Such a pity we chucked the idea of developing dive-bombers.' I specially wanted to make sure that DCAS knew that in my opinion this method of bombing was peculiarly well-suited to Army co-operation work.

'Now, look here, Victor,' he said, 'you've had as much as you can take for the time being. You must go home and have a good sleep. You're wrong about dive-bombers, and most people who can't think will agree with you. But it stands to reason that if a bomber dives straight on to a target, he is diving straight down the barrels of the defending guns – that is,' he corrected, 'if only the gunners and riflemen will continue to look steadily straight up their sights. That takes some doing. Trained men can do it. And if they *do*, dive-bombers are the easiest possible target for a steady shot. But although that is elementary knowledge to every British soldier in regard to stopping a charge of infantry or cavalry, for a reason I can only guess at, our soldiers have not yet learned that the same applies to a charge by dive-bombers.

'When the dive is over and they've lost all their height, what do they do? They can't fly all the way home at ground-level, can they? They would not get back. They've got to climb again. And that's when they become "easy meat" for a fighter. You'll see. The people in Fighter Command weren't born yesterday. They are learning fast. They'll have the dive-bombers whacked by the end of the next week. Now you go home and sleep it off.'

So we parted. Out in the passage, again, I recognised that there are some things which are better viewed from afar and assessed by a cool brain. In a few sentences, DCAS had removed my dive-bomber phobia. Within a week, Fighter Command had established mastery of the Stukas, and in that victory even the Defiants had a leading place.

As I walked along the passage into the region where my own office used to be, another recognition presented itself as a fact. I was deflated. I had, in ways that were totally disconcerting to me, discharged the two duties laid on me by Gort about twenty hours earlier. I had discharged them in such a manner that the result, too obviously to me, was that no one was taking up the two charges.

The capital letters, DMC, on a door I was passing caught my eye. Director of what? – I wondered; for the designation was new to me. Then I remembered; there had recently been formed a directorate exclusively for military co-operation; to look after the Air Force policy side of the perennially controversial problem.

A Director of Military Co-operation should be able to help me; he should know whether Gort had got through to Dunkirk; he might be able to get me through to Gort on an operation tie-line, to report that I had cut no ice with CIGS or Pound. Anyway, I ought to report to someone that I was at a loose-end. Presumably someone, and who better than DMC, should tell me to report at Hawkinge for duty with Back Violet? He at least should be able to fix me up with a railway warrant, or get me flown down, and tell Charles Blount that I was coming.

In the outer office I learned again what I had known. The Director was Air Commodore Hugh Frazer. I waited for no ceremony of permission to enter and, as I went in, found him telephoning. Looking up at me as he put the instrument down, he said, 'That was DCAS, about you – Good morning, by the way. Good to see you all in one piece, though apparently only just. He says that you are to go straight away on leave. He says that you are not to suppose that Charles Blount needs your help – there are enough people there already to do Violet's limited job of reconnaissance over the areas of retreat. Anyway, Vachell is standing in for you.'

I said, 'Oh . . . and good-morning to you. Congratulations on the broad stripe. What I want to know, first is, has Gort arrived?'

'Gort? Is he expected? You tell me.'

'Not in London,' I said, 'Dunkirk. He should be there by now, or at la Panne. I want to send him a message.'

I had to explain myself. Frazer was attentive but his common sense was operating. 'You feel pretty sure that your representation failed. But how do you know?' he asked. 'What you said may have sunk in. Better not cry out before you are hurt. Perhaps I can find out for you and see that the War Office advise GHQ, or rather, Gort's Command Post, wherever that may have got to. The planners must know and might tell me.'

'The planners! Yes!' I said, hope suddenly flooding back. 'Andrews would surely tell me. I might even persuade him to initiate something, himself. I'll go and see Andrews now. Can you

C/o War Office
18. VI. 40.

My dear Goddard

I am indeed grateful to you for all the good work you were able to accomplish on our behalf when you got home from Premesques. How lucky for us you got away with the forced landing as otherwise we might not have seen the vast assembly of vessels of all categories to get the troops away from the beaches.

Yours ever
Gort.

Gort's letter to the author, thanking him for his successful mission to the Chiefs-of-Staff.

fix me with a pass? Let me just do that, then I'll give you a message for Gort and will go home without any more fuss.'

Frazer did not demur. With his aid, I re-entered the Defence Committee offices and found Andrews in his upstairs office. He had a commander with him. I waited. The window overlooked St James's Park. Through the trees could be seen the tranquil blue lake with unconcerned ducks and pelicans plying their pleasant waterfare. Established England – green, beautiful in nature, serene.

The commander departed.

'I had to ferret you out,' I began, 'about this morning's effort. I'm afraid I made a bit of a fool of myself, and alarmed Vice-CAS.'

'But not me!' said Andrews. 'I wasn't there.' That astonished me. Whom had I mistaken for him? But he went on unchecked, 'You certainly caused a bit of a stir. And you've landed me in for an unusual job.'

'How's that?' I asked, hope redawning.

'Well, I've been told to lay on the staff-work for marshalling all kinds of odd shipping and craft not already ear-marked for service. That's what I am trying to put on paper, now. Never fear; you'll get your little boats. I have to send out signals to all the SNO's and Harbour Masters at our south-eastern ports and harbours ordering them to send every little ship and boat that volunteers to go, to fetch the Army back from the beaches of la Panne.'*

So, what I had inadvertently said had sunk in . . .

The pleasant rhythm of wheels over rail-joints soon charmed me away from the contemplation of England streaming by, with their persistent 'Go to sleep! Go to sleep! Go to sleep!'

My wife had been helping her sister to transplant her girls' school from Chislehurst to a noble Cotswold house near Chipping Campden. In a nearby inn where I 'slept it off' they heard something that I would have been glad to hear – the Admiralty's call to owners of yachts and motor boats to join in the Army's rescue across the Channel to the shallow beaches of la Panne.

---

*That day Captain Tennant, SNO for Vice-Admiral Ramsay at Dover, went himself to Dunkirk, and in the evening was reiterating my plea of the morning. Send every available craft, he signalled. He had seen the plight of the BEF for himself. As for destroyers, during that same day, the 27th, there were 11 destroyers at Dunkirk; and in the period 27th May to 4th June, no less than thirty-nine destroyers in all were in operation.

Epilogue

By dawn on 4th June, the last of the eastern British rearguard, stealthily withdrawn by night, had been embarked and borne away – all but a valiant remnant of wounded, captured or killed when on the brink of rescue. To be chosen as fighting units of a rearguard; to be the last guardians of retreat was honourable and was honoured by each unit chosen. To them as much as to any others, praise is due for the fact that, at that ending of their task, more than three hundred thousand Allied soldiers had been saved; two-thirds by way of the harbour, dry-footed into ships; one-hundred thousand by wading on sea-swept, fire-swept sands into the 'little boats'.

The western rearguard – the valiant and self-sacrificing French Army men – had in large measure also been embarked, but not all by any means when, at 3.30 a.m. heavy shelling began again, and the Admiralty called our Navy men away. The Germans had almost reached the harbour. Captain William Tennant, RN, and his assistants – the men who had conducted the whole escape 'repaired on board' with all decorum, and the last destroyer, already packed with French infantry, cast-off. Bidding farewell and thanks to French officials, navy and harbour men, and to a regiment of French soldiers standing in ranks for the rescue then denied, HMS *Shikari* steamed away for England and no bombs fell. Dunkirk in ruins was soon in German hands and Operation Dynamo was done.

Orders to disband Back Violet and close our headquarters reached me at Hawkinge in the afternoon. The task was easy; not worth mentioning in detail. Too late to worry about our personal postings, we deemed it best to dine together at the hotel where we had all been billeted: the Grand at Folkestone, down the hill and by the sea. Till then it had seemed normal peace-time, well-populated and well-served. We had not mixed with the guests. None knew what we were at – at Hawkinge or wherever, none enquired. And each night we had heard the rhythmic music of the dance band but none of us had danced.

By the time we had got our business done that final evening, driven back to the hotel, washed, changed and reached the palatial dining room, it was empty except for the waiters. So we dined alone, the ten of us. Pleasant it was, and friendly, that last meal together, but not spirited – not like our nonsense-talking evening meal at that old Château Écoive. At the end of dinner, a little self-consciously, we rose for the loyal toast. That done, we sat, fingering our wine glasses but no one had anything to say.

After a while, we moved off. The whole place was empty: every guest had gone. The season at the Grand had ended almost before it had begun. We parted from each other, then, and never met again as a group of men in Violet.

And that was the end of Violet. But not quite the end of the Violet epic.

My next assignment was to have been to command a wing of squadrons but hardly had I arrived at Odiham to take over command before I was ordered back to the Air Ministry to take over from Air Commodore Hugh Frazer who, as I have mentioned already, was the Director of Army Co-operation.

Charles Blount, once more commanding No 22 (Army Co-operation) Group came up from Farnborough on 27th October to a conference. I had not seen him since Hawkinge. I was then an Air Commodore and Director of Military Co-operation in the Air Ministry. He wanted to know how things had gone with me after he flew away from that deserted French airfield in the questionable Moth. At Hawkinge I had given him a resumé of Gort's final request to me and had told him what we did about it. But we hadn't talked over the action we had been able to take in conditions of near-total frustration and inferiority.

'You told me about the Ensign which brought you out,' said Blount, 'and you mentioned that it had brought in a full load of anti-tank ammunition. What happened to it all? Was it any good?'

'It provided,' I replied, 'so I've been told, for a most effective rearguard action that same night, on the Aachen road, east of Lille. A massive attack by German armour was repulsed by those four tons of ammunition fired by two batteries of anti-tank guns. That was surely Horsey's victory, though he may never hear of it. And it may have been the saving of Gort and many more besides.'

'Glad to hear that something was achieved by our so-called Air Power,' said Charles, ironically.

'Oh, come on, Charles! You know perfectly well that Peter

Fullard's 14 Fighter Group did wonders. God knows how many Huns the Hurricanes shot down. The Gladiators, too, did quite a lot of execution. And the much maligned Defiants, later, really had quite a bean feast of Stukas with their back guns, once they got the hang of it.'

Blount interposed, 'But that was over the Dunkirk area, when we were at Hawkinge. And, as you know, the Spitfires came into it at the finish. Yes . . . if the Germans do come this way – as they surely will – they're going to lose a lot of bombers to those eight-gun fighters of ours.'

We talked on like that for quite a while and during the course of our ruminations Blount remarked that we had gained something like air superiority over the Dunkirk area at the finish. 'The German Army generals, Haider and von Kleist,' Blount surmised, 'must have recognised that fact as a main reason for their failure to achieve the total destruction of our Army. Would to God that our generals had learnt that lesson, too!'

Blount than spoke with some delight about 'the little boats'. He mused that it was in little boats that our forebears came to England. Was it not in little boats that we who like to mess about in, chiefly learn our sailoring? 'Only in little boats,' he went on, 'do we ever put to sea from sandy shallows. Why then should it have been so far from the military logic for the rescue of a stranded army that hordes of little boats would be just the thing? A hundred thousand paddling soldiers must have taken quite a lot of ferrying,' he concluded.

I reminded him that after Peirse had sent me out of that meeting, the Chiefs of Staff themselves decided that that was the right thing to do.

'But what made you think of putting that notion to the Chiefs?' Blount asked.

'I didn't think of it, Charles; it just came out when I heard Pound say that he couldn't spare more destroyers, and that the cross-Channel steamers were all allocated and no more could be done about Dunkirk. The notion of the little boats was a gift. Anyway, Gort sent me to that meeting to get something done by CNS and he now knows what happened.'

Blount told me, too about the men of Violet whom we had known so well. 'Dizzy' Desoer had got a Lysander wing. Donald Hardman was doing the job which so ably he had helped to do with me; he was Blount's SOA. Blount also told me about many of the others; some who had come with him, some who had stayed with Cole-Hamilton, until middle of June commanding a re-vamped air component for the remnant of the BEF in central north-western France. 'Poor old "Coaly", as you know, went back,' said Blount, 'to do my job,' and added, wistfully, 'Then he had to fight a war on his own. Though not for long.'

'Why d'you say "poor old"?' I asked. 'You know you rather envy him. Although it was a forlorn hope, an endless retreat to the Atlantic, they did very well. Not too much opposition in the air.'

Blount replied, 'You didn't know that his wife died as he flew away?' I did not know that. Nor did I guess that I was soon to learn that Cole-Hamilton himself had died. Some said it was sheer exhaustion; others a broken heart. Strange for such a fire-eating, debonair, inspired leader. He and I had both left the Grand Fleet to go flying in 1915.

So we turned from the past to the immediate future on Blount telling me next morning he would be flying off to Northern Ireland.

'What takes you to Ulster, now?' I asked.

'I want to see Bob Stewart, the GOC. His division there,' said Blount, 'is the only large slice of the Army that is not all in tatters. They can do some useful tactical training as a division, right away. So I want him to let one of our Lysander squadrons – 16 Squadron – train with his division and get down to the evolution of a better system of support-communications than the old one – such a ghastly failure in France. The present army system,' he went on, 'for ordering support-bombing is just about as quick as that for getting daily rations.

'Of course, it wouldn't have made a fig of difference to the end result however quick we'd got our bombers on to targets. They'd most of them have been shot down just the same. But if Jerry brings off landings here, by air or sea, we'd have some hope of doing something, under the umbrella of our fighters; they at least can hold the ring! There'll be no excuse then for not getting the light bombers on to a fleeting target in a matter of minutes, like a fire brigade. But the Army's got to get a better way of saying what they want. They've got to make priority decisions without every demand for support going all the way in messages, right up to the GOC before the Air Force hears a word about it.'

'That's one of the things,' I said, 'this staff of mine has got to tackle with the War Office. I have Woodward with me, and he's already on to it.'

'Well, that's good to know. Send him to Ireland – and let him get a move on.' Then, doubtfully he asked, 'What exactly is your job?' That was something of a puzzle to me to answer. Everything was in the melting pot. The Army, disillusioned in regard to air co-operation, was crying out to have its own air force; some men highly placed were even demanding Spitfires for reconnaissance; others were asking for the control of our entire array of air power so soon as the invasion came, if not before. I told Blount what I thought the job was. But soon after that I was to have it put more pithily to me. Wilfred Freeman after helping Beaverbrook came in place of Peirse as Vice-CAS. Freeman was like his name, free of the bondage of convention, a free thinker and one free with his words. I asked him the question Blount had asked me, and he gave this reply: 'The Army is out, for the time being; the Navy can't do much to hit the Hun; that leaves only Bomber Command to do the hitting. That is fact – not fancy. But is it recognised? Once again, we have the same old outcry for the Army to be given a mighty air force of its own. The thing is childish but they don't yet understand. They've had a fearful pasting and have taken a total defeat. They blame it much on the air – and they are right. But they've got the culprits wrongly named.' He checked himself, looked straight at me – he had a natural twinkle when not annoyed – 'Your job? Your job is do everything you can to help the Army.' He said that with beaming generosity and compassion for hard-hit, needy friends. 'Everything!' he repeated with emphasis, quickly adding with mock ruthlessness, 'short of giving them anything.'

But that epitome of my duty came to me after Charles Blount had gone. To tell it, I diverged from his projected visit to Northern Ireland and his telling me what to give the Army. He wanted us to be the means for enabling the Army to make use of air power swiftly; to frame a system that would be child's play to operate, a scheme that everyone could quickly understand. And that in fact we did do. The system first went into action at El Alamein. It worked. Our victory there and in North Africa generally was largely due to swift air support in conditions of general air superiority.

'How are you going over to Ulster?' I asked.

'Flying, of course,' said Blount.

'Yes, but what in?'

'In that Moth of "ours",' he replied, and added with warmth and self-indulgent mirth, 'I love it!'

He told me in terms of 'glorious fun', about his flight home from

Lille to Hawkinge. That was the Moth he was going to use to fly himself to Northern Ireland, next day. He wanted my advice as a Moth devotee, about the route to take, whether by bee-line, or by the Isle of Man, or the coast of Wigtonshire.

I said, 'Charles, you're tired. Also, you are an AOC. Why fly yourself in a single-engined, draughty little kite over miles and miles of deserted sea? You'll go to sleep and fly into the drink. Can't you relax? Why not get yourself flown in something comfortable like other VIPs?'

'Evidently I am not as V.I. as I used to be,' said Blount. 'I no longer have a flight of Dominies to carry me and the generals about.' He said that in mock complaint, adding, 'You've collared them all for jobs in France. Besides, I much prefer my Moth. Keeps me busy all the time. Never a dull moment.'

'Look!' I said, 'Operation Dynamo is over. There's no need for you to go on flogging yourself to death. You seem to think you're a dynamo yourself – as though you only have to keep the "juice" turned on. Use the airline running from Hendon to Belfast. It runs every day, specially for people like you. Why not go by that?'

'All right,' he said, evidently wishing, for once, to please me more than to be rational, 'I have never before gone by a regular airline anywhere. I might as well see what it's like. How do I fix it?'

I said that I would fix it.

He got up, picked up his things – his 'sideways' cap, his brief case and his baton-length of polo stick – grinned back at me a gleeful smile as one about to go into a new adventure – as, indeed, he was. So that most gallant and most winning man departed.

He did not come again.

Next morning, I was telephoned from RAF Hendon. The commanding officer of that station, knowing that I had booked a place for Blount on that morning's Belfast flight rang me and said he had bad news. He said the Belfast plane had crashed and there was one survivor – a civilian.

Index

Index

Aachen, 201
Abyssinia, 13
Abbeville, 174
Adam, General, 119, 157
Admiralty, the, 108, 213, 232, 246
Africa, North, 86
Air Component see Royal Air Force
Air Ministry, 13, 15, 16, 20, 25, 26, 27, 31, 34, 35, 49, 63, 69, 104, 107, 160, 169, 176, 203, 239, 241, 258
Air Striking Force see Royal Air Force
Alfrey, Colonel, 173, 176, 177, 179, 188, 193, 194, 195, 209, 216, 218
Algeria, 86
Amiens, 158
Andrews, Captain, RN, 249, 250, 254, 256
Antwerp, 127
Appleyard, Brigadier, 60, 61
Ardennes, 115, 122, 130-1, 133
Arras, 57, 60, 61, 70, 84, 89, 112, 119, 121, 125, 129, 130, 137, 139, 143, 144, 145, 150, 152, 156, 157, 158, 159, 173, 216, 218
Atcherley, Wing Cdr D., 63
Atcherley, Wg Cdr R., 63
Austria, 132

BAFF, see Royal Air Force
Baldwin, Stanley, 31
Baltic, 109
Baring, 244
Barker, General, 119
Barratt, Air Chief Marshal Sir Arthur, 97, 122, 133, 137, 141, 150, 159, 169
Beatty, Admiral of the Fleet Viscount, 188
Beaverbrook, Lord, 261
Belfast, 262
Belgian Army, 45, 126, 173, 196, 198, 199, 210, 219
Belgium, 64, 65, 86, 100, 101, 102, 103, 104, 105, 110, 115, 126, 127, 128, 134, 140, 151, 163, 205, 210, 219, 220
Benskin, Mr and Mrs, 40, 41
Berlin, 25, 28
Biggin Hill, 235, 236
Bird, 145
Blount, Air Vice-Marshal Charles, 45, 47, 48-51, 69, 71, 72-5, 77, 82, 84, 85, 88, 89, 92, 93, 94, 97, 98, 102, 103, 105, 111-4, 119, 120, 122, 123, 133, 134-6, 144, 147, 150, 151, 153, 156, 157, 158, 159, 160, 161-7, 169, 170, 172, 174, 176, 179, 211, 235, 238, 241, 242, 245, 254, 258, 259, 260-2
Bomber Command see Royal Air Force
Bottomley, Air Commodore, 120, 121, 133, 138
Boulogne, 152, 153, 156, 174, 179, 185, 187, 190, 194, 214, 234, 237, 238
Bourget, Le, 152
Bourne, Walter, 39, 40
Boyle, Air Cdre Archibald, 25-33, 34, 35, 53, 107, 109, 110, 113, 116, 242, 243, 244, 246, 247, 248
Brassard see British Expeditionary Force
Brest, 53
Britain, Battle of, 16
British Expeditionary Force:
  GHQ (Brassard), 70, 129, 130, 131, 133, 143, 145, 146, 152, 156, 157, 158, 169, 171, 175, 179, 186
  Royal Corps of Signals, 55, 76, 102
  Royal Engineers, 60, 61
  et passim
Brittany, 55, 71
Broad, Henry, 180

266   Index

Brooke, General, 119, 157
Brook-Popham, Colonel 243
Brussels, 103, 201

Calais, 152-3, 156, 174, 179, 185, 187, 188, 190, 194, 214, 234, 238
Camberley, 186, 210
Capel, Air Commodore, Ben, 48, 50, 69, 73, 75, 88, 98, 102, 103, 111, 112, 129, 160
Chamberlain, Neville, 21, 27, 30, 32, 33, 34, 42, 43, 66, 95, 99, 108, 109, 116, 117, 118, 197
Chatham, 195
Chaume, Captain Bobbie la, 88, 238
Cherbourg, 153
Chipping Campden, 256
Chislehurst, 256
Churchill, Winston, 117, 175, 197, 199, 215, 216, 217, 219, 243, 246
Cochrane, Flight Lieutenant Ralph, 195
Cody, Colonel, 47
Cole-Hamilton, Air Commodore John, 102, 111, 124, 125, 145, 152, 218, 238, 260
Colyer, Group Captain Douglas, 152
Conde, 127, 129
Copenhagen, 109
Cossins, Aircraftman, 77, 86, 88, 125, 145, 150, 153, 160, 168, 170, 172, 177, 209, 212, 217, 218, 220, 221, 222, 223, 224, 226, 237
Cotton, Sidney, 104, 105, 140
Coulommiers, 97
Croydon, 15, 180, 198
Czechoslovakia, 13, 21, 186

Dagenham, 235
Daladier, 84, 85, 96, 99
Dartmouth, 80
Denmark, 108, 109, 110, 111, 112, 114, 115, 116, 117, 124, 132
Desoer, Wing Commander 'Dizzy', 98, 127, 129, 131, 133, 134, 137, 138, 139, 143, 150, 152, 153, 156, 160, 170, 172, 182, 191, 200, 207, 208, 209, 212, 215, 216, 217, 218, 220, 221, 222, 223, 224, 225, 227, 229, 259

Dill, General, 243, 244, 248, 249, 250, 251
Douai, 75, 76, 77
Douglas of Kirtleside, Lord, see Sholto Douglas
Dover, 213, 215, 236, 256
Dowding, Air Chief Marshal Sir Hugh, 63, 104, 135, 136
Dunkirk, 166, 174, 175, 179, 192, 194, 211, 212, 213, 214, 215, 226, 232, 234, 235, 236, 241, 245, 246, 249, 251, 254, 255, 256, 257, 259
Dutch Army, 126
Dyle, River, 103, 127, 135, 140, 141, 151
Dynamo, Operation, 175, 213, 215, 246 ff

Ecoive, Chateau, 85, 86, 87, 91, 98, 130, 240, 258
Eisenhower, General, 149
Escaut, R., 140, 150, 151

Farnborough, 45, 47, 50, 86, 172
Fields, Gracie, 89, 90, 240
Filtness, 160, 170, 212
Folkestone, 160, 257
Franklyn, General, 216
Frazer, Air Commodore Hugh, 254, 256, 258
Frederikshavn, 65
Freeman, Air Chief Marshal Wilfred, 261
French Air Force, 46, 63, 75, 96, 126, 127, 196
French Army, 45, 53, 54, 58, 59, 60, 101, 126, 127, 131, 137, 158, 161, 177, 196, 210, 212, 220, 257
  First Army: 57, 134, 143, 151, 158, 196
  Ninth Army: 134, 194
  Seventh Army: 57, 63, 66, 86, 87, 134, 174, 196
Fullard, Group Captain Peter, 136, 141, 259

Gallipoli, 219
Gamelin, General, 97

Garston, 35, -43, 171
Gaulle, General de, 87
George VI, HM, King, 74, 75-83, 198, 199
Georges, General, 122, 131, 176, 177
German Army, 53, 84, 86, 87, 95, 119, 120-123, 126, 128, 129, 130, 131, 132-3, 134, 138, 139, 143, 151, 200
Germany, 14, 16, 21, 32, 53, 59, 64, 65, 66, 68, 95, 96, 132, 186, 231 et passim
Giraud, General, 86, 87
Glasgow, 53
Gneisenau, 109
Goebbels, Josef, 46
Göring, Reichsmarschall Hermann, 14, 28, 31
Gort, General Viscount, 52, 54, 58, 75, 97, 106, 108, 119, 120, 122, 123, 124, 134, 135, 136, 143, 144, 145, 150-2, 156, 158, 164, 170, 173, 175, 176-80, 188, 198, 199, 200, 201, 209, 210-15, 218, 226, 234, 239, 240, 241, 243-8, 250, 251, 253, 254, 256, 258
Grey, Wing Commander 'Dolly', 92, 105, 106, 107

Halder, General von, 259
Halifax, Lord, 20
Hamburg, 106
Hardman, Wing Commander Donald, 49, 52, 54, 60, 70, 111, 112, 125, 145, 147, 149, 152, 153, 259
Havre, Le, 153
Hawkinge, 160, 169, 170, 172, 235, 245, 257, 258, 262
Hazebrouck, 143, 144, 145, 146-152, 155-157
Hendon, 185, 237, 262
High Wycombe, 121, 138
Hitler, Adolf, 13, 19, 20, 21, 23, 24, 25, 26, 28, 30, 31, 32, 33, 44, 46, 53, 60, 65, 66, 67, 84, 96, 99, 108, 117, 189, 196, 209
Holland, 64, 86, 115, 126, 127
Hore-Belisha, Leslie, 122, 214
Hornchurch, 235, 237
Horsey, Captain, 227, 228, 229, 230, 235, 258
Hungary, 132, 186

Iraq, 44, 173
Ireland, 260, 261, 262
Ironside, General, 136, 158, 213, 240, 244, 248
Ismay, General, 249

Jamaica, 180
Japan, 13, 159
Jarvis, Wing Commander Louis, 73, 88, 145, 147, 152, 153, 238, 239

Kattegat, 109
Keitel, Field Marshal Wilhelm, 28, 32
Keyes, Admiral, Roger, 188, 197, 198, 199, 200
Kiel, 65, 106, 110, 116
Kleist, General von, 259
Kimmins, Major Brian, 173, 174, 176, 178, 179, 186, 193, 194, 209, 216, 218, 220
Knutsford, Lord and Lady, 41, 42, 43
Kordt, Acting Ambassador, 33
Kurdistan, 173

La Panne, 213, 232, 236, 250, 251, 254, 256
Leconfield, 106
Le Mans, 52, 53, 55, 56, 57
Leopold III, HM King, 198, 199, 200, 210, 224
Lille, 57, 75, 122, 135, 136, 153, 173, 181, 206, 215, 219, 262
Lille-Seclin, 75, 105
Lindbergh, Col Charles, 13-16, 118
Lithuania, 108
Liverpool, 37
Lloyd George, David, 153
London, evacuation of, 34-43
Ludlow-Hewitt, Air Marshal, 237
Luftwaffe, 46, 84, 122, 126, 128, 136, 137, 204 et passim
Luxembourg, 110, 119, 120, 131, 133, 134

Madrid, 186

268   Index

Mafeking, 246
Maginot Line, 45, 60, 96, 115, 120, 131, 134, 197
Man, Isle of, 262
Manston, 233, 234, 235
Maroeuil, 60, 63, 65, 66, 70, 73, 84, 85, 87, 113, 119, 125, 127, 145, 152, 156
Mason-Macfarlane, General, 110, 216
Medhurst, Charles, 29, 36
Mein Kampf, 19, 23, 24, 196
Meuse, River, 122, 143
Moscow, 19, 20, 21, 22, 26
Mosul, 240
Munich, 21, 35
Musgrave-Whitham, Group Captain Bob, 56
Mussolini, Benito, 31

Nantes, 53, 71
Newall, Air Vice-Marshal, 108, 109, 117, 135, 136, 169, 241, 243, 244, 249
North Sea, 68, 108, 115
Norway, 107, 108, 109, 110, 111, 114, 115, 116, 118, 124, 132

Osborne, 80
Oslo, 109

Paris, 55, 67, 88, 152, 157, 177, 178, 180, 181, 182, 200
Pearl, Flying Officer, Leonard, 150, 160, 170, 171, 172, 179, 180, 201, 202, 203, 204, 205, 206, 207, 212, 217
Pegwell Bay, 235
Peirse, Air Chief Marshal Sir Richard, 241, 248, 249, 251, 252, 259, 261
Pelly, Wing Commander Claud, 49, 65, 66, 98, 122, 127, 131, 140, 143, 145, 147, 150, 152, 153, 160, 174, 175, 179, 216, 234
Philip, Prince, 13
Philippines, 13
Playfair, Air Vice Marshal Pip, 97
Poland, 19, 21, 22, 23, 24, 25, 27, 28, 32, 34, 46, 53, 54, 59, 99, 100, 102, 107, 124, 132
Polzeath, 190
Portal, Air Marshal 108

Pound, Admiral of the Fleet Sir Dudley, 213, 215, 240, 243, 248, 249, 250, 254, 259
Pownall, Lt General H., 122, 133, 134, 135, 136, 143, 173, 174, 175, 178, 181, 197, 209, 210, 211, 214
Premesques, 170, 171, 177, 182, 190, 195, 206, 216, 246

Ramsay, Vice-Admiral, 175, 215, 256
Rheims, 45, 97, 118, 126
Ribbentrop, Frau, 20, 25
Ribbentrop, J. von, 19, 20, 28, 32
Rotterdam, 103
Royal Air Force:
    Air Component: 44, 46, 54, 58, 61, 62, 70, 72, 74-83, 90, 97, 99, 100, 125, 128, 152, 153, 156, 158, 160, 162, 179, 218, 238 et passim HQ (Violet) 49, 70, 73, 120, 121, 129, 130, 132, 141, 145, 150, 152, 153, 156, 157, 160, 171, 174, 178, 185, 217, 234, 237, 238, 242, 245, 254, 257, 258 *et passim*
    Squadrons: No 85: 46
                    87: 46
                    607: 46
                    615: 46
    Air Striking Force: 97, 121, 126, 128, 141, 143, 218, 238
    70 Wing: 119, 134, 137, 141
    60 Wing: 132
    14 Group, 134, 136, 137
    BAFF: 97-98, 120, 121, 122, 136, 141, 150, 159, 169
    Fighter Command: 67, 97, 104, 128, 134, 135, 141, 253
    Bomber Command: 45, 67, 97, 107, 108, 116, 120, 121, 133, 138, 139, 140, 141, 158, 159, 197, 238, 241, 261
Royal Scots Fusiliers, 25
Rugg, Wing Commander 145, 152, 238
Ruhr, 96
Rundstedt, General, von, 149, 186
Russia, 21, 53, 59, 85, 107

St Nazaire, 53
Scapa, 39

Scharnhorst, 109
Sedan, 126, 143
Sholto Douglas, Air Marshal Sir, 36, 38, 214, 241, 244, 245, 246, 252
Siegfried Line, 115
Silvertown, 195
Slessor Air Cdre Jack, 158
Smuts, General, 153
Somme, Battle of, 44, 84, 98, 243
Sorley, Squadron Leader Ralph, 237
Southampton, 53
Spain, 13, 100, 146, 150
Spanish Civil War, 64, 149, 186
Stalin, Josef, 19, 20, 26, 28
Stanton, George, 56
Stewart, Bob, 260
Strugnell, Group Captain, 235
Sweden, 108

Tennant, Captain W, RN, 256, 257
Teruel, 186
Torch, Operation, 86
Trenchard, Marshal of the RAF Viscount, 25, 26, 117, 153, 243

Ukraine, 23, 24, 107
Ultra Secret, The, 101

Vachell, Group Captain John, 30, 31, 254
Vanlaer, Lieutenant Pierre, 87, 88, 226, 238
Vansittart, Sir R., 107
Verdun, 44
Violet see Royal Air Force

Warsaw, 100
Watford, 35, 43
Watson-Watt, Dr, 189
Watts, Peter, 93
Wenninger, Frau, 20, 22, 25
Wenninger, General, 14, 20-33
West Malline, 235
Whitehall, 239, 240, 242
Whitfield, Group Captain, 133, 137, 138
Wigglesworth, Wing Commander, 13
Wilhelmshaven, 109
Windsor, Duke of, 112
Winterbotham, Wing Commander Frederick, 95, 101, 104

Zeebrugge, 188